ISBN: 9781314248982

Published by:
HardPress Publishing
8345 NW 66TH ST #2561
MIAMI FL 33166-2626

Email: info@hardpress.net
Web: http://www.hardpress.net

Page 131 *[illegible]*

Page 181 *[illegible]*

PERSONAL SKETCHES

OF

HIS OWN TIMES,

BY

SIR JONAH BARRINGTON,

AUTHOR OF

"THE HISTORY OF THE IRISH UNION," &c. &c.

IN THREE VOLUMES.

VOL. III.

LONDON:

HENRY COLBURN AND RICHARD BENTLEY,
NEW BURLINGTON STREET.

1832.

PRINTED BY A. J. VALPY, RED LION COURT, FLEET STREET.

DEDICATION.

TO THE

RIGHT HONOURABLE THE LORD STOWELL,
&c. &c.

January 1st, 1832.

My Dear Lord,

To experience the approbation of the public in general must ever be gratifying to the author of any literary work, however humble may be its subject: such has been my fortunate lot as to the first two volumes of these light sketches of incident and character.

But when my attempt also received the unqualified approbation of one of the most able, learned, and discriminating official personages that England has, or probably will have to boast of, my vanity was justly converted into pride, and a value stamped upon my production which I durst not previously have looked to.

Greatly indeed was my pleasure enhanced when your Lordship informed me that my

Sketches had " given me much repute here, were read with *general avidity,* and considered as giving much insight into the original character of the Irish."

Yet a still stronger testimonial of your Lordship's favour was reserved to augment my pride and pleasure—your Lordship's note to me, stating, that my volumes " had afforded him much amusement, and had given very general satisfaction; and that he was tempted to wish for a third volume composed of similar materials."

Your wish, my Lord, is obeyed. A third volume is composed, and if it should have the good fortune to afford your Lordship an hour's amusement, my gratification will be consummated.

After more than threescore and ten winters have passed over the head of man, any increase of mental faculty, or intellectual powers in a writer can never be expected; at the very best he may be stationary. I can, therefore, only offer you this volume, such as it is: receive it, then, my Lord, as the last and only *souvenir* I can now tender to mark the sincerity, respect, and attachment, with which I am your Lordship's faithful servant,

JONAH BARRINGTON.

PREFACE.

THE Introduction prefixed to the first volume of these Sketches somewhat developes the origin of the work, and the source of its materials. Commenced to wear away the tedium of a protracted winter, it continued, for nearly three months, the amusement of my leisure hours. During that short space the entire of the two first volumes was collected and composed.

I do not allude to this as any proof of literary expertness : on the contrary, I offer it as some apology for the inaccuracies incidental to so hasty a performance. In common with all biographical and anecdotical compositions, mine cannot affect to be exempt from small errors; but whatever they may be, I alone am responsible. Not one anecdote—character—sentence—observation—line—or even thought, was contributed or suggested to me by any living person; nor was a single page of the MS. even seen by any friend save one (and that but very partially), on whose suggestion it had been commenced, and on whose recommendation I transmitted the two first volumes to my present publisher, but with (I own) very great diffidence as to their catastrophe. On that point, however, I was most agreeably disappointed. The flattering excitement which originated the present volume appears in the dedication.

In deference to the *goût* of the present fashionable class of readers, I deeply regret that these volumes are not the florid children of fiction and of fancy. Unfortunately, they are only embellished recitals of actual facts and incidents, extracted from authentic sources, and forming an *Olla Podrida* of variegated materials—some, perhaps, too cheerful for the grave—others too *sombre* for the cheerful, and, on the whole, I fear, rather too *ordinaire* for refinement, or insufficiently *languid* for modern sensibility—particularly of the softer sex, whose favour, of all things, I should wish to cultivate.

I cannot deny also my presumption in having garnished these Sketches here and there with my own crude or digressive observations; but my *ensemble* being altogether a whimsical composition, without sequence or connexion, minor errors may merge in the general confusion, and the originator of them be screened under the gabardine of his singularity.

The only merit which I actually claim is, that the principal sketches somewhat illustrate the native Irish character at *different epochas* in different grades of society, and furnish some amusing points of comparison between the more *remote* and the *modern* manners and habits of that eccentric people;—and there my irregularities are perfectly appropriate. But a far more dangerous ordeal lies glowing hot before me;—I fear my fair readers will never pardon me for introducing so small a proportion of true love into my anecdotes—an omission for which I am bound, so far as in me lies, to give the very best apology I can. But when I reflect on the exquisite tenderness of the female heart, and its intrinsic propensity to imbibe that most delicious of the passions on every proper opportunity, I almost despair of being able to conciliate the lovely spinsters who may deign to peruse my lucubrations; and if the ladies of an *age mûr* do not take my part, I shall be a ruined author. Trembling, therefore, I proceed to state some matters of fact, which, if dispassionately considered and weighed, may prove that, from the rapid movements of love in Ireland, there can be but very scant materials for interesting episodes in that country.*

Ireland has been ever celebrated by every author who characterised it, as the most amatory of islands; and the disinterestedness of its lovers, and their inveterate contempt of obstacles, and abhorrence of any species of procrastination, has been a subject of general eulogium.

Love is the only object of liberty and equality as yet enjoyed by the Irish people. Even among the better orders, *money*, not being in general there the circulating medium of matrimony, is always despised when it does not attend, and abused behind its back as inveterately as if it was a sub-sheriff.

A love-stricken couple seldom lose their precious moments practising idle sensibilities, and waiting for bank-notes that won't come, or parchments that have not one word of truth in them. Such illusory proceedings were very sensibly dispensed with, and a justifiable impatience generally, because quite natural, sent formality about its business. The lovers themselves came to the real point; a simple question and categorical reply settled the *concours* at once; and marriage and possession occupied not unfrequently the second or third evening after a first acquaintance, whilst the first of a honey-moon, and the commencement of a new family, dated sometimes from the first evening of acquaintance. After that knot was tied, they always had an indefinite time and unrestrained opportunities to cultivate their love, or what remained of it, for the remainder of their existence.

This rapid, but rational consummation of love-matches in Ireland, however, left no opportunity or field for amatory adventures, as in countries where love, jealousy, and murder are often seen bubbling in the same cauldron!

No doubt the Irish manner of courtship plunders love of its episodes, romance of its refinements, and consequently my fair English readers of those sentimentalities which so beautifully garnish the produce of imagination-workers. Take it all for all, however, Irish love is found to answer very well for domestic purposes, and, making allowances for wear and tear, to be, I believe, to the full, as durable as in any other country.

In a plainer way, I now frankly confess that during the composition of the three volumes, my *inventive* genius, (if I have any,) like one of the

seven sleepers, lay dormant in my *occiput*, and
so torpid, that not one fanciful anecdote or brilliant hyperbole awakened during the whole of
that ordinary period ; and I fear that there is
not an incident in the whole which has any just
chance of melting down my fair sensitives into
that delicious trickle of pearly tears, so gratifying
to the novel writers, or even into one soft sigh of
sympathetic feeling, so naturally excited by exploits in aerial castles, or the embroidered scenery
of fancy and imagination.

Of the egotistical tone of these volumes I am
also most gravely accused.   The best reply I can
make, (and it seems rather a decisive one,) is,
that it would be a task somewhat difficult for the
wisest author that ever put pen to paper, to
separate egotism from autobiography ; indeed, I
believe it has never yet been practically attempted.   Were I to leave myself out of three
volumes of my own *personal* anecdotes, I rather
think I should be consigned to Miss Edgeworth for
the destiny of increasing her volume of Irish
Blunderers.   I fancy also that with most ladies
and gentlemen in these civilized parts of this
terrestrial globe, the *amour propre (alias egotism)*
holds a very considerable rank amongst their

intellectual gallantries; and, as in *garçon* Cupid's amours, it would be no easy matter for either sex to enforce profound silence on the matter of their adoration; and I apprehend the singular number will hardly be turned out of service in the English grammar to gratify my commentators by making me write nonsense.

These observations are addressed to my good-humoured and playful critics; but there is another class of a very different description. I have been honoured by the animadversions of as many of these sharp-set gentry as any uncelebrated author could possibly expect, or indeed any reasonable writer could possibly wish for; and, though the comparison may be considered as out of course, I shall nevertheless add it to the rest of my *errata,* and compare my orchestra of cavillers to the performers in a Dutch concert, where every musician plays his own tune, and no two of their airs or instruments are in harmony.

Literary works may be fairly termed literary chopping-blocks; like the human species, they never fail to have plenty of snarlers to cut up the reputation of the author, and probably the very best parts of his production. However, it is consolatory to perceive that many of those ingenious gentry who have done me that honour may with convenience and economy pluck their *own wings* to make their pens of; and I am satisfied that if the Roman gander who saved the Capitol were permitted to return to earth, and visit the metropolis of England, he would feel infinite gratification at finding that so many of his family have been raised to the rank of critics, and are now flourishing amongst the human species.

By some of my most inveterate cavillers I have been accused of personality. Never was an imputation worse founded. I feel incapable of leaning on any fair or worthy person. But it is impossible for any biographical writer to avoid topics of general allusion, which the equivocal good-nature of *intimate friends* seldom fails to find out an appropriate application for. Should the proprietors of shallow egotism or arrogant folly, however, (and such things *are*,) please to fit caps on their own heads, and look at general allusion through a microscope, I do not feel myself bound either to undeceive or confirm their applications —the *qui capit ille facit* is their own act, not my aphorism.

In truth, the multiplicity of inaccuracies, fibs, bounces, and impossibilities imputed to me are

of so many families and ranks, that I scarcely
know how to arrange their table of precedence;
but as all manner of things connected with theology, from the days of Jupiter Ammon to Pope
Joan, and thence to our own episcopacy, take
place of temporal concerns, so I rather think I
should adopt the same course of procedure; and
therefore, as the doctrine of spirits and ghosts is
incontestably connected with theological dogmas,
so I conceive it most decorous to begin with that
very supernatural subject.

The article as to Lord Rossmore's Bansheen,
(in the first volume,) has been the favourite subject of general animadversion, incredulity, and
inveterate impeachment of my orthodoxy, common sense, religion, and morality. Yet, strange to
say, I absolutely persist unequivocally as to the
matters therein recited, and shall do so to the day
of my death, after which event I shall be able to
ascertain individually the matter of fact to a
downright certainty, though I fear I shall be
enjoined to absolute secrecy.

To-give new food to my cavillers, I now re-
assert what has been already read with expressed surprise at my heterodoxy—namely, that
no man or woman, old or young, *professing* Chris-

tianity, and yet denying the possible appearance
of apparitions in the world, can be a genuine, or
indeed any Christian at all; nay, not even an
unadulterated Deist, and most certainly not a
member of the Jewish persuasion, as this can be
his only argument. Nor shall I omit in my following challenge every member of the 104 sects
that have, like suckers, sprouted out of and
weakened the established Church of England,
(which, I think, might, after reforming the clergy,
have served people very well, without the assistance of any hair-splitters, unless they were
unconscionable epicures in theology); to all such
folks I here throw down my glove—and by these
presents, I invite any preacher, teacher, priest,
bishop, deacon, fat dignitary, or lank curate, who
disclaims my said doctrine, to reply to it if he
can—otherwise I shall crow over him, reasonably considering that " silence gives consent,"
and set down my doctrines as admitted fully and
unanimously by the *nil dicits* of all the Christian
clericals and pious labourers in the holy vine-
yards, and all the singers at the Meeting Houses
in the British Empire.

Consistently with my rank as a goblin *cha-
perone*, I should consider myself guilty of great

impoliteness did I not notice one or two of the
lectures I have received from lay disputants since
the two first volumes have been published, but
which other occupations have heretofore prevented me from duly noticing.

The most formidable, because the most rational,
of my avowed contraventionists, has attacked me
on a point which I admit to be the most assail-
able of my anecdotes, and to constitute the most
plausible ground he could pitch his scepticism
on : I allude to his dogma as to my Rossmore
Bansheen, in which he asserts that all supernaturals are now-a-days as much out of fashion and as
scarce as miracles. I admit that miracles, *eo nomine,*
have diminished very considerably (without any
good reason that I know of) for some centuries past,
and consequently, that my assertion of modern
supernaturals has, in the opinion of many wise
persons, lost the advantage of that scriptural confir-
mation, which it certainly would have had eighteen
hundred years ago. But that is only begging the
question without the candour of admitting that
if miracles *ever* existed, the same Omnipotence
which created may *revive* them, particularly as all
these matters are decided in a world that not a
priest in Europe has any communication with.

Prejudices—whether natural or transplanted—
have long roots : they shoot deep and strong,
and are most difficult to eradicate. Out of a hundred pertinacious argumentators, I verily believe
there is seldom even one of the debaters, who at
the conclusion admits a single *scintilla* of diminution in his original hypothesis. So prone is
man to prejudice, that I have known clerical
rhetoricians argue, on points of their own trade,
very *nearly* that black was white ; and I really
believe all the Saints in the calendar could not
make any impression on their sentiments ; therefore, yielding all argument deducible either from
the Witch of Endor, or the Weird Sisters, &c., I
found my tenet upon proven facts and causes, of
which the (assailed) anecdote of Lord Rossmore
is only as a vanguard.

This plausible and ingenious antagonist, to whom
I allude, is a gentleman universally considered to
be in his sound senses, and of high respectability;
and one who, I believe, both individually and professionally, generally *looks* before he *leaps :* this
gentleman has so billeted his scepticism on his
brain, that it lives at free quarters, and shuts its
door against all reasoning; and I much fear his
incredulity will retain its post, till he becomes a

goblin himself, and learns the fallacy of his prejudices by actual demonstration.

Some other intolerant correspondents, of much personal consideration, are fully entitled to my proper observation ; and I regret that, a preface being inappropriate to any controversy in detail, I am obliged to postpone paying my *devoirs* to them. But this above-named gentleman having favoured me with a letter of many pages, expressing his unqualified disbelief of Lord Rossmore's Bansheen and all ghosts in general, and his extreme *surprise* that I could venture to support so exploded a doctrine, I should act unhandsomely if I did not acknowledge the receipt of it, and assure him that I shall take the earliest opportunity I can of putting in my rejoinder.

I admit that the reasoning of this respectable intolerant (Mr. T—— of Gray's Inn) appeared so moral, rational, religious, pious, and plausible, that even an idiot, or a soft country gentleman with a blank mind, might, without any further imputation against his understanding, be actually convinced by it. However, as I do not boast of these latter qualities, I retain my own doctrine inflexibly,—and so does Mr. T—— ; and lamentable it is to say, that there is not the most remote probability of either of us yielding his hypothesis, or any human possibility of finding any person in the whole world who could decide as an arbitrator. Mr. T—— conceives that I cannot be a Christian if I believe in supernaturals, and I am as steadily convinced that he cannot be a true Christian if he does not. The majority of society, who seldom take the trouble of looking deeper than the surface in matters of theology, except when they are text-puzzled on Sundays, are mostly on his side; profound philosophers, theoretical moralists, and all delicate ladies, are on mine. However, there being no mathematical demonstration on either, well authenticated supernaturals are the sole mode of deciding the question in this part of the firmament. On this enigmatical subject my good friends the clergy are rather awkwardly circumstanced. They may be very excellent casuists, so far as their knowledge *extends;* yet, being only simple mortals themselves, they can know no more about the matter than the most ignorant of their parishioners. Though my Lords Spiritual, the Bishops of England, are by far the most temporal, sleek, and comfortable covey of prelates on the surface of this globe—whatever they may do in their poli-

tical capacities, it would be profane to suppose
they could have private audiences either in the
upper or lower department of the other world,
until their *post obitums* fall in, and give them
the *entrée*. The fattest prelate of the land, therefore, can know no more of supernaturals than
the hungriest curate of his diocese ; the happy
translation, however, must take place, (and nobody
can tell how soon,) and no doubt its approach
must be hailed by these parties with great pleasure, as the only tranquil catastrophe they can be
absolutely certain of during this ticklish epoch.

I have already mentioned that my reasoning on
this subject in detail appears in the first volume
of this work ; where, though I profess no enthusiastic adoration of Dr. Johnson's morality, I
certainly am proud to have the advantage of his
coincidence on the subject of supernaturals. I
therefore refer my respectable antagonist, Mr.
T——, (whom, by-the-by, I never had the honour
of speaking to or seeing,) to that volume.

I have also received, amongst many other favours upon the same subject, a letter under the
signature of R. H., Brompton ; but, though on
thick gilt paper, of a very different complexion,
and in very different language from that of my

last-named correspondent.   Mr. R. H. accuses me
of publishing *absolute falsehoods,* and putting *dangerous* doctrines into the heads of *silly people,*
which he illustrates by the example of his *own
wife and daughter,* who, " naturally nervous," ever
since reading my argument in favour of ghosts,
&c., fall into " twitters" if they hear any noise
in the house after nightfall, which they cannot
instantly account for.   His life is a torment to him !
Even a kitten, which was locked up accidentally
in a cupboard, and began to rattle the tea-things
after the candles were put out, threw Mrs. H.
into strong hysterics, and nearly cost Miss H.
her reason, besides the expense of drugs and
attendance.   This Mr. H., of Brompton, describes
himself " a *rational* gentleman," (*credat Judæus
Apelles !*) I suppose in contradistinction to me; but,
whether gentle or simple, he has in his commentary
on my anecdote been so far impartial, that he has
shown no greater respect for his own composition
than he has for mine.   To do him justice, he has
not attempted reasoning : therein he was perfectly
right ; reason does not seem to be his forte, or in
unison with either his temper or intellect, and the
retort courteous with which he has favoured me is
vastly better adapted to both the manners and

capacity of that gentlemanly personage. To increase his troubles, I have referred him to a
decided ghost story ycleped the " Tapestry
Chamber," from the celebrated pen of Sir Walter
Scott, directing my letter " dead office, Brompton." That story was vouched by Miss Seward,
the most learned and religious of the *bas-bleus*.
It has been swallowed by the public at large with
a greedy avidity, as a genuine undoubted apparition ; nor has a single reviewer, commentator,
periodical, or other species of critic, ever ventured
to call it a *bounce*, or to express the slightest
doubt of its absolute authenticity. Whilst Sir
Jonah Barrington's " Bansheen of Lord Rossmore," vouched by three living persons, has
experienced all manner of ugly epithets, the
" Tapestry Chamber," so vouched, remains in full
blow, with scarcely an unbeliever. It is observable also that Sir Walter's apparition, coming a
year after my " Bansheen," and the public stric-
tures thereupon, proves and exemplifies his coincidence in my belief; and (Miss Seward having
been for some time a ghost herself) I trust Sir
Walter, not being defunct, will, on his return from
his travels, do me the justice of confirming my
tenet by his own, and the authority of Miss

Seward. In the mean time, as for Mr. H. R. of Brompton, whom I *strongly* suspect to be an M.P. and a saint—*requiescat in pace!* unless I can trace the writing, and, if I can, he may be assured the public shall have a garnished edition of it.

The Irish mower cutting his *own* head off has also afforded a multiplicity of amusing comments, both from my friends and the periodicals; the former call it *ingenious*, the latter a *bounce*. However, I refer my sceptics to the second edition of the former portion of these Sketches, where that incident is repeated and enlarged upon. That anecdote, not being in any degree *supernatural*, is susceptible of testimony; and it is rather fortunate for me that the very same respectable gentleman, Mr. T., who is so inflexible an anti-Bansheen, was also an avowed disbeliever of my self-decapitation anecdote, until his friend, Lord Mountnorris, *vouched* to him decidedly the *truth* of Dennis's cutting his own *head* off, though his lordship would not give him the same corroboration as to the *ear* of his comrade: however, as to that, *exceptio probat regulam*, and I am contented.

So numerous have been the comments I have read in print, and received in MS., as to different articles of those Sketches, that a rejoinder to one half of them would be more than food for a tolerable quarto, and of course my notices must be very limited.

The letter which I received, marked *private*, by post from London, under the signature Z. Y., though long in my possession, I had no clue to answer, or any *à-propos* opportunity of noticing; and I regret that the limits of a Preface do not even now admit me to go much further than to advert to the subject of it. That subject, could I here dilate on it, would afford myself a very agreeable field for general as well as individual comment; and indeed, not being devoid of a popular interest, it deserves a distinct, and not limited consideration : such (I intend) it shall receive hereafter on a different occasion. At present I only wish the persons therein alluded to, and particularly the one who, Z. Y. insinuates, " has felt *no pleasure* at my observations," to be assured that I should consider myself much to blame, had I intended to draw any *invidious comparisons*, or lean either by irony, ridicule, or satire, on either of two persons so justly and highly estimated by the public, for whom I feel the sentiments of private friendship, and whom I have known before they could either know or forget themselves.

One observation, however, I may venture, and (though singular) I have very generally found it a true one, namely, that the best writers are the most thin-skinned, and become jealous of comment, *pari passu* with the march of their celebrity. Even when their literary reputation has been popularly established beyond the power of "reviewing" injury, they feel more ticklish at criticism than scribblers in the fifth degree of comparison; and, as if they were afflicted with the disease called "noli me tangere," they consider even the approach of a quill as injurious to their tranquillity. Such species of impression on either a party or a partizan has no doubt procured me the honour of the letter I have alluded to;—it is palpably the work of no ordinary penman. I regret that I must persist in my opinion both as to the lady and gentleman, and cannot relinquish my consistency as to the principle of distinction between genius and talent, though with modification, and perhaps according to *my* more minute *view* of these modern rarities.

I never found these gifts of intellect completely amalgamated in any one modern writer either in prose or poetry. Heavens and earth—flights of fancy, and matters of fact, *savans* and rainbows, angels, and ladies of quality, &c. &c. &c. afford very different touchstones whereby to assay the extent of human intellect.

The personages that Z. Y. has alluded to may rest assured that not a friend of theirs, either old or new, has a greater pride in their compatriot-ship than the composer of this terrestrial baga-telle ; the one works in prose, and dresses in poetry, the other makes Irish petticoats with fo-reign flounces to them. Both are good artists—yet I confess myself so very worldly and unrefined a being that I should, under the circumstances of Ireland, prefer one sound, unexaggerated, unagi-tating true matter-of-*fact* essay on the real con-dition of my countrymen. The most lovely subjects of madrigal and sonnet, after a curt exhibition of their charms, wax old and ugly, and in some time enjoy little more than a florid epitaph. Time with his extinguisher soon puts out all flames of an amatory description, and reduces both the poet and his muse—the first (if he lives) to a state of dotage, the other to the enjoyment of some "newer lover." But the love of a country blooms for ever : it defies the power of time and the lapse of ages ; and I should like to see the produce of some proud and emulative talent or genius, to decide which is best adapted to descant upon that subject. Two attempts on that matter I have seen ; the one has lost reputation by danger—diving too deep ; the other gained none by being too superficial. Of all themes, *absenteeism*, if handled strongly, would give great credit, if its writer would take a fair, clear, and comprehensive view of that existing cause of national misfortune.

CONTENTS

OF

THE THIRD VOLUME.

PERPLEXITIES OF A BARONET.

The Author apologises for ending, instead of commencing, his former volumes, with an inquiry into his pedigree—How to improve a family name—The cognomen of Alderman Sir W. Stammer—Vowel *versus* Consonant—The lady of " masculine understanding"—The Alderman's conditions on altering his surname — Unsuspected presidency of *King James* at the Dublin municipal meetings—Ulster king-at-arms—George the Fourth's visit to Dublin—Various heraldic bearings .

DANGERS OF REFLECTION.

Personal description of Counsellor Conaghty — Singular contrast of physical roughness and mental suavity—A legal costume—The Counsellor's marriage—The bride described— Her plan for inducing her husband to sacrifice to the Graces —The fatal mirror—The Counsellor views himself in a new light — His consternation and false persuasion — The devil unjustly accused—Conaghty's illness and death . .

THE FARRIER AND WHIPPER-IN.

THE RIVAL PRACTITIONERS.

TRANSFUSION OF BLOOD.

SWEARING NO VICE.

A BARRISTER BESIEGED.

GEORGE ROBERT FITZGERALD.

RECRUITING AT CASTLEBAR.

A NIGHT JOURNEY.

MARTIAL LAW.

BULLETIN EXTRAORDINARY.

BREAKFASTS AT BALLINROBE.

NEW MODE OF SERVING A PROCESS.

DONNYBROOK FAIR.

THE WALKING GALLOWS.

CONVERSION AND INVERSION.

REBEL PORTRAITS.

REMINISCENCES OF WIT.

COUNSELLOR LYSIGHT.

FATALITIES OF MARRIAGE.

A WEDDING IN OLDEN DAYS.

THE LAST OF THE GERALDINES.

HANGING AN ATTORNEY BY ACCIDENT.

FLOGGING THE WINE-COOPERS.

THE ENNISCORTHY BOAR.

PERSONAL SKETCHES.

PERPLEXITIES OF A BARONET.

The Author apologises for ending, instead of commencing, his
   former volumes, with an inquiry into his pedigree—How to
   improve a family name—The cognomen of Alderman Sir W.
   Stammer—Vowel *versus* Consonant—The lady of " masculine
   understanding "—The Alderman's conditions on altering his
   surname—Unsuspected presidency of *King James* at the
   Dublin municipal meetings—Ulster king-at-arms—George
   the Fourth's visit to Dublin—Various heraldic bearings.

THE concluding the second volume of my Biographical Sketches with the recital of a laborious
search after my progenitors, doubtless savours
somewhat of our national perversions. But those
who know the way in which things are done in
Ireland, will only call it a " doughan dourish,"
or " parting drop "—which was usually admi-

nistered when a man was not very sure which end of him was uppermost.

The English, in general, though not very exquisite philologists, and denominated " Bulls " in every known part of the world, have yet a great aversion to be considered " *blunderers ;*" an *honour* which their own misprisions of speech fall short of, owing to the absence of point in their humour (as they call it).

When an English ·dramatist wants a *good blunder*, he must send to Ireland for it. A few *English.* blunders would damn the best play ; and I have known some pieces actually saved by a profusion of Irish ones. As to my misplacing my pedigree, I can only say, that though an English writer, speaking of his origin, would say he was born and bred at London, &c. &c.—an Irishman always places his acquirements before his birth, and says he was bred and born at Drogheda, &c. My mistake is not quite so bad as this; and I shall endeavour to recompense my readers for having made it, by transporting them to the city of Dublin, where, so long as a thing has *fun in it,* we set all cold-blooded critico-cynicals at defiance, and where we never have a lack of families and of good pedigrees—at least for home consumption.

· The sketch which I thus introduce has certainly nothing whatever in it connected with myself. However, it is so far in point, that it proves how very differently gentlemen may furbish up

families ;—one by traversing foreign parts to discover the old cavaliers, arms, and quarterings of
his race ;—another by garnishing a new coach
with new quarters, shields, and bearings, such as
no family, ancient or modern, had ever seen or
heard of till they appeared emblazoning the pan-
nels of an alderman's landau.

In the year of our Lord 1809, after his late Majesty King George the Third had expended forty-
nine years of his life in ruling the state, it pleased
his royal fancy to order a universal jubilee, and to
elevate his Lord Mayors into Imperial Baronets.
At this propitious era, William Stammer, Esquire,
Alderman of Dublin, and likewise of Skinners'
Alley, wine-merchant, do. consumer, dealer and
chapman, freemason, orangeman, and friendly
brother, happened, by Divine Providence and
the good-will of the Common Council, to be seated
on the civic throne as " the Right Honourable the
Lord Mayor of the King's good city of Dublin."
He ruled with convivial sway the ancient, loyal,
joyous, moist, and vociferous municipal corps of
the said celebrated city, and its twenty-four fe-
derated corporations :—consequently he was, in
point of dignity, the second *Lord Mayor* in all
Christendom, though unfortunately born a few centuries too late to be one of its seven *champions*.
However, being thus enthroned at that happy
festival time, he became greater than any of
these, and found himself, suddenly, as if by ma-

gic, (though it was only by patent,) metamorphosed into *Sir* William Stammer, Baronet of the United Kingdoms of England, Scotland, and Ireland.

Sir William Stammer, Bart., being (as he himself often informed me, and which I believe to be true,) an excellent, good-hearted kind of person, and having by nature an even, smooth-trotting temper, with plenty of peace and quietness in it, bore his rank with laudable moderation : but as he was the first genuine corporator the Union had honoured by this *imperial* dignity, he felt a sort of loyal fervor, which urged him to make some particular acknowledgment to his gracious Majesty for so unprecedented a mark of distinction. But in what way a sober British king should be complimented by an Irish wine-merchant was a matter which required much ingenuity and profound consideration. At length, it was suggested and strongly urged by several of his civic friends, (especially those of the feminine gende ,) that his Lordship had it actually within his power to pay as loyal and handsome a compliment as ever was paid to any king of England by an Irish gentleman with a twang to his surname ; *videlicet*, by sacrificing the old Irish pronunciation thereof, ameliorating the sound, and changing it in such sort, that it might be adapted to the court language, and uttered without any difficulty or grimace by the prettiest mouths of the highest classes of British society ; it was, in fact, strenuously argued that, instead of the old hacknied family name commonly pronounced Stam-mer, the word *Steem-er* (being better vowelled and Anglicised) would sound far more genteel and modern, and ring more gratefully in the ear of royalty. It was also urged, how Mrs. Clarke's friend, the Rev. Dr. O'Meara, unfortunately lost the honour of preaching before royalty by his pertinacity in retaining the abominable *O*, and that had he dropped that hideous prefixture, and been announced plainly as the Rev. Doctor Meera, his doctrines might probably have atoned for his Milesianality, and a stall in some cathedral, or at least a rural deanery, might have rewarded his powers of declamation.

"Having begun so well, who knows what famous end you may arrive at, Sir William?" said Sir Jemmy Riddle, the then high sheriff (a very good man too), who was be-knighted on the same occasion. "When we all go to St. James's," continued Sir Jemmy, " to thank our Sovereign and kiss his hand in *his own metrolopus*, sure the name of our Lord Mayor, Sir W. Steemer, will sound every taste as harmonious if not *harmoniouser*, than that of the great Sir Claudius Hunter, or our own Claudius Beresford, or any Claudius in Europe!—and sure, changing *am* for *ee*, to please his Majesty, is neither a sin nor a shame in any family, were they as old as *Mathuslin :*—besides, old White, the schoolmaster, the greatest scholar,

by odds, that ever was in Dublin, told me that
one vowel was worth two consonants any day in
the year ; and that the alteration would make a
great difference in the sweetness of the odes he
was writing on your promotion."

Sir William, however, being fond of the old
proper name which had stuck to him through
thick and thin, in all weathers, and which he
and his blood relations had been so long accustomed to spell, did not at all relish the proposed
innovation. Besides, he considered that any thing
like the assumption of a new name might bring
him too much on a level with some *modern* corporators, who not having any particular cognomen of
their own at the time of their nativity, or at least
not being able to discover it, but being well
christened for fear of accidents, very judiciously
took only provisional denominations for their ap-
prenticeship indentures, and postponed the adop-
tion of any immutable surname until they had considered what might probably be most attractive to
customers in their several trades.

The grand measure was nevertheless so strongly
pressed—the ladies so coaxed the alderman to
take the *pretty* name, and they were so well sup-
ported by Sir Charles Vernon, then master of the
ceremonies, (and of course the best judge in Ireland of what was good for Sir William at the Castle of Dublin,) that his resolution gradually softened, wavered, and gave way. He became con-

vinced against·his will, and at last, with a deep
sigh and a couple of imprecations, ungratefully
yielded up his old, broad, national *Stammer*, to
adopt an Anglicised mincemeat version thereof;
and in a few nights, Sir William *Steemer's* landau
was announced as stopping the way at the breaking up of the Duchess of Richmond's drawing-
room.

'Tis true, some very cogent and plausible reasons were suggested to Sir William, pending the
negotiation, by a lady of excellent judgment, and
what was termed in Dublin " masculine understanding." This lady had great weight with his
lordship. " You know, my Lord Mayor," said
she, sententiously, " you are now nine or ten
pegs (at the lowest computation) higher than you
were as a common alderman, and a pronunciation
that might sound quite in unison with ' sheriff's
peer,' would be mere discord in the politer mouths
of your new equals."

" Ah ! what would Jekey Poole say to all this,
if he were alive?" *thought* Sir William, but was
silent.

" Consider, also,"—pursued the lady,—" consider
that Stammer is a very common kind of word; nay,
it is a mere verb of Dutch extraction (as that great
man Doctor Johnson says), which signifies stutter-
ing ; and to articulate which, there is a graceless
double chopping of the under jaw—as if a person

was taking a bite out of something :—try now, try, Stammer—Stammer!"

"Egad, its—its very true," said Sir William : "I—I never remarked that before."

"But," resumed the lady with the masculine understanding, "the word Steemer, on the contrary, has a soft, bland, liquid sound, perfectly adapted to genteel table-talk. To pronounce Steemer, you will perceive, Sir William, there is a slight tendency to a lisp : the tip of the tongue presses gently against the upper gums, and a nice extension of the lips approaching toward a smile, gives an agreeable sensation, as well as a polite complacency of countenance to the addresser.— Now, try!"

Sir William lisped and capitulated—on express condition; first, that the old County Clare tone of Stammer, in its natural length and breadth, should be preserved when the name was used by or to the Corporation of Dublin."

"Granted," said the lady with the masculine understanding.

"Secondly, amongst the aldermen of Skinners' Alley."

"Granted."

"Thirdly, in the Court of Conscience."

"Granted."

"Fourthly, in my own counting-house."

"Granted—according to the rank of the visitor."

" Fifthly, as to all my *country* acquaintance."

" Granted, with the exception of such as hold any offices, or get into good company."

The articles were arranged, and the treaty took effect that very evening.

Sir William no doubt acquired one distinction hereby, which he never foresaw. Several other aldermen of Dublin city have been since converted into baronets of the United Kingdom, but not one of them has been able to alter a single syllable in his name, or to make it sound even a semitone more *genteel* than when it belonged to a common-place alderman. There was no lack of jesting, however, on those occasions. A city punster, I think it was a gentleman called, by the Common Council, Gobbio, waggishly said, " That the Corporation of Dublin must be a set of incorrigible Tories, inasmuch as they never have a feast without *King-James** being placed at the head of their table."

It is said that this joke was first cracked at the Castle of Dublin by a gentleman of the long robe,

* Two Dublin aldermen lately made baronets; one by his Majesty on his landing in Ireland (Alderman King); and the other by the Marquess of Wellesley on *his* debarkation (Alderman James), being the first public functionary he met. The Marquess would fain have *knighted* him; but being taken by surprise, he conferred the same honour which Aldermen Stammer and King had previously received.

There are now four baronets amongst that hard-going corporation.

and that Mr. Gobbio gave one of the footmen
(who attended and *took notes*) half a guinea for it.
Though a digression, I cannot avoid observing that
I hear, from good authority, there are yet some
few wits surviving in Dublin ; and it is whispered
that the butlers and footmen in genteel families
(*vails* having been mostly abolished since the
Union) pick up, by way of substitute, much ready
money by taking notes of the " *good things* " they
hear said by the lawyers at their masters' dinner
parties, and selling them to aldermen, candidates
for the sheriffry, and city humourists, wherewith
to embellish their conversation and occasionally
their speeches.   Puns are said to sell the best,
they being more handy to a corporator, who has
no great vocabulary of his own : puns are of easy
comprehension ; one word brings on another, and
answers for two meanings, like killing two birds
with one stone, and they seem much more natural
to the memory of a common councilman than wit
or any thing classical—which Alderman Jekey
Poole used to swear was only the d—'d *garbage*
(gibberish) of schoolmasters.

Had the Jubilee concern ended here, all would
have been smooth and square:—but as events in
families seldom come alone, Providence had de-
creed a still more severe trial for Sir William
Steemer—because one of a more important character, and requiring a more prompt as well as expensive decision.

Soon after the luxurious celebration of the Jubilee throughout the three united kingdoms (except among such of the Irish as happened to have nothing in their houses to eat or drink, let their loyalty be ever so greedy), I chanced to call at the Mansion House on official business ; and Sir William, always hospitable and good-natured, insisted on my staying to taste (in a family way) some "*glorious turtle*" he had just got over from the London Tavern, and a bottle of what he called " old Lafitte with the red nightcap," which, he said, he had been long preserving wherewith to *suckle* his Excellency the Duke of Richmond.

I accepted his invitation : we had most excellent cheer, and were busily employed in praising the vintage of 1790, when a sealed packet, like a government dispatch, was brought in by the baronet's old porter. We all thought it was something of consequence, when Sir William, impatiently breaking the seal, out started a very beautiful painting on parchment or vellum, gilded and garnished with ultramarine, carmine, lapis caliminaris, and all the most costly colours.

" Heyday !" said Sir William, staring : " what the deuce have we here ? Hollo! Christopher— Kit—I say Kit—who—who—or where the devil did this come from ?"

" By my sowl, my lord," replied Christopher, " I dunnough who that same man was that fetched it ; but he was neat an' clean, and had good apparel on his body, though it was not a livery like mine, my lord."

" Did—did—he say nothing, Kit?" said Sir William, surprised.

" Oh yes, plenty my lord ; he desired me on my peril to give the thing safe and sound to your lordship's own self.   He swore, like any trooper, that it was as good as a ten thousand pound bank of Ireland note in your pocket any how.   So I curdled up at that word, my lord ; I towld him plain and plump he need not talk about peril to me ; that I was nothing else but an honest sar-vant ; and if the said thing was worth *fifty* pounds in *ready money*, it would be as safe as a diamond stone with me, my lord."

" And was that all, Christopher?" said Sir Wil-liam.

" Oh no, my lord," replied Kit, " the man grinned at me all as one as a monkey ; and said that, maybe, I'd be a master myself one of these days. ' By my sowl, maybe so, Sir,' says I, ' many a worse man arrived at being an attorney since I came into service ;' and at the word, my lord, the said man held his hand quite natural, as if he'd fain get something into it for his trouble ; but the devil a cross I had in my fob, my lord, so I turned my fob inside out to show I was no liar, and he bowed very civilly and went out of the street-door, laughing that the whole street could hear him ; though I could swear by all the books in your lordship's office, that he had nothing to laugh at : and that's all I had act or part in it, my lord."

Sir William now seemed a little puzzled, desired Christopher to be gone, and throwing the painting on the table, said, " I didn't want any arms or crests. I had very good ones of my own, and I don't understand this matter at all. My family had plenty of arms and crests since King William came over the water."

" So have mine—a very nice lion rampant of their own, my lord," said her ladyship, as excellent a woman as could be : " I'm of the Rawins's," continued she, " and they have put me into your arms, Sir William :—look !"

" Oh that is all as it should be, my dear," said his lordship, who was a very tender husband.. But regarding it more closely, her ladyship's colour, as she looked over his shoulder, mantled a few shades higher than its natural roseate hue, and she seemed obviously discontented.

" I tell you, Sir William," said she, " it is a malicious insult ; and if you were out of the mayoralty, or my boy, Lovelace Steemer, had arrived at full maturity, I have no doubt the person who sent this would be made a proper example of. I hope you feel it, Sir William."

" Feel !—feel what, my love ?" said Sir William, calmly, he being not only a courteous, but a most peaceful citizen. " Don't be precipitate, my darling !—let us see—let us see."

" See!" said her ladyship, still more hurt, " ay,
see with your own eyes!" pointing to the *insult:*
" the fellow that painted that (whoever he is) has
placed a pair of enormous horns just over your
head, Sir William!—a gross insult, Sir William—
to me, Sir William—indeed to both of us."

I was much amused, and could not help observing " that the horns were certainly enormous
horns, to be sure; but as the joke must be intended
against Sir William himself—not her ladyship—I
hope—" said I.

" No, no, Sir Jonah," said the lady interrupt-
ing me.

" I see now," said Sir William, looking at the
bottom, " this comes from Ulster."

" Read on, Sir William," said I, " read on."

" Ay, Ulster king-at-arms: and who the deuce
is *Ulster king-at-arms?*"

" I suppose," said I, " some blood relation to
the Escheator of Munster, and—"

" And who—who the d—l is the *Escheator of
Munster?*" said Sir William (who had never vaca-
ted a seat in the Irish Parliament).

" He is of the same family as the Chiltern hundreds," quoth I.

" Chiltern hundreds! Chiltern hundreds! By
Jove, they must be an odd family altogether,"
said the Lord Mayor, still more puzzled, his lady
sitting quite silent, being now altogether out of
her depth,—till a small letter, to that moment over-

looked, was taken up and read by the Lord Mayor, and was found to be connected with a bill furnished, and wanting nothing but a receipt in full to make it perfect. The countenance of Sir William now became less placid. It proved to be a very proper and fair intimation from his Majesty's herald-at-arms, to the effect that, as the baronetcy originated with the Jubilee, and was granted in honour of King George the Third having ruled half a century, an amplification of the new baronet's heraldry by an additional horn, motto, ribbon, &c., was only a just tribute to his Majesty's longevity! and, in truth, so properly and professionally was the case stated, that Ulster's clear opinion may be inferred that every family in the empire might, in honour and loyalty, take a pair of horns, motto, and ribbon, as well as Sir William, if they thought proper so to do, and on the same terms.

How the matter was finally arranged, I know not; but the arms came out well emblazoned and duly surmounted by a more moderate and comely pair of horns; and Sir William, in regular season, retired from office with due *éclat*, and in all points vastly bettered by his year of government. Though he retired, like Cincinnatus—but not to the plough—Sir William reassumed his less arduous duties of committing rogues to Newgate—long corks to Chateau Margaux—light loaves to the four Marshalsea Courts—and pronouncing thir-

teen-penny decrees in the Court of Conscience :*
every one of which occupations he performed cor-
rectly and zealously, to the entire satisfaction of
the nobility, clergy, gentry, and public at large,
in the metropolis of Ireland.

An incident appertaining to the same body, but

* Every lord mayor of Dublin becomes judge of a " Court
of Conscience " for twelve months after the expiration of his
mayoralty ; each decree costing a shilling ; many of the causes
are of the most comical description ; but never would there have
arisen so great a judge as Sancho Panza of Barataria, from
presiding in our Court of Conscience.

I cannot omit stating, that Sir William, when lord mayor,
gave the most numerous, brilliant, and complete masquerade
ever seen in Dublin, or, I believe, any where else. There were
fourteen or fifteen hundred persons, and I am sure not more
than one hundred dominoes ; every body went in character, and
every person tried to keep up the character he adopted. Ireland, of all places in the world, is, perhaps, best adapted to a
masquerade, as every Irishman is highly amused when he can
get an opportunity of assuming, by way of freak, any new character.

It was the custom for the mob, on those occasions, to stop
every carriage, and demand of each person, " What's your
character ?" I was dreadfully tired of them in the street on
the night in question ; but fairly put into good-humour by the
jeu d'esprit of a mob-man, who opened the carriage-door.
After I had satisfied him as to character, he desired to know,
where I was going? " Shut the door," said I. " Ah, but
where are you going ?" I was vexed. " I'm going to the
Devil," said I. " Ough, then, *God* send you safe !" replied the
blackguard.

with a termination by no means similar, occurred a few years afterward, which, among other matters, contributes to show what different sort of things the Irish at different times rejoice in. In 1809, they rejoiced in full jubilee on the memorable event of his Majesty King George the Third having entered the fiftieth year of his reign, without ever paying one visit to, or taking the least notice of, his loyal Corporation of Dublin : and after he was dead (*de facto*, for the King never dies *de jure*), they celebrated another jubilee on account of his Majesty George the Fourth honouring them with a visit *the very earliest opportunity.* This was the first time any king of England had come to Ireland, except to cut the throats of its inhabitants ; and his present Majesty having most graciously crossed over to sow peace and tranquillity among them, if possible, and to do them any and every kindness which they would *submit to,* it was not wonderful each man in Ireland hailed the event as forming a most auspicious commencement of his Majesty's reign, not only over his subjects at large, but, in particular, over that glorious, pious, immortal, and uproarious body, the Corporation of Dublin city. Events have proved how ungratefully his Majesty's beneficent intentions have been requited.

His Majesty having arrived at the hill of Howth, to the universal joy of the Irish people, was received with unexampled cordiality, and in due form, by the Right Honourable the Lord Mayor, on the very field of battle where O'Brien Borun had formerly acquired undying fame by cutting the Danes into slices (an operation which we have since repeated on them at Copenhagen, though with different instruments). That Right Honourable Lord Mayor was Sir Abraham Bradley King, then one of the best looking aldermen in Europe. On this occasion he obtained, not military honour, but, on the other hand, a more tranquil one than the said King O'Brien Borun ever arrived at;—he was actually *imperialised* as a baronet in very superior style to his brother corporator *Steemer*, on the loyal demi-century occasion.

I have since heard that an effort was made somewhat to transform the armorial bearings of the Bradley King family, also, in commemoration of this auspicious event; and that it was intended to give him, as an addition to his crest, Sir John Skinner's steam packet, out of which his Majesty had landed just previous to bestowing the baronetcy on Sir Abraham. Here the city punsters began again with their vulgar insinuations; and, omitting the word *packet*, gave out that Alderman King wanted to put Alderman *Steemer* as a supporter to his arms, instead of a griffin rampant or unicorn, as customary on these occasions; but this vile play upon words Sir Abraham peremptorily and properly checked with the same constitutional firmness and success wherewith he had previously refused to " tell tales out of school " about the Orangemen to the House of Commons.*

On this occasion, Sir Abraham proudly and virtuously declared that all the heralds in Europe should never *ravish* him as they had done his brother Steemer; and that if any alteration was to be made in his shield by Ulster-at-arms, or any Ulster in Europe, he would permit nothing but an emblematic crown to be introduced therein, in honour and commemoration of his sovereign; and though our national poet, Mr. Thomas Moore, and Sir Abraham, never coalesced upon any point whatsoever (except the consumption of paper), yet on this conciliatory occasion, Sir Abraham declared his willingness to forgive and forget the religion and politics of the poet for eight and forty hours. This was as it should be; and a crown, with a posy or nosegay in its neighbourhood (instead of a cut and thrust) are accordingly embodied in the armorial bearings of Sir Abraham, the cruel idea of a bloody hand being now softened down and qualified by the bouquet which adorns it.

Again the indefatigable corporation wags, who could let nothing pass, began their jocularities : the worthy Baronet's name being *King,* and the shield having a *crown* in it, the Common Council began to hob-nob him as, *Your Majesty,* or the

* This was the first instance I recollect of pertinacity conquering privilege.

Crown Prince, or such like. But Sir Abraham had been an officer in the King's service, and being a spirited fellow to boot, he declared open and personal hostility against all low and evil-minded corporate punsters. These *titles* were therefore relinquished; and the whole affair ended, to the real satisfaction of every staunch Protestant patriot from Bray to Balbiggen, and as far westward as the College of Maynooth, where I understand the rejoicings terminated—for Sir Abraham found the road *too bad* to travel any farther.

Having endeavoured somewhat to divert the reader's criticism on my pedigree blunder, I have, in compliance with the wish of one of the ablest, wisest, and steadiest public personages of Great Britain (whose title heads this volume), reopened my old trunks, and made a further attempt at amusing myself and other folks—and at depicting, by authentic anecdotes, the various and extraordinary habits and propensities of the Irish people, with their gradual changes of national character for the last fifty or sixty years,—which (to my grief I say it) will be the work, not of a *novelist,* but a *contemporary.* I fancy there are very few of those who flourished so long ago, who could procure pen, ink, and paper, either for love or money, where they sojourn at present; and of those who still inhabit the same world with the stationers, some have lost one half of their faculties, at least,

and scarce any among the remainder possess sufficient energy to retrace by description the events
that took place during a long and, perhaps, active
career.   I shall take Time by the forelock ; and,
ere the candle goes out, draw as many Sketches
of my past day as I may have time to record, before I wish the present generation a good morning
—which adieu cannot now be long distant :—*tant
pis !*

DANGERS OF REFLECTION.

Personal description of Counsellor Conaghty—Singular contrast of physical roughness and mental suavity—A legal costume—The Counsellor's marriage—The bride described—
Her plan for inducing her husband to sacrifice to the Graces
—The fatal mirror—The Counsellor views himself in a new
light—His consternation and false persuasion—The devil unjustly accused—Conaghty's illness and death.

THE most extraordinary instance I recollect
of a sudden affection of the mind being fatal
to the body was presented by an old acquaintance of mine, Counsellor Conaghty, a gentleman
of the Irish bar, who pined and died in consequence of an unexpected view of his own person;
but by no means upon the same principle as Nar-
cissus.

Mr. Conaghty was a barrister of about six feet
two inches in length; his breadth was about three
feet across the shoulders; his hands splay, with
arms in full proportion to the rest of his members.
He possessed, indeed, a set of limbs that would

not have disgraced a sucking elephant; and his body appeared slit up two-thirds of its length, as if Nature had originally intended (which is not very improbable) to have made twins of him—but finding his *brains* would not answer for *two*, relinquished her design. His complexion, not a disagreeable fawn-colour, was spotted by two good black eyes, well intrenched in his head, and guarded by a thick *chevaux de frise* of curly eyebrows. His mouth, which did not certainly extend, like a john-dory's, from ear to ear, was yet of sufficient width to disclose between thirty and forty long, strong, whitish tusks, the various heights and distances whereof gave a pleasing variety to that feature. Though his *tall* countenance was terminated by a chin which might, upon a pinch, have had an interview with his stomach, still there was quite enough of him between the chin and waistband to admit space for a waistcoat, without the least difficulty.

Conaghty, in point of disposition, was a quiet, well-tempered, and, I believe, totally irreproachable person. He was not unacquainted with the superficies of law, nor was he without professional business. Nobody, in fact, disliked him, and he disliked nobody. In national idiom, and Emerald brogue, he unquestionably excelled (save one) all his contemporaries. Dialogues sometimes occurred in Court between him and Lord

Avonmore, the Chief Baron, which were truly ludicrous.

The most unfortunate thing, however, about poor Conaghty, was his utter contempt for what fastidious folks call *dress*.—As he scorned both garters and suspenders, his stockings and small-clothes enjoyed the full blessings of liberty. A well-twisted cravat, as if it feared to be mistaken for a cord, kept a most respectful distance from his honest throat—upon which the neighbouring· beard flourished in full crops, to fill up the interstice. His rusty black coat, well trimmed with peeping button-moulds, left him, altogether, one of the most tremendous figures I ever saw, of his own profession.

At length it pleased the Counsellor, or old Nick on his behalf, to look out for a ‹wife; and, as dreams go by contraries, so Conaghty's perverse vision of matrimonial happiness induced him to select a *sposa* very excellent internally, but in her exterior as much the reverse of himself as any two of the same species could be. ·

Madam Conaghty was (and I dare say still is) a neat, pretty, dressy little person : her head reached nearly up to her spouse's hip ; and if he had stood wide, to let her pass, she might' (without much stooping) have walked under him as through a triumphal arch. ·

He was quite delighted with his captivating

fairy, and she equally so with her good-natured giant. Nothing could promise better for twenty or thirty years of honey-moons, when an extraordinary and most unexpected fatality demonstrated the uncertainty of all sublunary enjoyments, and might teach ladies who have lost their beauty the dangers of a looking-glass.

The Counsellor had taken a small house, and desired his dear little Mary to furnish it to her own dear little taste. This, as new-married ladies usually do, she set about with the greatest zeal and assiduity. She had a proper taste for things in general, and was besides extremely anxious to make her giant somewhat smarter; and, as he had seldom in his life had any intercourse with looking-glasses larger than necessary, just to reflect his chin whilst shaving, she determined to place a grand *mirror* in her little drawing-room, extensive enough to exhibit the Counsellor to himself from head to foot—and which, by reflecting his loose, shabby habiliments, and tremendous contour, might induce him to trim himself up.

This plan was extremely promising in the eyes of little Mary; and she had no doubt it would be entirely consonant with her husband's own desire of Mrs. Conaghty's little drawing-room being the nicest in the neighbourhood. She accordingly purchased, in Great George Street, at a very large price, a looking-glass of sufficing dimensions, and it was a far larger one than the Counsellor had ever before noticed.

When this fatal reflector was brought home, it was placed leaning against the wall in the still unfurnished drawing-room,—and the lady, having determined at once to surprise and reform her dear giant, did not tell him of the circumstance. The ill-fated Counsellor, wandering about his new house—as people often do toward the close of the evening—that interregnum between sun, moon, and candlelight, when shadows are deep and figures seem lengthened—suddenly entered the room where the glass was deposited. Unconscious of the presence of the immense reflector, he beheld, in the gloom, a monstrous and frightful Caliban— wild, loose, and shaggy,—standing close and direct before him; and, as he raised his own gigantic arms in a paroxysm of involuntary horror, the goblin exactly followed his example, lifting its tremendous fists, as if with a fixed determination to fell the Counsellor, and extinguish him for ever.

Conaghty's imagination was excited to its utmost pitch. Though the spectre appeared larger than any d—l on authentic record, he had no doubt it was a genuine demon sent express to destroy his happiness and carry him to Belzebub. As his apprehensions augmented, his pores sent out their icy perspiration : he tottered—the fiend too was in motion ! his hair bristled up, as it were like pikes to defend his head. At length his blood recoiled, his eyes grew dim, his pulse ceased, his long limbs quivered—failed ; and down came poor Conaghty with a loud shriek and a tremendous crash. His beloved bride, running up alarmed by the noise, found the Counsellor as inanimate as the boards he lay on. A surgeon was sent for, and phlebotomy was resorted to as for *apoplexy*, which the seizure was pronounced to be. His head was shaved ; and by the time he revived a little, he had three extensive blisters and a cataplasm preparing their stings for him.

It was two days before he recovered sufficiently to tell his Mary of the horrid spectre that had assailed him—for he really thought he had been felled to the ground by a blow from the goblin. Nothing, indeed, could ever persuade him to the contrary, and he grew quite delirious.

His reason returned slowly and scantily ; and when assured it was only a *looking-glass* that was the cause of his terror, the assurance did not alter his belief. He pertinaciously maintained, that this was only a kind story invented to tranquillise him. " Oh, my dearest Mary !" said poor Conaghty, " I'm gone !—my day is come—I'm called away for ever. Oh ! had you seen the frightful figure that struck me down, you could not have survived it one hour ! Yet why should I fear the d—l ? I'm not wicked, Mary ! No, I'm not *very* wicked !".

A thorough Irish servant, an old fellow whom

the Counsellor had brought from Connaught, and
who *of course* was well acquainted with supernatural appearances, and had not himself seen the
fatal mirror,—discovered, as he thought, the real
cause of the goblin's visit, which he communicated to his mistress with great solemnity, as she
afterward related.

" Mistress," said the faithful Dennis Brophy,
:" Mistress, it was all a *mistake*. By all the books
in the master's study, I'd swear it was only a
mistake!—What harm did ever my master do
nobody? and what would bring a d—l overhauling
a Counsellor that did no harm? What say could
he have to my master?"

"Don't teaze me, Dennis," said the unhappy
Mary.; " go along!—go!"

" I'll tell you, mistress," said he; " it was a
d—l sure enough that was in it!"

" Hush! nonsense!" said his mistress.

" By J—s! it *was* the d—l, or one of his gos-
soons," persisted Dennis ; " but he mistook the
house, mistress, and that's the truth of it!"

" What do you mean ?" said *the mistress*.

" Why, I mane that you know Mr. —— lives
on one side of us, and Mr. —— lives at the other
side, and they are both *attornies*, and the people
say they'll both go to *him :* and so the d—l, or his
gossoon, mistook the door, and you see he went off
again when he found it was my master that was
in it, and not an attorney, mistress."

All efforts to convince Conaghty he was mistaken were vain. The illusion could not be removed from his mind; he had received a shock which affected his whole frame; a constipat on of the intestines took place; and in three weeks, the poor fellow manifested the effects of groundless horror in a way which every one regretted.

FORMER STATE OF MEDICINE IN IRELAND.

Remarks on Sir Charles Morgan's account of the Former State
of Medicine in Italy—The author's studies in the Anatomical
Theatre of Dublin University—Dr. Burdet—Former importance of farriers and colloughs—Jug Coyle, and her powers of
soliloquy—Larry Butler, the family farrier, described—Luminous and veritable account of the ancient colloughs—The
- *faculty* of the present day—Hoynhymms and Yahoos—Hydrophobia in Ireland, and its method of cure.

DOCTOR SIR CHARLES MORGAN has given us,
at the conclusion of his lady's excellent work
" Italy," the state of " medicine " in that country.
Our old cookery books, in like manner, after
exquisite receipts for all kinds of dainties, to suit
every appetite, generally finished a luxurious volume with *remedies* for the " bite of a mad dog—for
scald heads—ague—burns—St. Anthony's fire—
St. Vitus's dance—the tooth-ache," &c. &c. Now,
though the Doctor certainly did not take the
cooks by way of precedent, that is no reason why
I should not indulge my whim by citing both ex-

amples, and garnishing this volume with " the
state of medicine in Ireland " fifty years ago.

I do not, however, mean to depreciate the state
of medicine in these days of " new lights " and
novelties, when old drugs and poisons are *nick-
named*, and every recipe is a rebus to an old
apothecary. Each son of Galen now strikes out
his own system; composes his own syllabus; and
finishes his patients according to his own proper
fancy. When a man dies after a consultation
(which is generally the case—the thing being
often decided by *experiment*)—there is no particular necessity for any explanation to widows,
legatees, or heirs-at-law ; the death alone of any
testator being a sufficient apology to his nearest
and dearest relatives for the failure of a consultation—that is, if the patient left sufficient property
behind him.

. My state of Irish medicine, therefore, relates to
those " once on a time " days, when sons lamented their fathers,* and wives could weep over

* In these times it may not, perhaps, be fully credited when
I tell—that four of my father's sons carried his body *themselves*
to the grave : that his eldest son was in a state bordering on
actual distraction at his death ; and in the enthusiastic paroxysms
of affection which we all felt for our beloved parent at that cruel
separation, I do even now firmly believe there was not one of
us who would not, on the impulse of the moment, have sprung
into, and supplanted him in his grave, to have restored him to
animation. But we were all a family of nature and of heart,
and decided enemies to worldly objects.

expiring husbands ; when every root and branch of
an ancient family became as black as rooks for the
death of a blood relation, though of almost incal-
culable removal. In those times the medical old
woman and the surgeon-farrier—the bone-setter
and the bleeder—were by no means considered
contemptible practitioners among the Christian
population—who, in common with the dumb
beasts, experienced the advantages of their miscellaneous practice.

An anatomical theatre being appended to the
University of Dublin, whenever I heard of a *fresh*
subject, or remarkable corpse, being obtained for
dissection, I frequently attended the lectures, and
many were the beauteous women and fine young
fellows then carved into scraps and joints *pro bono
publico.** I thereby obtained a smattering of information respecting our corporeal clockwork ;
and having, for amusement, skimmed over " Cullen's First Lines," " Every Man his Own Doctor,"
" Bishop Berkeley on Tar Water," and " Sawny
Cunningham on the Virtues of Fasting Spittle," I
almost fancied myself qualified for a diploma. A

---

* I never saw a young woman brought into the dissecting-
room but my blood ran cold, and I was immediately set a-
moralising. The old song of " Death and the Lady " is a
better lecture for the fair sex than all the sermons that ever were
preached, including Mr. Fordyce's. 'Tis a pity that song is
not *melodised* for the use of the fashionables during their campaigns in London.

Welsh aunt of mine, also; having married Doctor Burdet, who had been surgeon of the Wasp sloop of war, and remarkable for leaving the best stumps of any naval practitioner, he explained to me the use of his various instruments for tapping, trepanning, raising the shoulder-blades, &c. &c. : but when I had been a short time at my father's in the country, I found that the farriers and old women performed, either on man or beast, twenty cures for one achieved by the doctors and apothecaries. I had great amusement in conversing with these people, and perceived some reason in their arguments.

As to the farriers, I reflected, that as man is only a mechanical animal, and a horse one of the same description, there was no reason why a drug that was good for a pampered gelding might not also be good for the hard-goer mounted on him. In truth, I have seen instances where, in point both of intellect and endurance, there was but very little distinction between the animals—save that the beverage of the one was *water*, and that of the other was *punch*—and, in point of *quantity*, there was no great difference between them in this matter either.

At that time there was seldom more than one regular doctor in a circuit of twenty miles, and a farrier never came to physic a gentleman's horse that some boxes of pills were not deducted from his balls, for the general use of the ladies and gentlemen of the family; and usually succeeded vastly better than those of the apothecary.

The class of old women called colloughs were then held in the highest estimation, as understanding the cure (that is if God pleased) of all disorders. Their *materia medica* did not consist of gums, resins, minerals, and hot iron,—as the farriers' did; but of leaves of bushes, bark of trees, *weeds* from *churchyards*, and mushrooms from *fairy grounds;* rue, garlic, rosemary, birds'-nests, foxglove, &c.: in desperate cases they sometimes found it advisable to put a *charm* into the bolus or stoop, and then it was sure to be " firm and good." I never could find out what either of their charms were. They said they should die themselves if they disclosed them to any body. No collough ever could be a *doctor* whilst she had one tooth remaining in her head, as the remedy was always reduced to a pulp or paste by her own mumbling of its materials, and the contact of an old grinder would destroy the purity of the charms and simples, and leave the cure, they would say, no better than a farrier's.

Our old collough, Jug Coyle, as she sat in a corner of the hob, by the great long turf fire in the kitchen, exactly in the position of the Indian squaws, munching and mumbling for use an apron-full of her morning's gatherings in the fields, used to talk at intervals very *sensibly* of her art. " Ough! then, my dear sowl, (said she one evening,) what would the poor Irishers have done in owld times but for their colloughs? Such brutes as you!" continued she, (looking at Butler, the farrier of the family, who was seated fast asleep on a bench at the opposite end of the hearth,) " 'tis you, and the likes of you, a curse on you, root and branch! that starved the colloughs by giving your poisons to both cows and quality. Sure its the farriers' and pothecaries' drugs that kills all the people—ay, and the horses and cattle too," and she shook her claw-like fist at the unconscious farrier.

" Jug Coyle," said I, " why are you so angry?"

Jug:—" Sure its not for myself, its for my calling," said she: " a thousand years before the round towers were built (and nobody can tell *that* time), the colloughs were greater nor any lady in the country. We had plenty of charms in those days, Master Jonah, till the farriers came, bad luck to the race! Ough! may the curse of Crummell light on yees all, breed, seed, and generation, Larry Butler! not forgetting Ned Morrisy of Clapook, the villanous cow-doctor, that takes the good from the colloughs likewise, and all—"

Here Jug Coyle stopped short, as the farrier opened his eyes, and she knew well that if Larry Butler had a sup in, he would as soon beat an old woman as any body else. She therefore resumed munching her herbs, but was totally silenced.

Larry Butler was one of the oldest and most indispensable *attachés* of our family. Though nobody remembered him a *boy*, he was as handy, as fresh, and as *rational*, perhaps more so, than half a century before. Short, broad, and bow-legged, bone and muscle kept his body together—for flesh was absent. His face, once extremely handsome, still retained its youthful colouring—though broken and divided : his sharp eye began to exhibit the dimness of age : the long white hair had deserted his high forehead, but fell, in no scanty locks, down each side of his animated countenance. He is before my eye at this moment—too interesting, and, at the same time, odd a figure ever to be forgotten.

I had a great respect for old Butler : he was very passionate, but universally licensed : he could walk any distance, and always carried in his hand a massive firing-iron. I have thus particularly described the old man, as being one of the most curious characters of his class I ever met in Ireland.

Larry soon showed signs of relapsing into slumber ; but Jug, fearing it was a *fox's sleep* (an old trick of his), did not recommence her philippic on the farriers, but went on in her simple praise of the collough practice. " Sure, " said she, " God never sent any disorder into a country that he did not likewise send something to cure it with."

" Why, certainly, Jug," said I, " it would be rather bad treatment if we had no cures in the country."

" Ough! that saying is like your dear father," said she, " and your grandfather before you, and your great-grandfather who was before him agin. Moreover," pursued Jug, " God planted our cures in the fields because there was no pothecaries."

" Very true, Jug," said I.

" Well, then, Master Jonah," resumed she, " if God or the Virgin, and I'm sure I can't say which of them, planted the cures, sure they must have made people who knew how to pick them up in the fields, or what good is their growing there?"

. " There's no gainsaying that, Jug," gravely observed I.

" Well, then, it was to the colloughs, sure enough, God gave the knowledge of picking the cures up—because he knew well that they were owld and helpless, and that it would be a charity to employ them. When once they learned the herbs, they were welcome every where; and there was not *one* man died in his bed (the people say) in owld times for *twenty* now-a-days."

" Of that there is no doubt, Jug," said I, " though there may be other reasons for it."

" Ough! God bless you agin, avourneen! any

how," said Jug. " Well, then, they say it was Crummell and his troopers, bad luck to their sowls, the murdering villains! that brought the first farriers (and no better luck to *them!*) to Ireland, and the colloughs were kilt with the hunger. The craturs, as the owld people tell, eat grass like the beasts when the cows were all kilt by the troopers and farriers—avourneen, avourneen!"

Modern practitioners will perceive, by these two specimens of our ancient *doctors,* that the state of medicine in Ireland was totally different from that in Italy. Surgery being likewise a branch of the healing art, no doubt also differed in the two countries, in a similar degree. I shall therefore give a few *instances* of both medico-surgical and surgico-medical practice fifty years ago in Ireland; and if my talented friend, Lady Morgan, will be so good as to inquire, she will find, that though she has left medicine so entirely to her lord, she may get an admirable *doctor* or two to introduce into her next Irish *imaginations*—which I hope will be soon forthcoming—certainly not sooner than agreeable and welcome.

I must here notice a revolution ; namely, that of late, since farriers have got a " step in the peerage," and are made commissioned officers in the army, they think it proper to refine their pharmacopeia so as to render it more congenial to their new rank and station, and some horses are now not only theoretically but practically placed on more than a level with the persons who mount them.

.The practice of horse medicine is indeed so completely revolutionised, that gas, steam, and the chemistry of Sir Humphrey Davy, are resorted to for the morbid affections of that animal in common with those of a nobleman. The horse, now, regularly takes his hot bath like my lord and lady, James' powders, refined liquorice, musk, calomel, and laudanum, with the most " elegant extracts " and delicate infusions. As if *Gulliver* were a prophet, he literally described, in the reign of Queen Anne, both the *English horse* and the *Irish peasant* as they exist at the present moment. If the lodging, clothing, cleaning, food, 'medicine, and attendance of the modern Hoynhymm, be contrasted with the pig-sty, rags, filth, neglect, and hunger of the Yahoo, it must convince any honest neutral that Swift (that greatest of Irishmen) did not overcharge his satire. The sum lavished upon the care of one Hoynhymm for *a single day*, with little or nothing to do, is more (exclusive of the farrier) than is now paid to five Irish Yahoos for *twelve hours'* hard labour, with to feed, clothe, lodge, and nourish *themselves*, and probably five wives and twenty or thirty children, for the same period, into the bargain.

· A few very curious cases may elucidate our ancient practice of cure—a practice, I believe, never even heard of in any other part of Europe. The bite of a mad dog was to the Irish peasantry of all things the most puzzling and terrific ; and I am sure I can scarcely guess what Doctor Morgan will think of my veracity when I state the two modes by which that horrible mania was neutralised or finally put an end to.

When the bite of a dog took place, every effort was made to kill the beast, and if they succeeded, it was never inquired whether he actually *was*, or (as the colloughs used to say) *pretended to be* mad : his liver was immediately taken out, dried by the fire till quite hard, then reduced to powder, and given in frequent doses with a draught of holy or blessed water, to the patient for seven days. If it happened that the saliva did not penetrate the ⸳sufferer's clothes, or if the dog was *not* actually mad, it was then considered that the patient was *cured* by drinking the dog's liver and holy water ;—and if it so happened that the bite set him barking, then the priest and farrier told them it was the will of God that he should bark, and they were contented either to let him die at his leisure, or send him to heaven a little sooner than was absolutely necessary.

The herbs of the colloughs were sometimes successfully resorted to ; whether accidental or actual preventives or antidotes, it is not easy to determine : but when I detail the ulterior remedy to cure the hydrophobia in Ireland, or at least to render it *perfectly innoxious*, I am well aware that

I shall stand a good chance of being honoured by the periodicals with the appellation of a "bouncer," as on occasion of the former volumes: but the ensuing case, as I can personally vouch for the fact, I may surely give with tolerable confidence.

KILLING WITH KINDNESS.

Illustration of the Irish horror of hydrophobia—Thomas Palmer, of Rushhall, Esquire, magistrate and land-agent, &c.—A substantial bill of fare—Dan Dempsey, of the Pike, is bitten by a mad dog—Application to the magistrate for legal permission to *relieve* him of his sufferings—Mode of relief proposed—Swearing scholars—Permission obtained—Dan regularly smothered, by way both of *cure* and *preventive*—Fate of Mr. Palmer himself—Allen Kelly, of Portarlington —" New Way to Pay Old Debts."

SUCH a dread had the Irish of the bite of a mad dog, that they did not regard it as murder, but absolutely as a legal and meritorious act, to smother any person who had arrived at an advanced stage of hydrophobia. If he made a noise similar to barking, his hour of suffocation was seldom protracted.

In this mode of administering the *remedy*, it was sometimes difficult to procure proper instruments; for they conceived that *by law* the patient should be smothered between two *feather*-beds, — one being laid cleverly over him, and a sufficient number. of the neighbours lying on it till he was " out of danger."

The only instance I am able to state from my own knowledge occurred about the year 1781. Thomas Palmer, of Rushhall, in Queen's County, was then my father's land-agent, and at the same time a very active and intelligent magistrate of that county. He was, *gratis*, an oracle, lawyer, poet, horse—cow—dog and man doctor, farmer, architect, brewer, surveyor, and magistrate of all work. He was friendly and good-natured, and possessed one of those remarkable figures now so rarely to be seen in society. I feel I am, as usual, digressing;—however, be the digression what it may, I cannot deny myself the pleasure of depicting my old friend, and endeavouring to render him as palpable to the vision of my reader as he is at this moment to my own.

. Palmer was one of that race of giants for which the rich and extensive barony of Ossory, in Queen's County (now the estate of the Duke of Buckingham), was then and had long been celebrated. His height was esteemed the *middle* height in that county—namely, about six feet two inches; he was bulky without being fat, and strong, though not very muscular. He was, like many other giants, *split up* too much, and his long dangling limbs appeared still longer from their clothing, which was invariably the same :—a pair of strong buck-skin breeches, never *very* greasy, but

never free from grease; half jack-boots; massive;
long silver spurs, either of his own or of somebody's
grandfather's; a scarlet waistcoat with long skirts;
and a coat with " *all the cloth* in it." These habiliments rendered him altogether a singular but not
other than respectable figure. His visage made
amends for both his *outré* boots and breeches; it
was as well calculated as could be for a kind-
hearted, good-humoured, convivial old man. His
queue wig, with a curl at each side, had his griz-
zle hair combed smoothly over the front of it; and
he seldom troubled the powder-puff, but when he
had got the "skins whitened," in order to " dine in
good company." He was the *hardest-goer* either at
kettle or screw (except Squire Flood of Roundwood) of the whole grand-jury, for whose use he
made a new song every summer assize: and it
was from him I heard the very unanswerable argument, " that if a man fills the bottom of his glass,
there can be no good reason why he should not
also fill the top of it; and if he empties the top of
his glass, he certainly ought in common civility to
pay the bottom the same compliment:"—no man
ever more invariably exemplified his own the-
orem.

Thomas Palmer was hale and healthy;—his
fifty-seventh year had handed him over safe and
sound to its next neighbour: his property was
just sufficient (and no more) to gallop side by side
with his hospitality. When at home, his boiler

was seldom found . bubbling without a corned round withinside it; and a gander or cock turkey frequently danced at the end of a string before the long turf fire. Ducks, hares, chickens, or smoked ham, often adorned the sides of his table; whilst apple-dumplings in the centre and potatoes at cross corners completed a light snack for five or six seven-feet Ossoronians, who left no just reason to the old cook and a couple of ruddy ploughmen, (who attended as *butlers,*) to congratulate themselves upon the *dainty* appetites of their masters, or the balance of nourishment left to liquidate the demand of their own stomachs. But, alas! those pleasurable specimens of solid fare have passed away for ever! As age advances, Nature diminishes her weights and measures in our *consumption,* and our early *pounds* an d Scotch *pints (two bottles)* are at length reduced to the miserable rations of *ounces* and *glassfuls.*

At this magistrate's *cottage,* which had as stout a roof to it as any mansion in the county, I once dined, about the year 1781, when the state of medicine in Ireland was exemplified in a way that neither Cullen, Darwin, Perceval, James, or any other learned doctor ever contemplated, and which I am convinced—had it been the practice in Italy—Doctor Morgan would not have passed over in total silence.

We had scarcely finished such a meal as I have particularised, and " got into the punch," when a

crowd of men, women, and children, came up to
the door in great confusion, but respectfully took
off their hats and bonnets, and asked humbly to
speak to his worship.

Tom Palmer seemed to anticipate their business,
and inquired at once " if Dan Dempsey of the
Pike (turnpike) was in the same way still ?"

" Ough ! please your worship," cried out twenty voices together, " worse, your worship, worse
nor ever, death's crawling upon him—he can't
stop, and what's the use in leaving the poor boy
in his pains any longer, your worship ?   We have
got two good feather-beds at the Pike, and we
want your worship's leave to smother Dan Dempsey, if your worship pleases."

" Ough avourneen ! he growls and barks like
any mastiff dog, please your worship," cried a
tremulous old woman, who seemed quite in terror.

" You lie, Nancy Bergin," said her older husband, " Dan Dempsey does *not* bark like a *mastiff;*—its for all the world like your worship's
white lurcher, when she's after the rabbits, so it
is !"

" He snapped three times at myself this morning," said another humane lady, " and the neighbours said it were all as one, almost, as biting
me."

" Hush ! hush !" said the magistrate, waving
his hand : " any of you who can read and write,
come in here."

" Ough ! there's plenty of that sort, please your worship," said Maurice Dowling, the old schoolmaster. " Sure its not ignorance I'd be teaching my scholards every day these forty years, except Sundays and holidays, at the Pike. There's plenty of swearing scholards here any how, your worship."

" Come in any three of you, then, who can clearly' swear Dan Dempsey barks like a dog,— no matter whether like a mastiff or a lurcher—and attempts to bite."

The selection was accordingly made, and the affidavit sworn, to the effect that " Dan Dempsey had been bit by a mad dog ; that he went mad himself, barked like any greyhound, and had no objection to bite whatever Christian came near him. Squire Palmer then directed them to go back to the Pike, and said they might smother Dan Dempsey if he barked any more in the morning ; but told them to wait till then.

" Ah, then, at what hour, please your worship ?" said Nan Bergin, accompanied by several other female voices, whose owners seemed rather impatient.

" Three hours after day-break," said the magistrate : " but take care to send to Mr. Calcut, the coroner, to come and hold his inquest after Dan's smothered. Take care of that, at your peril."

" Never fear, please your worship," said Ned Bergin.

They then gathered into a sort of consultation before the door, and bowing with the same respect as when they came, all set off, to smother Dan Dempsey of Rushhall Turnpike.

The magistrate's instructions were accurately obeyed : Daniel barked, and was duly smothered between two feather-beds, three hours after day-break next morning, by the schoolmaster's watch. Mr. Calcut came and held his coroner's inquest, who brought in their verdict that the said " Daniel Dempsey died *in consequence of a mad dog !*"

The matter was not at that day considered the least extraordinary, and was, in fact, never mentioned except in the course of common conversation, and as the subject of a paragraph in the Leinster Journal.

It is a singular circumstance, that the termination of poor Palmer's life resulted from his consistency in strictly keeping his own aphorism which I have before mentioned. He dined at my father's Lodge at Cullenagh ; and having taken his *quantum sufficit,* (as people who dined there generally did,) became obstinate, which is frequently the consequence of being pot-valiant, and insisted on riding home, twelve or thirteen miles, in a dark night. He said he had a couple of songs to write for the high sheriff, which Mr. Boyce from Waterford had promised to sing at the assizes ;— and that he always wrote best with a full stomach. It was thought that he fell asleep ; and that his

horse, supposing he had as much right to drink
freely as his master, had quietly paid a visit to his
accustomed watering-place, when, on the animal's
stooping to drink, poor Palmer pitched over his
head into the pond, wherein he was found next
morning quite dead—though scarcely covered with
water, and grasping the long branch of a tree as if
he had been instinctively endeavouring to save
himself, but had not strength, owing to the over-
powering effect of the liquor. His horse had not
stirred from his side. His loss was, to my father's
affairs, irreparable.

- It is very singular that nearly a similar death
occurred to an attorney, who dined at my father's
about a month afterward—old Allen Kelly of Portarlington, one of the most keen though cross-grained
attorneys in all Europe. He came to Cullenagh to
insist upon a settlement for some bills of costs he
had dotted up against my father to the tune of
fifty pounds. It being generally, in those times,
more convenient to country gentlemen to pay by
bond than by ready money—and always more
agreeable to the attorney, because he was pretty
sure of doubling his costs before the judgment was
satisfied, Allen Kelly said, that, out of *friendship*, he'd take a *bond and warrant of attorney* for his
fifty pounds; though it was not taxed, which he
declared would only *increase* it wonderfully. The
bond and warrant, which he had ready filled up
in his pocket, were duly executed, and both par-

ties were pleased—my father to get rid of Allen
Kelly, and Allen Kelly to get fifty pounds for the
worth of ten.   Of course he stayed to dine, put the
bond carefully into his breeches pocket, drank
plenty of port and hot punch, to keep him warm
on his journey, mounted his nag, reached Portarlington, where he watered his nag (and *himself*
into the bargain).   Hot punch, however, is a bad
balance-master, and so Allen fell over the nag's
head, and the poor beast trotted home quite lonesome for want of his master.   Next day Allen
was found well bloated with the Barrow water;
indeed, swollen to full double his usual circum-
ference.   In his pockets were found divers documents which *had been* bonds, notes, and other
securities, and which he had been collecting
through the country : but unfortunately for his
administrators, the Barrow had taken pity on the
debtors, and whilst Allen was reposing himself in
the bed of that beautiful river, her naiads were
employed in picking his pocket, and there was
scarcely a bill, bond, note, or any acknowledgment, where the fresh ink had not yielded up its
colouring ; and neither the names, sums, dates, or
other written matters, of one out of ten, could be
by any means decyphered.   In truth few of the
debtors were very desirous, on this occasion, of
turning *decypherers*, and my father's bond (among
others) was from that day never even suggested
to him by any representative of Allen Kelly, the
famous attorney of Portarlington.

SKINNING A BLACK CHILD.

Lieutenant Palmer and his black servant—The Lieutenant's sister marries Mr. George Washington, a " blood relation" of the American president—This lady presents her husband with a son and heir—Awkward circumstance connected with the birth of the infant—Curious and learned dissertation respecting " fancy-marks," &c.—A *casus omissus* — Speculations and consultations — Doctor Bathron, surgeon and grocer—His suggestion respecting little Washington—Doctor Knaggs called in — Operation begun — Its ill success — " Black and all Black"—The operator's dismay and despair —Final catastrophe of Master Washington.

ANOTHER, and a not unpleasant, because not fatal, incident may serve to illustrate the " state of medicine and surgery," between forty and fifty years ago, in Ireland. It occurred near my brother's house, at Castlewood, and the same Lieutenant Palmer, of Dureen, was a very interested party in it. The thing created great merriment among all the gossiping, tattling old folks, male and female, throughout the district.

The lieutenant having been in America, had brought home a black lad as a servant, who resided in the house of Dureen with the family. It is one of the mysteries of nature, that infants sometimes come into this world marked and spotted in divers fantastical ways and places, a circumstance which the faculty, so far as they know any thing about it, consider as the sympathetic effect either of external touch or ardent imagination ;—or, if neither of these are held to be the cause, then they regard it as a sort of *lusus* with which Dame Nature occasionally surprises, and then (I suppose) laughs at the world, for marvelling at her capriciousness,—a quality which she has, as satirists pretend, plentifully bestowed on the fairest part of the creation. Be this as it may, the incident I am about to mention is in its way unique ; and whether the occasion of it proceeded from sympathy, fancy, or touch, or exhibited a regular *lusus Naturæ*, never has, and now never can be unequivocally decided.

A sister of the lieutenant, successively a very good maiden, woman, and wife, had been married to one Mr. George Washington, of the neighbourhood, who, from his name, was supposed to be some distant blood relation to the celebrated General Washington ; and, as that distinguished individual had no children, all the old women and other wiseacres of Durrow, Ballyragget, Ballyspellen, and Ballynakill, made up their minds that his Excellency, when dying, would leave a capital legacy in America to his blood relation, Mr. George Washington, of Dureen, in Ireland; who was accordingly advised — and, with the aid of the Rev. Mr. Hoskinson, clergyman of Durrow (father to the present Vice Provost of Dublin University), he took the advice—to write a dignified letter to his Excellency, General George Washington of Virginia, President, &c. &c. &c. stating himself to have the honour of entertaining hopes that he should be enabled to show his Excellency, by an undeniable pedigree (when he could procure it) that he had a portion of the same blood as his Excellency's running in his humble veins. The letter went on to state, that he had espoused the sister of a British officer, who had had the honour of being taken prisoner in America; and that he, the writer, having reasonable expectation of shortly fathering a young Mr. Washington, his Excellency's permission was humbly requested for the child to be named his god-son : till the receipt of which permission, the christening should be kept open by his most faithful servant and distant relation, &c.

This epistle was duly despatched to his Excellency, at Mount Vernon, in Virginia, and Mrs George Washington, of Dureen, lost no time in performing her husband's promise. No joy ever exceeded that which seized on Mr. Washington,

when it was announced that his beloved wife had
been taken ill, and was in excessive torture.   The
entire household, master included, were just seated
at a comfortable and plentiful dinner; the first
slices off the round, or turkey, were cut and tasted;
some respectable old dames of the neighbourhood
had just stepped in to congratulate the family on
what would occur, and hear all that was going
forward at this critical, cheerful, and happy moment
of anticipation, when Mrs. Gregory (the *lady's
doctor*), who was, in her own way, a very shrewd,
humorous kind of body, and to whom most people in that country under thirty-five years of age
had owed their existence, entered the apartment
to announce the happy arrival of as fine a healthy
little boy as could be, and that Mrs. Washington
was as well, or indeed rather better, than might
be expected *under the circumstances*.   A general
cheer by the whole company followed, and bum-
pers of hot punch were drunk with enthusiasm to
the success and future glory of the *young* General
Washington.

Mrs. Gregory at length beckoned old Mrs.
Palmer to the window with a mysterious air, and
whispered something in her ear; on hearing
which, Mrs. Palmer immediately fell flat on the
floor, as if dead.   The old dames hobbled off to
her assistance, and Mrs. Gregory affected to feel
strongly herself about something,—ejaculating, loud
enough to be generally heard, and with that sort

of emphasis people use when they wish to persuade us they are praying in downright earnest, " God's will be done!"

" What about ?" said the lieutenant, bristling up :—" I suppose my mother has taken a glass too much : it is not the first time !—she'll soon come round again, never fear. Don't be alarmed, my friends."

" God's will be done !" again exclaimed the oracular Mrs. Gregory.

" What's the matter ? What is all this about ?" grumbled the men. " Lord bless us ! what can it be ?" squalled the women.

" There cannot be a finer or stronger little boy in the 'varsal world," said Mrs. Gregory : " but, Lord help us !" continued she, unable longer to contain her overcharged grief, " Its—its not so— so *white* as it should be !"

" Not white ?" exclaimed every one of the company simultaneously.

" No,—O Lord, no !" answered Mrs. Gregory, looking mournfully up to the ceiling in search of heaven. Then casting her eyes wistfully around the company, she added—" God's will be done ! but the dear little boy is—is—quite *black!*"

" *Black! black!*" echoed from every quarter of the apartment.

" As black as your hat, if not *blacker*," replied Mrs. Gregory.

" Oh ! Oh—h !" groaned Mr. Washington.

" Oh! Oh—h!" responded Mrs. Gregory.

" Blood and ouns!" said the lieutenant.—" See how I am shaking," said the midwife, taking up a large glass of potsheen and drinking it off to settle her nerves.

What passed afterward on that evening may be easily surmised : but the next day Mrs. Gregory, the *sage femme*, came into Castle Durrow to " prevent *mistakes*," and tell the affair to the neighbours in her own way ; that is, partly in whispers, partly aloud, and partly by nods and winks—such as old ladies frequently use when they wish to divulge more than they like to speak openly.

Sufficient could be gathered, however, to demonstrate that young Master Washington had not one white, or even *gray* spot on his entire body, and that some *frizzled* hair was already beginning to show itself on his little pate ; but that no nurse could be found who would give him a drop of nourishment, even were he famishing—all the women verily believing that, as Mrs. Washington was herself an unexceptionable wife, it must be a son of the d—l by a dream, and nothing else than an imp. However, Mr. Hoskinson, the clergyman, soon contradicted this report by assuring the Protestants that the day for that sort of miracle had been for some centuries over, and that the infant was as fine, healthy, natural, and sprightly a little negro as ever came from the coast of Guinea.

Never was there such a buzz and hubbub in any

neighbourhood as now took place in and about the town of Castle Durrow. Every body began to *compute periods* and form conjectures ; and though it was universally known that red wine, &c. &c. cast on the mamma, often leaves marks upon children, yet censorious and incredulous people persisted in asserting, that such marks only came in spots or splashes, when the person of a lady happened to be actually touched by the colouring matter : but that no child could be black, and *all* black, unless in a *natural* way. Among the lower orders, however, the thing was settled at once in the most plausible and popular manner, and set down as downright witchcraft and nothing else : and suspicion fell on old Betty Hogan of the Seven Sisters, near Ballyspellen, who was *known* to be a witch, and able to raise the devil at Hallow Eve, to turn smocks, and tell fortunes ; and she was verily seen by more than one to go into the Cave of Dunmore with a coal-black cur dog (without tail or ears), after her, the very night and minute Mrs. Washington was delivered of the devil ; and nobody ever saw the cur dog before or since.

Mr. Washington and the lieutenant were, however, by no means at ease upon the subject of this freak of Nature, and were well warranted in their dissatisfaction ; as at length all the old women agreed in believing, that the black lad from America was nothing else but the devil disguised, who had followed the lieutenant as a servant boy, to gain over the family, and particularly Mrs. Washington, as Satan did Eve;—and that he ought to be smothered by the priests, or at least transported out of the country, before he did any more mischief—or there would not be a white child in the whole barony the next season.

Lieutenant Palmer was of course high in blood for the honour of his sister, and Mr. Washington cock-a-hoop for the character of his wife : and so great was their ire, that it was really believed the black boy would have been put down a draw-well, as the people threatened,—that being the approved method of getting rid of a devil whenever he showed his face in that part of the country : but as, possibly, Betty Hogan might be a better judge of him than themselves, they suspended the execution till they should bring the old witch and confront her and *the devil* together—when of course he would show his cloven foot, and they might both be put into the well, if they did not take every *taste* of the black off *Master Washington.*

The father and uncle decided more calmly and properly to lay the whole affair before a consultation of doctors, to know if it was not a regular *imagination mark*—whether a child might not be marked by mere fancy, without the marking material (such as grapes, currants, or the like,) touching the mother; and lastly, why, as children in general are only partially marked, this child was not *spotted* like others, but as black as ebony every inch of it.

All the doctors in the neighbourhood were called in to the consultation. Old Butler, the farrier (heretofore mentioned), came with all expedition to Dureen, and begged leave to give his opinion and offer his services, wishing to see Master Washington before the doctors arrived, as he had a secret for turning any skin ever so brown as white as milk!

On seeing Master Washington, however, he declared he was *too* black *entirely* for his medicines, or any body else's. " The devil so black a crethur," says he, " ever I saw, except Cornet French's *Black and all Black,* that beat the Pandreen mare for the King's hundred at the races of Gort:—the devil a white hair had *he* from muzzle to tail, good, bad, or indifferent. By my sowl! its a neat crust poor George Washington has got to mumble any how! I never saw luck or grace come of the negers, bad luck to them all!"

The day for the consultation being fixed, several apothecaries and bone-setters attended at the house of Mr. George Bathron, of Dureen, grocer, wine-merchant, surgeon, apothecary, druggist, and physician.

The first point stated and unanimously agreed on, was, " that the child was black." The reasons for that colour being universal on the young gentleman were not quite so clear. At length Dr.

Bathron, finding he had the lead, and having been
some years at school when a boy, and likewise
apprenticed to a grocer and apothecary at Ballyragget, where he learned several technical words
in the Latin tongue; finding, besides, that he had
an excellent opportunity to prove his learning to
those less educated,—declared with great gravity
that he had read many authors upon the subject
of *marks*, and could take upon himself positively
to assert that the child was (according to all
authority on such matters) a *casus omissus*. The
others, not being exactly sure either of the shape,
size, or colour, of a *casus omissus*, thought it
better to *accede* to what they did not *comprehend*,
and all subscribed to the opinion that the child
was a *casus omissus*. It was immediately circulated outside the house, that all the doctors
found the child to be a *casus omissus*; and old
Skelton, who had been a trooper in Germany, declared that a doctor there told him that was
the true surname of a devil incarnate. And the
prevailing notion then was, that the black lad,
old Betty Hogan, the witch, and Master Washington, should all be put down the draw-well together, to save the other married women of the
country from bearing devils instead of children.

The *doctors*, however, having given their opinion, were extremely ticklish in taking any step
with a *casus omissus*; and not wishing to pitch
themselves against any infernal personification,

left future proceedings to the entire management of Dr. Bathron.

Doctor Bathron was a smart, squat, ruddy, jovial apothecary, and he was also a professed poet, who had made some celebrated odes on the birthday of Miss Flower, Lord Ashbrooke's sister, when she visited Castle Durrow; and on this occasion he required a fortnight to make up his mind as to the best proceedings to bring the skin to its proper colour. Having, by search of old bookstalls in Dublin (whither he went for the purpose), found an ancient treatise, translated from the work of the high German Doctor Cratorious (who flourished in the fourteenth century), on *skinning* certain parts of the body to change the colour or complexion, or effectually to disguise criminals who had escaped from prison;—by which means, likewise, disfiguring marks, freckles, moles, &c. might be removed,—Doctor Bathron decided, that if this could be done partially, why not on the entire body, by little and little, and not skinning one spot till the last should be healed? He therefore stated to Mr. Washington, and all the good family of Dureen, that he would take upon himself to *whiten* the child—as he was perfectly satisfied the black skin was merely the outside, or scarf-skin, and that the real skin and flesh underneath were the same as every body else's.

The mode of operating was now the subject of difficulty. It was suggested, and agreed on, to call in Mr. Knaggs, the doctor of Mount Meleck, who, though he had injured his character as a practitioner of judgment by attempting to cut off the head of Sam Doxy of the Derrys, as hereinafter mentioned, had at the same time proved himself a skilful operator, having gashed boldly into the nape of Mr. Doxy's neck without touching the spinal marrow, which a bungler needs must have done. He had also acquired the reputation of science by writing a treatise on the Spa of Ballyspellen, which the inn-keeper *there* had employed him to compose, in order to bring customers to his house to drink the waters as " a specific for numerous disorders, when mixed in due proportion with excellent wines, which might be had very reasonable. at the sign of the Fox and Piper, at Ballyspellen," &c.

This man, in fine, together with Doctor Bathron, undertook to bring Master Washington to a proper hue by detaching the exterior black *pelt* which was so disagreeable to the family, and letting the natural white skin, which they had no doubt was concealed under it, come to light—thereby restoring the boy, as he ought to be, to his happy parents.

" You'll gain immortal honour," said the grandmother : " I am sure they will all be bound to pray for you!"

. The state of practice in Ireland suggested but two ways of performing this notable operation—

one purely surgical, the other surgico-medical : namely, either by gradually flaying with the knife, or by blisters.

It was at length settled to begin the operation the ensuing week, previously preparing the heir-at-law by medicine to prevent inflammation ; the first attempt was to be on a small scale, and the operation to be performed in Doctor Bathron's own surgery ;—and he being still undecided whether the scalpel and forceps, or Spanish flies, would be the most eligible mode of skinning Master Washington, determined to try both ways at once, one on each arm, and to act in future according as he saw the skin yield easiest.

Most people conceived that, as a blister always raises the skin, it would be the readiest agent in loosening and carrying off the black one that had created so much uneasiness in the present in- stance :—the doctor's doubts as to which, were, that the blister alone might not rise regularly, but operate at one place better than at another—in which case the child might be piebald, which would make him far worse than before.

The operation at length proceeded, and Lieu- tenant Palmer himself recounted to me every part of the incident. A strong blister, two inches by three, was placed on the child's right arm, and being properly covered, remained there without inflicting any torture for above an hour. The left arm was reserved for the scalpel and forceps, and the operator entertained no doubt whatever of complete success.

The mode he pursued was very *scientific;* he made two parallel slashes as deep as he could in reason, about three inches down the upper part of the arm, and a cross one, to introduce the forceps and strip the loose black skin off, when he could snip it away at the bottom, and leave the white or rather red flesh underneath, to generate a new skin, and show the proper colouring for a godchild of General Washington.

All eyes were now rivetted to the spot. The women cried in an under key to Master George, who roared. " Hush, hush, my dear," said the Doctor, " you don't know what's good for you, my little innocent !" whilst he applied the forceps, to strip off the skin like a *surtout.* The skin was tight, and would not come away cleverly with the first tug, as the doctor had expected ; nor did any thing *white* appear, though a sufficiency of red blood manifested itself.

The doctor was greatly surprised. " I see," said he, " it is somewhat deeper than we had conceived. We have not got deep enough." Another gash on each side; but the second gash had no better success. Doctor Bathron seemed desperate; but conceiving that in so young a subject one short cut—be it ever so deep—could do no harm, his hand shook, and he gave the scalpel its full force, till he found it touch the bone.' The experiment was now complete; he opened the wound, and starting back, affected to be struck with horror, threw down his knife, stamped and swore the child was in fact either the devil or a *lusus Naturæ*, for that he could see the very bone, and the child was actually coalblack *to* the bone, and the bone black also, and that he would not have taken a thousand guineas to have given a single gash to a thing which was clearly supernatural—actually dyed in grain. He appeared distracted; however, the child's arm was bound up, a good poultice put over it, the blister hastily removed from the other arm, and the young gentleman, fortunately for Doctor Báthron, recovered from the scarification, and lived with an old dry-nurse for four or five years. He was then killed by a cow of his *father's* horning him, and died with the full reputation of having been a devil in reality, which was fully corroborated by a white sister of his, and his mother, (as I heard,) departing about the very same time, if not on the next day. It was said he took their souls away with him, to make his peace with his master for staying so long.

Doctor George Bathron, who was the pleasantest united grocer and surgeon in the county, at length found it the best policy to tell this story himself, and by that means neutralise the ridicule of it. He often told it to me, whilst in company with Mr. Palmer; and by hearing both versions, I obtained full information about the circumstance, which I relate as a very striking example of the mode in which we managed a *lusus Naturæ* when we *caught* one in Ireland five and forty years ago.

THE FARRIER AND WHIPPER-IN.

Tom White, the whipper-in of Blandsfort—An unlucky leap—
Its consequences—Tom given over by the *Faculty*—Handed
to the farrier—Larry Butler's preparations—New way to
stand fast—The actual cautery—Ingredients of a " charge "
—Tom cured *intirely.*

TOM WHITE, a whipper-in at my father's at
Blandsfort, had his back crushed by leaping his
horse into a gravel pit, to pull off the scut of a
hare. The horse broke his neck, the hare was
killed, and the whipper-in, to all appearance, little
better ; and when we rode up, there lay three
carcases " all in a row."—However (as deaths
generally confer an advantage upon some survivor), two of the *corpses* afforded good cheer next
day :—we ate the hare, the hounds ate the horse,
and the worms would certainly have made a meal
of Tom White, had not old Butler, the farrier,
taken his cure in hand, after Doctor Ned Stapleton, of Maryborough, the genuine bone-setter of
that county, had given him up as broken-backed

and past all skill.   As has been already seen, our
practice of pharmacy, medicine, and surgery in
Ireland, fifty years ago, did not correspond with
modern usages; and though our old operations
might have had a trifle more of *torture* in them—
either from bluntness of knives or the mode of
slashing a patient;   yet, in the end, I conceive that
few more lives are saved by hacking, hewing, and
thrusting, *scientifically*, according to modern practice, than there were by the old trooper-like
fashion.

I was in Blandsfort House when Mr. Jemmy
Butler, our hereditary farrier, who had equal skill
—according to the old school—in the treatment
of dogs, cows, and horses, as well as in rat-catch-
ing, began and concluded his medico-surgical cure
of Tom White : I can therefore recount with tolerable   fidelity   the   successful   course   adopted
toward that courageous sportsman.

Tom's first state of insensibility soon gave way ;
and incontrovertible proofs of his existence followed, in sundry deep groans, and now and then
a roaring asseveration that ·his back was broke.
He entreated us to send off for his *clergy* without
any delay, or the reverend father would not· find
him in this world.   However, Mr. Butler, who
had no great belief in any world either above or
below the Queen's County, declared, " that if the
clergy came, he'd leave Tom White to die, as he
well knew Tom was a thief; and if any clergy

botheration was made about his sowl, it would
only tend to irritate and inflame his hurt." But
he undertook to give him a better *greasing* than all
the priests in the barony, if they should be seven
years anointing him with the best salvation oil
ever invented.

Tom acquiesced; and, in fear of death, acknowledged " he was a great thief, sure enough, but if
he recovered, he would *take up*, and tell all he had
done, without a word of a lie, to Father Cahill of
Stradbally, who was always a friend to the poor
sarvants."

Mr. Butler now commenced his cure, at the
performance of which, every male in the house,
high and low, was called on to be present. The
farrier first stripped Tom to his shirt, and then
placed him flat on the great kitchen table, with his
face downward; and having (after being impeded
by much roaring and kicking) tied a limb fast to
each leg of it—(so as to make a St. Andrew's cross
of him) he drew a strong table-cloth over the
lower part of the sufferer's body; and tying the
corners underneath the table, had the pleasure of
seeing Tom White as snug and fast as he could
wish, to undergo any degree of torture without
being able to shift a quarter of an inch.

Mr. Butler then walked round in a sort of
triumph, every now and then giving the knots a
pull, to tighten them, and saying, " Mighty well,—
mighty good! Now *stand fast*, Tom."

Tom's back being thus duly bared, the *doctor* ran his immense thumb from top to bottom along the spine, with no slight degree of pressure; and whenever the whipper-in roared loudest, Mr. Butler marked the spot he was touching with a lump of chalk. Having, in that way, ascertained the tender parts, he pressed them with all his force, as if he were kneading dough—just, as he said, to *settle the joints* quite even. No bull in the midst of five or six bull-dogs tearing him piece-meal could, even in his greatest agonies, amuse the baiters better, or divert them with more tremend-ous roars, than the whipper-in did during the greatest part of this operation.

The operator, having concluded his *reconnoitring*, proceeded to real action. He drew parallel lines with chalk down Tom's back—one on each side the back-bone; at particular points he made a cross stroke, and at the *tender parts* a *double* one; so that Tom had a complete ladder delineated on his back, as if the doctor intended that something should mount by it from his waistband to his cravat.

The preliminaries being thus gone through, and Mr. Butler furnished with a couple of red-hot irons, such as maimed horses are fired with, he began, in a most deliberate and skilful manner, to fire Tom according to the rules and practice of the *ars veterinaria*. The poor fellow's bellowing, while under the actual cautery, all the people

said, they verily believed was the loudest ever
heard in that country since the massacre of Mullymart.* This part of the operation, indeed, was
by no means superficially performed, as Mr. Butler *mended* the lines and made them all of a uniform depth and colour, much as the writing-mas-
ter mends the letters and strokes in a child's copy-
book : and as they were very straight and regular,
and too well *broiled*, to suffer any effusion of red
blood, Tom's back did not look much the worse for
the tattooing. In truth, if my readers recollect
the excellent mode of making a cut down each
side of a saddle of mutton, just to elicit the brown
gravy, they will have a good idea of the longitudinal cauteries in question. On three or four of
the tender places before mentioned Mr. Butler
drew his transverse cross bars, which quite took
off the uniform appearance, and gave a sort of
garnished look to the whole drawing, which seemed
very much to gratify the operator, who again walked round and round *the body* several times with a
red-hot iron in his hand, surveying, and here and
there retouching the ragged or uneven parts.
This *finishing* rendered the whipper-in rather
hoarse, and his first roars were now changed to

* A massacre of the Irish at a place called Mullymart, in
the county of Kildare, which is spoken of by Casaubon in his
Britannia as a thing prophesied : the prophesy did actually take
effect; and it is, altogether, one of the most remarkable traditionary tales of that country.

softer notes—somewhat as an opera singer occasionally breaks into his falsetto.

" Howld your bother," said Mr. Butler, to whom Tom's incessant shrieking had become very disagreeable : " howld your *music*, I say, or I'll put a touch* on your nose as tight as yourself did on Brown Jack, when I was firing the ring-bone out of him : you're a greater beast yourself nor ever Brown Jack was."

Mr. Butler having partly silenced the whipper-in through fear of the *touch*, the second part of the process was undertaken—namely, depositing what is termed by farriers the cold charge, on the back of Tom White. However, on this occasion the regular *practice* was somewhat varied, and the *cold* charge was nearly boiling hot when placed upon the raw *ladder* on the whipper-in's back. I saw the *torture* boiled in a large iron ladle, and will mention the ingredients, just to show that they were rather more exciting than our milk-and-water charges of the present day :—viz. " Burgundy pitch, black pitch, diaculum, yellow wax,

---

* An instrument used in the practice of farriers. It is a piece of cord passed round the nose of a horse (being the most sensitive part of that animal) ; and being twisted tight by a short stick, it creates a torture so exquisite, that all other tortures go for nothing. Therefore, when a horse is to have his tail cut off, or his legs burned, &c., a touch is put upon his nose, the extreme pain whereof absorbs that of the operation, and, as they term it, makes the beast " *stay easy*."

white wax, mustard, black resin, white resin, sal
ammoniac, bruised hemlock, camphor, Spanish
flies, and oil of origanum, boiled up with spirits
of turpentine, onion juice, and a glass of whisky;
it was kept simmering till it became of a proper
consistence for application, and was then *laid on*
with a painter's brush, in the same way they calk
a pleasure-boat. Four coats of this savoury substance did the farrier successively apply, each
one as the former began to cool. But, on the first
application, even the dread of the touch could
not restrain Tom White's vociferation. After this
had settled itself in the chinks, he seemed to
be quite stupid, and tired of roaring, and lay
completely passive, or rather insensible, while
Mr. Butler *finished* to his taste ; dotting it over
with short lamb's-wool as thick as it would .stick,
and then another coat of the unction, with an
addition of wool ; so that, when completed by
several layers of charge and lamb's-wool, Tom's
back might very well have been mistaken for a
saddle of Southdown before it .was skinned. A
thin ash board was now neatly fitted to it down
Tom's spine by the carpenter, and made fast with
a few short nails driven into the charge. I believe
none of them touched the quick, as the 'charge
appeared above an inch and a half thick, and it was
only at the blows of the hammer that the patient
seemed to feel extra sensibility. Tom was now
untied and helped to rise : his woolly carcase was

bandaged all round with long strips of a blanket, which being done, the operation was declared to be completed, in less than three quarters of an hour.

The other servants now began to make merry with Tom White. One asked him, how he liked purgatory?—another, if he'd "stop thieving," after that *judgment* on him?—a third, what more could Father Cahill do for him? *Doctor* Butler said but little : he assumed great gravity, and directed " that the whipper-in should sit up stiff for seven days and nights, by which time the *juices would be dried on him;* after that he might lay down, if he could."

This indeed was a very useless permission, as the patient's tortures were now only in their infancy. So soon as the charge got cold and stiff in the nitches and fancy figures upon his back, he nearly went mad; so that for a few days they were obliged to strap him with girths to the head of his bed to make him " stay easy;" and sometimes to gag him, that his roars might not disturb the company in the dining parlour. Wallace the piper said that Tom's roarings put him quite *out:* and an elderly gentleman who was on a visit with us, and who had not been long married to a young wife, said his bride was so shocked and alarmed at the groans and " pullaloes" of Tom White, that she could think of nothing else.

When the poor fellow's pains had altogether subsided, and the swathing was off, he cut one of the most curious figures ever seen : he looked as if he had a stake driven through his body ; and it was not till the end of four months that Mr. Butler began to pour sweet oil down his neck, between his back and the charge, which he continued to do daily for about another month, till the charge gradually detached itself, and broken-backed Tom was declared cured : in truth, I believe he never felt any inconvenience from his fall afterward.

This mode of cauterising the people was then much practised by the old farriers, often with success; and I never recollect any fatal effects happening in consequence.

The farriers' rowelling also was sometimes had recourse to, to prevent swellings from coming to a head : and I only heard of two fatalities arising herefrom ; one, in the case of a half-mounted gentleman at Castle Comber, who died of a locked jaw ; and another, in that of a shopkeeper at Borris, in Ossory, who expired from mortification occasioned by a tow and turpentine rowell being used to carry off an inflammation.

THE RIVAL PRACTITIONERS.

Dr. Fletcher, Dr. Mulhall, and the author's father—Interesting
particulars of a medical consultation—Family recollections
— Counsellor, afterward Judge Fletcher — First meeting
between him and the author—Catching a Tartar—Sam
Doxy of the Derrys—Breaks his neck in riding to a Turnpike-Board dinner—Pronounced dead by Mr. Knaggs, the
apothecary—That eminent practitioner's judgment disputed
by Lieut. Jerry Palmer—The apothecary proceeds to show
that the patient *must*, or at least *ought* to be, dead—An in-
- cision, and its consequences—Lieut. Palmer's successful mode
of treatment—Recovery of the corpse.

In addition to my preceding illustrations of the
former state of medicine and surgery in Ireland,
I cannot omit a couple of convincing proofs of the
intuitive knowledge possessed by Irish practitioners
in my early days. They present scenes at which
I was myself present, and one of which was the
most distressing I had witnessed, while the other
was more amusing at its conclusion than any
operation I ever saw performed by any, either of
the farriers or colloughs of Ireland.

Doctor Knaggs, the hero of the second incident, was a tall, raw-boned, rough, dirty apothecary; but he suited the neighbours, as they said he had " the skill in him," and was " mighty successful." Sam Doxy, his patient, was, on the contrary, a broad, strong, plethoric, half-mounted gentleman. He had his lodge, as he called it, in the midst of a *derry* (a bog), drank his gallon of hot punch to keep out the damp, and devoured numerous cock turkeys, and cows that were past *child-bearing*, to keep down the potsheen. Every neighbour that could get to him was welcome, and *the road* was seldom *in a fit state* to permit their going away again quickly.

The first of these anecdotes I still relate with some pain, though forty-five years and more have of course blunted the feeling I experienced on its occurrence; and as I shall soon be in the same situation myself as the parties now are, I can, comparatively speaking, look lightly on an event which, in youth, health, and high blood, was quite chilling to my contemplation.

The father of the late Judge Fletcher of the Common Pleas was an *actual* physician at Mount Melec, about seven miles from my father's. He was a smart, intelligent, and very humorous, but remarkably diminutive doctor. He attended my father in his last moments, in conjunction with the family practitioner, Doctor Dennis Mulhall, whose appearance exactly corresponded with that

of Doctor Slop, save that his paunch was doubly
capacious, and his legs, in true symmetry with his
carcase, helped to *waddle* him into a room. He was
a matter-of-fact doctor, and despised *anatomy*.
His features had been so confused and entangled
together by that unbeautifying disorder, the small-
pox, (which I have so often alluded to,) that it
almost required a chart to find their respective
stations.

These two learned gentlemen attended my poor
father with the greatest assiduity, and daily pre-
scribed for him a certain portion of every drug the
Stradbally apothecary could supply : but these
were not very numerous ; and as every thing loses
its vigour by age, so the Stradbally drugs, having
been some years waiting for customers (like the
landlord of the Red Cow in " John Bull"), of
course fell off in their efficacy, till at length they
each became, what the two doctors ultimately
turned my poor father into—a *caput mortuum*.
Notwithstanding the drugs and the doctors, indeed,
my father held out nearly ten days; but finally,
as a matter of course, departed this world. I was
deeply and sincerely grieved. I loved him affec-
tionately, and never after could reconcile myself
to either of his medical attendants. I had over-
heard their last consultation, and from that time to
this, am of opinion, that one doctor is as good as,
if not better than, five hundred. I shall never forget the dialogue. After discussing the weather and

prevalence of diseases in the county, they began to *consult*.—" What do you say to the *pulveres Jacobi?*" said Dr. Mulhall (the family physician).

" We are three days two late," smirked Doctor Fletcher.

" What think you then of cataplasmus, or the *flies?*—Eh! Doctor, eh! the flies?" said Mulhall.

" The flies won't rise in time," replied Doctor Fletcher :—" too late again!"

" I fear so," said Mulhall.

" 'Tis a pity, Doctor Mulhall, you did not suggest blistering breast and spine sooner : you know it was not my business, as I was only *called in* :—I could not duly *suggest*."

" Why," replied Doctor Mulhall, " I thought of it certainly, but I was unwilling to *alarm the family* by so definitive an application, unless in *extremis*."

" We're in *extremis* now," said Doctor Fletcher —" he! he !"

" Very true—very true," rejoined Doctor Mulhall; " but Nature is too strong for art; she takes her way in spite of us !"

" Unless, like a wife, she's kept down at first," said Fletcher—" he ! he ! he !"

" Perhaps I was rather too discreet and delicate, doctor; but if the colonel can still get down the *pulveres Jacobi*—" said Mulhall.

" He can't!" said Fletcher.

" Then we can do no more for the patient,"
replied Mulhall.

" Nothing *more*," said Fletcher; " so you had
better break your ' *give-over* ' to the family as ten-
derly as possible. That's your business, you
know : there is no use in my staying." And so,
as the sun rose, Doctor Fletcher jumped into his
little cabriolet, and I heard him say in parting,
" This is no jest, I fear, to his family."

The next day I lost my father; and never did
grief show itself more strong, or general, than on
that mournful occasion. There was not a dry eye
amongst his tenantry. My mother was distracted :
for more than thirty years that they had been
united, a single difference of opinion was never
expressed between them. His sons loved him as
a brother; and the attachment was mutual. His
person was prepossessing—his manners those of a
man of rank—his feelings such as became a man of
honour. He had the mien of a gentleman, and
the heart of a philanthropist; but he was careless
of his concerns, and had too rustic an education.
He left large landed estates, with large incumbrances to overwhelm them; and thirteen children
survived to lament his departure.

After I was called to the bar, Counsellor Fletcher,
the doctor's son (already mentioned in a former
Vol.), was in the best of practice. On my first circuit, I did not know him, and of course wished to
make acquaintance with my seniors. Lord Norbury

went circuit as judge at the same time I went first as barrister; he therefore can be no *juvenile* at this time of day.

Fletcher was, as has already been mentioned, of very uncertain humour, and when not pleased, extremely repulsive. The first day I was on circuit he came into the bar-room, perhaps tired, or —what was far worse to him—hungry, for nothing ruffled Fletcher so much as waiting for dinner. Wishing to lose no time in making acquaintance, with any countryman and brother barrister, and supposing he was endowed with the same degree of urbanity as other people, I addressed him in my own civil, but perhaps over-vivacious manner. He looked gruff, and answered my first question by some monosyllable. I renewed my address with one of the standing interrogatories resorted to by a man who wishes to fall into conversation. —Another monosyllable.

I was touched:—" You don't know me, perhaps, Counsellor Fletcher?" said I.

" Not as yet, sir," said Fletcher.

I was angry:—" Then I'll refresh your memory," said I. " Your father *killed* mine."

The barristers present laughed aloud.

" I hope you don't mean to revenge the circumstance on *me*, sir?" said Fletcher, with a sardonic smile.

" That," said I, " depends entirely on your

making me an apology for your father's ignorance.
I forgive *your own*."

He seemed surprised at the person he had to
deal with, but no increase of ire was apparent.
He looked, however, rather at a loss. The laugh
was now entirely against him, when Warden
Flood (my predecessor in the Admiralty), who was
then father of the circuit bar, happened to come
in, and formally introduced me as a new member.

After that time Fletcher and I grew very intimate :—he had several good qualities, and these
induced me to put up with many of his humours.
He was a very clever man, possessing good legal
information ; had a clear and independent mind,
and never truckled to any one because he was
great. He often wrangled, but never quarrelled
with me, and I believe I was one of the few who
maintained a sincere regard for him. He was intimate with Judge Moore, who now sits in his
place, and was the most familiar friend I had at
Temple. I have alluded to Judge Fletcher inci-
dentally, as a public character who could not be
bribed to support the Union, and was appointed a
judge by the Duke of Bedford during his short
viceroyalty.

I have introduced Doctor Fletcher's medical
practice in my glance at the Irish *faculty*, the
more particularly, because I was present at another consultation held with him, which was (as I

hinted at the commencement of this sketch) connected with as droll an incident as any could be,
little short of terminating fatally.

I rode with Mr. Flood, of Roundwood, to the
meeting of a turnpike-board, held at Mount Rath,
a few miles from my father's house. One of the
half-mounted gentlemen already described, Sam
Doxy of the Derrys, being on his way to the same
meeting, just at the entrance of the town his
horse stumbled over a heap of earth, and, rolling
over and over (like the somerset of a rope-
dancer), broke the neck of his rider. The body
was immediately—as usual when country gentlemen were slain in fox-hunting, riding home drunk
at nights, or the like—brought on a door, and laid
upon a bed spread on the floor at the next inn. Mr.
Knaggs, the universal prescriber, &c. for the town
and vicinity, was sent for to inspect *the corpse,* and
Doctor Fletcher being also by chance in the place,
was called into the room to consult as to the *dead
man,* and vouch that the breath was out of the
body of Mr. Samuel Doxy of the Derrys.

The two practitioners found he had no pulse,
not even a single *thump in his arteries* (as Doctor
Knaggs emphatically expressed it). They therefore both shook their heads. His hands being felt,
were found to be cold. They shook their heads
again. The doctors now retired to the window,
and gravely consulted : first, as to the danger of
stumbling horses ; and second, as to the proba-

bility of the deceased having been sober. They then walked back, and both declared it was "all over" with Mr. Doxy of the Derrys. His neck was broken—otherwise dislocated; his marrow-bones (according to Dr. Knaggs) were disjointed; and his death had of course been instantaneous. On this decisive opinion being promulgated to the turnpike-board, Dr. Fletcher mounted his pony, and left the town, to *cure* some other patient.

The coroner, Mr. Calcut, was sent for to hold his inquest before Sam's body could be "forwarded" home to the Derrys; and Mr. Knaggs, the apothecary, remained in the room, to see if any *fee* might be stirring when his relations should come to carry away the dead carcase; when, all of a sudden, an exclamation of "by J—s!" burst forth from Mr. Jerry Palmer (already mentioned) of Dureen, near Castle Durrow, an intimate acquaintance of Sam Doxy: "I don't think he's dead at all:—my father often made him twice *deader* at Dureen, with Dan Brennan's double-proof, and he was as well and hearty again as any dunghill cock early in the morning."

"Not dead!" said Knaggs with surprise and anger. "Is not dead, you say?—Lieutenant Jer Palmer, you don't mean to disparage my skill, or injure my business in the town, I hope? There is no more life left in Sam Doxy than in the leg of that table."

The lieutenant bristled up at the doctor's contradiction. " I don't care a d—n, Pothecary Knaggs, either for your skill, your business, or yourself; but I say Sam Doxy is *not* dead, and I repeat that I have seen him *twice as dead* at Dureen, and likewise, by the same token, on the day Squire Pool's tenants of Ballyfair had a great dinner in Andrew Harlem's big room at Maryborough."

" Pothecary Knaggs" was now much chagrined. " Did you ever hear the like, gentlemen of the turnpike-board ?" said he. " Is it because the lieutenant was in the American wars that he thinks he knows a corpse as well as I do ?"

" No I don't do that same," said Palmer : " for they say here that you have *made* as many dead bodies yourself as would serve for a couple of battles, and a few skirmishes into the bargain. But I say *Sam* is not dead, by J—s !"

" Well now, gentlemen," said Knaggs, appealing to public candour from the rough treatment of the lieutenant, " you shall soon see, gentlemen, with all your eyes that I am no *ignoramus,* as the lieutenant seems to say." Then opening his case of instruments and strapping a large operation knife on the palm of his fist, " now, gentlemen of the turnpike-board," pursued he, " I'll convince you all that Sam Doxy is as dead as Ballaghlanagh.*

* Ballaghlanagh was the name of an old Irish bard (by tra- dition), whose ghost used to come the night before to people who were to be killed fighting in battle on the morning : and as

Its a burning shame for you, Lieutenant Jer Palmer, to be after running down a well-known practitioner in this manner, in his own town. Gentlemen, look here, now, I'll show you that Sam is dead. Living, indeed! Oh, that's a fine story!"

We all conceived that Doctor Knaggs only intended to *try* to bleed him; and with this impression flocked round the body. Doctor Knaggs turned *the corpse* on one side, took off the cravat, and the neck appeared to have somewhat of a bluish look on one side. "Now, gentlemen," said he, "here's the spot (pressing it with his finger): the spinal marrow is injured, perhaps in more places than one, or two either; the bones are dislocated, and the gristle between them is knocked out of its place. The formation of a gentleman's neck is just the same as that of a horse's tail; and as most of you have either yourselves docked and nicked, or been present at the docking and nicking of the tail of a hunter, you'll understand precisely the structure of Sam Doxy's vertebre. Now, gentlemen, (all this time placing Sam's head in a convenient position to make an incision, or, had the coroner been present, to *cut the head off*, for clearer demonstration,) see, now, I'll just make a slight

---

a *ghost* offers the most convincing proof that the mortal it represents is no longer living, the term *Ballaghlanagh*, came, figuratively, to signify a " dead man." I learnt this explanation from the old colloughs, who all joined exactly in the same tradition.

longitudinal gash along the back joints of the neck,
and by withdrawing the skin and the covering of
fat on either side, I'll show as clear as his nose the
fatal fracture of the spinal cord."

Every person in company now began instinctively to feel the nape of his own neck for the
spinal cord which, the doctor was speaking of.
" No man," resumed Doctor Knaggs, " ever recovered when this cord was fairly cracked, and
that's the real secret of hanging, I assure you ; and
it has been remarked that no culprit at Maryborough has ever given a kick after he was duly
strung and the shelf fell, for these three last years,
since I humanely taught the hangman the proper
way. The *jerk* is the thing, gentlemen ; and whether the spine is broken by its being pulled up from
a man's shoulders by a cord, or thrust down into
his shoulders by a fall on the head, makes no sort of
difference. Not dead !" resumed he, with a sneer
at the lieutenant : " Gentlemen, (every body came
close) now, you see, the gristle which we call
cartilage lies between those two bones, and the
cord runs over and within also :—when cut through,
then, the head, gentlemen, having no support, bobs
forward, and the dislocation will appear quite
plain. See, now," and as he spoke he gave a
pretty smart gash from the nape of Sam's neck
downward toward his shoulders ; and proceeding
to draw back the skin and fat on each side, to get
a view of the bones, to the surprise of the turn-

pike-board, the amazement of Doctor Knaggs himself, and the triumph of Lieutenant Jer Palmer,
a stream of warm red blood instantly issued from
the gash, and a motion appeared in one eyelid of
the corpse.

"By J—s!" shouted the lieutenant, "I told
you the man was not dead—not a taste of it. Oh!
you diabolical pothecary, if you attempt to give
another slash, I'll cut your own wezand; and if
the poor follow dies *now*, of this cutting, which I
think he may, I'll prosecute you for the murder of
Sam Doxy of the Derrys—a fair honest man, and
a friend of my father's!"

Doctor Knaggs stood petrified and motionless.

"Gentlemen," continued Jer Palmer, "lend
me your cravats. (An immense jug of hot punch
was smoking on the hearth ready made for the
proposed dinner.) I know well enough what to
do," said the lieutenant: "my father's own neck
was broken two years ago, coming home drunk one
night from Ballyspellen Spa, at the widow Maher's
house-warming: his horse tumbled over at the
Seven Sisters; but Dr. Jacob soon brought him to
again.—I recollect now all about it. Here, gentlemen, stir, give me your *cravats*; you have no
handkerchiefs I suppose."

They all obeyed the lieutenant, who immediately plunged the cravats into the hot punch, and
lapped one of them round the *dead man's* neck,
then another over that, and another still, and kept

dropping the hot punch on them, whereat the blood flowed freely. He then, putting his knees to the dead man's shoulder, gave his head two or three no very gentle lugs, accompanying them in the manner of a view holloa, with " Ough! Hurra! Hurra! By J—s he's alive and kicking! Oh! you murdering thief of a pothecary, get off, or I'll cut your throat!"

The poor apothecary stood motionless at the window; for Palmer (whom, in his paroxysm, he durst not go near) was between him and the door; but he wished himself a hundred miles off. The lieutenant then put a spoonful of the punch into Sam Doxy's mouth, and down it went, to the surprise of the turnpike-board. In a short time a glassful was patiently received the same way. A groan and a heavy sigh now proved the fallibility of Pothecary Knaggs; and the lieutenant's superior treatment was extolled by the whole board. The dead man at length opened one eye, then the other; in about half an hour he could speak; and in the course of an hour more the broken-necked Doxy was able to sit up. They then got some mulled wine and spices for him, and he was quite recovered, with the exception of a pain in his head and neck; but he could bear no motion, so they fixed him in an upright position in an arm-chair, and Palmer remained with him to perfect his miraculous cure. We dined in another room.

Mr. Flood and myself called on Doxy next day, and brought him and Lieutenant Palmer home to Roundwood; and poor Dr. Knaggs' wanting to cut off the head of Mr. Sam Doxy of the Derrys became a standing jest, with a hundred embellishments, till both have been forgotten. I know not if Knaggs is living. Sam Doxy was at last choked by the drumstick of a turkey sticking in his throat whilst he was picking it.

TRANSFUSION OF BLOOD.

The Irish on the continent—Slow travelling of remittances—Inconveniences thereof—Sir John Burke, of Glinsk—Reasonable points of curiosity—Prompt satisfaction—*Messieurs les Créanciers*—Sir John's health declines—Given over by the faculty generally—Doctor T—'s perseverance—Its success—A game at cross purposes—Custodiums in Ireland—New mode of liquidating a debt—Galway gore—Receipt for ennobling the *bourgeois* of Paris—Sir John Burke's marriage and visit to Rome—His return—Lady Burke—Glinsk Castle.

It has been generally observed, that our fellow-subjects who sojourn long on the continent often lose many of their national traits, and imbibe those of other countries. The Irish, however, present an exception to this rule. I have scarce ever met a thorough-paced Irishman whose oddities totally deserted him; the humorous idiom of his language, and the rich flavour of his dialect, are intrinsic, and adhere as steadily to his tongue as *fancy* does to his brain, and eccentricity to his actions.

An Irishman is *toujours* an Irishman, and where-soever he " puts up " seldom fails to find one in-veterate enemy—" himself." This observation is not confined to the lower or middle classes of Hibernians, but occasionally includes the superior orders. Like the swine, when the demon got into them, Irishmen on the continent keep frisking, pirouetting, galloping, and puffing away, till they lose their footing; and there is scarcely a more entertaining spectacle than that afforded by the schemes, devices, and humours of a true son of Erin, under these circumstances.

I was greatly amused by an incident which took place at Paris some time since;—it possesses as much of the Irish *flavour* as any bagatelle anecdote I recollect to have met with; and as the parties are above the medium class, well known, all alive, and still on the same *pavé* in perfect harmony, the thing is rendered more entertaining.

An Irish baronet of very ancient family (an honour which he never suffered any person to be ignorant of after twenty minutes' conversation), proprietor of a large Galway territory, garnished with the usual dilapidated chateau, brogueless tenantry, managing attorneys, and mis-managing agents, having sufficiently squeezed his estate to get (as he terms) the *juice* out of it, determined to serve a few campaigns about St. James' Street, &c., and try if he could *retrench* at the several club-houses and " hells " to be met with amidst

what is called " high life " in our economical metropolis.

After having enacted with *éclat* all the parts in
the various scenes usually performed on that great
theatre,, he at length found, that the place was
not much *cheaper* than *sweet* Glinsk, or any old
principality of his own dear country. He therefore resolved to change the scene for a more
diverting and cheerful one; and by way of a
finish, came over to Paris, where any species of
ruin may be completed with a taste, ease, and despatch unknown in our boorish country.

The baronet brought over three or four thousand pounds in his fob, just (as he told me) to try,
by way of comparison, how long that quantity of
the dross would last in Paris *——on which point his
curiosity was promptly satisfied :—" Frascati" and
the " Salon des Etrangers," by a due application
of spotted bones, coloured pasteboard, and painted
whirligigs, under the superintendence of the Marquis de Livere, informed him at the termination
of a short novitiate, that nearly the last of his

---

* Last year, the son of a very great man in England came
over to Paris with a considerable sum in his pocket for the very
same purpose. The first thing he did was gravely to ask his
banker (an excellent and sensible man), " How long six thousand pounds would last him in Paris ?" The reply was a true
and correct one, " If you play, three days; if you don't, six
weeks."

" Empereurs" had been securely vested in the custody of the said Marquis de Livere.

Though this seemed, *primâ facie*, rather *inconvenient*, yet the baronet's dashing establishment did not immediately suffer diminution, until his valet's repeated answer, *pas chez lui*, began to alarm the crew of grooms, goddesses, led captains, &c.

Misfortune (and he began to fancy this was very like one) seldom delays long to fill up the place of ready money when that quits a gentleman's service : and it now seemed disposed to attach itself to the baronet in another way. Madam Pandora's box appeared to fly open, and a host of bodily ills beset Sir John, who, having but indifferent nerves, was quite thrown on his back.

Such was the hapless situation of Sir John Burke, while exercising his portion of the virtue of patience, in *waiting for remittances*—a period of suspense particularly diagreeable to travellers abroad—every post-day being pretty certain to carry off the *appetite;* which circumstance, to be sure, may be sometimes considered *convenient* enough.

Families from the interior of Hibernia are peculiarly subject to that suspense ; and where their Irish agent happens to be an old *confidential solicitor*, or a *very dear friend*, or a near relation of the *family*, the attack is frequently acute. An instance, indeed, occurred lately, wherein the *miscarriage* of an Irish letter actually caused the very same accident to a new-married lady!

The baronet, however, bore up well; and being extremely good-humoured, the surliest *créanciers* in Paris could not find in their hearts for some time to be angry with him; and so, most unreasonably left him to be angry with himself, which is a thousand times more tormenting to a man, because *sans* intermission.

At length, some of his most *pressing* friends, who a short time before had considered it their highest honour to enjoy the *pratique* of Monsieur le Chevalier, began to show symptoms of losing temper; —as smoke generally forebodes the generation of fire, something like a blaze seemed likely to burst forth; and as the baronet most emphatically said to me—" The d—d duns, like a flock of jack snipes, were eternally thrusting their *long bills* into me, as if I was a piece of *bog!*"

Complaisance and smooth words very rarely fail to conciliate a Frenchman; and, after all, the baronet never experienced more civil or kinder friends in Paris than some of these very *snipes* who stuck their long bills into him. But "remittances" from the county of Galway have been, time immemorial, celebrated for the extreme slowness of their movements; and though in general very *light*, they travel more deliberately than a broad-wheel waggon. Hence, Sir John Burke's

"corporal ills" were both perpetuated and height-
ened by his mental uneasiness.

Doctors were called in, in hopes that one or
other of them might *by chance* hit upon a remedy;
and Sir John submitted to their prescriptions (to
use his own words), like a lamb going to the
slaughter.—" I knew very well," said he, " that
one *banker* could do me more good by a single
dose, than all the *doctors* in Paris put together ;—
but as my friends Messrs. ***** had declined to
administer any more *metallic* prescriptions, I really
feared that my *catastrophe* was not very distant."

And, indeed, the doctors, neither jointly nor
severally agreeing as to the nature of his symptoms, nor to the necessary mode of treatment, after
several *consultations* respecting the *weather* and the
war (as customary), gave Sir John's case up as
desperate: and having showed the palms of their
hands without any favourable result, shook their
heads, made each three low and lingering bows,
and left the baronet to settle affairs himself with
Madam Pandora as well as he could.

One of these medical gentlemen, however,—
a fair, square, straightforward, skilful nosologist,—
could not bring himself so easily to give up the
baronet: he returned ; and by dint of medica-
menta, phlebotomy, blistering, leeching, cupping,
smothering in vapour, &c. &c. (the pains of the
patient's mind, meanwhile, being overcome by the
pains of his body) the doctor at last got him

thorough the thing (as they say in Ireland). He was not, however, quite free from the danger of a relapse; and an unlucky flask *extraordinary* of "Epernay sec" (taken to celebrate his recovery) set Sir John's solids and fluids again fermenting, knocked down his convalescence, which Dr. T—— had so indefatigably re-established, and introduced a certain inflammatory gentleman called fever.

. The clergy were now summoned, and attended with an extra quantity of oil and water to lighten and prepare the baronet's soul for speedy transportation; some souls, they said, and I believe truly, being much easier put into dying order than others. The skill of Doctor T——, however, once more preserved his patient for further adventures, and both physician and baronet agreed that, as the priests had done his body none, and his soul no *perceptible* service, and as holy men were of course above all lust of lucre, there was no necessity for cashing *them;* so that the contemplated fees for masses should in strict justice be transferred to prescriptions. A few more plenteous bleedings were therefore substituted for extreme unction: with the aid of a sound natural constitution, Sir John once more found himself on his legs; and having but little flesh, and no fat, his shanks had not much difficulty in carrying his body moderate distances. "

: At the last bleeding, the incident occurred to

which the foregoing is but matter of induction. The blood which the doctor had just extracted from the baronet was about twenty ounces 'of genuine ruby Galway gore, discharged unadulterated from the veins of a high-crested, aboriginal Irishman. It lay proudly basking and coagulating before the sun in china basins, at the chamber-window. Sir John seeming still rather weak, the physician determined to bring all his skill into a focus, discover the latent source of indisposition, and if possible at once root it out of the baronet's constitution, thereby gaining the double advantage of increasing professional fame and the amount of his fees. Now, at precisely the same point of time, the baronet was inventing an apology for *not paying* the doctor.

After musing some time, as every physician in the world does, whether he is thinking of the patient or not, Doctor T——— said, " Pray, let me see your tongue, Sir John." .

" My *tongue!*" exclaimed the baronet, "ah ! you might be greatly disappointed by *that* organ ; there's no depending on *tongues* now-a-days, doctor !"

" Yet the tongue is very symptomatic, I can assure you, Sir John," pursued the doctor gravely.

" Possibly, in *your* part of the world," replied the baronet. " But I do assure you, we place very little reliance on tongues in my country."

" You know ' best," said the doctor coolly :

" then, pray let me feel your pulse, Sir John,"
looking steadfastly on his stop-watch, counting the
seconds and the throbs of the Milesian artery.
" Heyday! why, your pulse is not only irregular,
but *intermits!*"

" I wish my remittances did not," remarked
Sir John, mournfully, and thinking he had got an
excellent opportunity of apologising to the doctor.

The latter, however, had no idea of any round-
about *apologies* (never having been in Ireland), and
resumed : " your remittances! ah, ah, Sir John !
But seriously, your pulse is all astray ; pray, do
you feel a pain any where ?"

" Why, doctor," said Sir John, (sticking in like
manner to *his* point,) " whenever I put my hand
into my breeches-pocket, I feel a confounded
twitch, which gives me very considerable uneasiness, I assure you."

" Hah !" said the doctor, conceiving he had now
discovered some new symptom about the femoral
artery—" are you sure . there's nothing *in* your
pocket that hurts you, Sir John ?—Perhaps some—"

" O no, doctor," said the baronet rather impatiently ; " there's *nothing at all* in my pocket,
Doctor T———."

" Then the twitch may be rather serious," and
the doctor looked *knowing,* although he was still
at fault concerning the *éclaircissement.* " It is a
singular symptom. Do you feel your head at all
heavy, Sir John—a sensation of weight ?"

" Not at all," replied the other :—" my head is (except my *purse*) the lightest thing I possess at present."

The disciple of Galen still supposed Sir John was jesting as to his purse, inasmuch as the plum-coloured vis-a-vis, with arms, crests, and mant-lings to match—with groom, geldings, and the baronet's white Arabian, still remained at the Hotel de Wagram, Rue de la Paix.

" Ha! ha! Sir John," cried he, " I am glad to see you in such spirits."

Nothing, however, either as to the malady or the fees being fully explained, it at length flashed across the doctor's comprehension that the baro-net might *possibly* be in downright *earnest* as to his *remittances*. Such a thought must, under the cir-cumstances, have a most disheartening effect on the contour of any medical man in Europe. On the first blush of this fatal suspicion the doctor's features began to droop—his eyebrows descended, and a sort of *in utrumque paratus* look, that many of my readers must have borne when expecting a money letter, but not quite sure it may not be an *apology*, overspread his countenance, while his nasal muscles puckering up (as in the tic dou-loureux), seemed to quaver between a smile and a sardonic grin.

Sir John could scarcely contain himself at the doctor's ludicrous embarrassment. " By Jove," said he, " I am serious!"

" Serious! as to what, Sir John?" stammered the physician, getting out of conceit both with his patient and himself.

" The fact," said Sir John, " is this : your long and indefatigable attention merits all my confidence, and you shall have it."

" Confidence!" exclaimed the doctor, bowing, " you do me honour ; but——"

" Yes, doctor, I now tell you (*confidentially*) that certain papers and matters called in Ireland *custodiums*,* have bothered both me and my brother

---

* A *custodium* is a law proceeding in Ireland, not practised much any where else, and is vastly worse than even an " extent in aid." By one fiction the debtor is supposed to owe money to the king :—by another " fiction," the king demands his money ;—and the debtor, by a third " fiction," is declared a rebel, because he does not pay the king.—A commission of rebellion then issues in the name of the king against the debtor ; and by a fourth " fiction," he is declared an outlaw, and all his estates are seized and sequestered to pay *his majesty.* A receiver of every shilling belonging to the debtor is then appointed by the king's chief baron of the exchequer ; every tenant on the estates is served with the " fictions," as well as the landlord ; and a *debt* of *one hundred pounds* has been frequently ornamented with a bill of costs to the amount of *three thousand* in the name of his majesty, who does not know the least circumstance of the matter.

There was scarcely a gentleman in the county of Galway, formerly, but was as great an *outlaw* as Robin Hood ; with this difference, that Robin Hood might be *hanged*, and his majesty could only *starve* the gentleman.

Joseph, notwithstanding all his exertions for me as agent, receiver, remitter, attorney, banker, auditor, and arranger-general; which said custodiums have given up all my lands, in spite of Joe, to the king, as trustee for a set of horse-jockies, Jews, mortgagees, gamblers, solicitors, and annuity-boys—who have been tearing me to pieces for twenty years past without my having the slightest suspicion of their misdemeanors;. and now, doctor, they have finally, by divers law fictions, got *his majesty* to patronise them."

"But, sir! sir!" interrupted the doctor.

"I assure you, however," continued Sir John, placidly, "that my brother Joe (whose Christian name — between you and me, doctor—ought to have been Ulick, after Ulick the Milesian, if my mother had done him common justice at his christening) is a long-headed fellow, and will promptly bring those infernal custodium impostors into proper order."

"But, sir, sir!" repeated the doctor.

"One fellow," pursued the baronet, "hearing that Joe intended to *call him out* for laying on his papers, has stopped all law proceedings already, and made a proper apology. The very name of Burke, of Glinsk, doctor, is as sounding as *Waterloo*, in the county of Galway.

"Pardon me, Sir John," said Doctor T——, " but what can all this have to do with—"

" Never mind," again interrupted the baronet, catching hold of one of the doctor's coat-buttons,* " never mind ; I give you my word, Joe is a steady, good, clever fellow, and looks two ways at every thing before he does it—I don't allude to the cast in his eye : a horse with a wall-eye, you know, doctor, is the very lad for hard work!—ha! ha! ha!"

The doctor could stand this no longer, and said, " I know nothing about wall-eyed horses, Sir John."—Indeed, being now hopeless, he made the second of the three bows he had determined to depart with; but he found his button still in custody between Sir John's fingers, and was necessitated to suspend his exit, or leave it behind him.

." A plan has occurred to me, doctor," said the baronet, thoughtfully, " which may not only liquidate my just and honourable debt to you for attendance and operations, but must, if you are as skilful as I think you are, eventually realise you a pretty fortune."

·This in a moment changed the countenance of the doctor, as a smouldering fire, when it gets a

---

* How admirably does Horace describe the grievance of a *bore* catching hold of your button, and making the proprietor a prisoner till his speech is expended. Doctor T—— told me that the satire came into his head whilst Sir John had him in hold, and that in his hurry to emancipate himself, he made a large cut in a new surtout, and quite spoiled its beauty.

blast of the bellows, instantly blazes up and begins to generate its hydrogen. " And, pray, sir," asked the impatient physician, " what plan may this be? what new *bank* are you thinking of?"

" 'Tis no *bank*," said Sir John ; " its a much better thing than any bank, for the more you *draw*, the richer you'll be."

The doctor's eyelids opened wide ; his eyebrows became elevated, and he drew his ear close to the proposer, that he might not lose a single word of so precious an *exposé*.

" You know," said Sir John, " though you are a Sarnion (Guernsey-man) by birth, you *must* know, as *all the world* knows, that the name of the Burkes or O'Bourkes (Irlandois), and their castle of Glinsk, have been established and celebrated in Ireland some dozen centuries."

" I have heard the name, sir," said the doctor, rather peevishly.

" Be assured 'tis the very first cognomen in Ireland," said Sir John.

" Possibly," said the doctor.

" Nay, *positively*," rejoined the baronet: " far more ancient than the O'Neils, O'Briens, O'Flahertys, who indeed are comparatively *moderns*. We were native princes and kings several centuries before even the term Anno *Domini* was used."

" I will not dispute it, sir."

" Nay, I can prove it. I had six and twenty

quarters on my shield without a blot upon either—
save by one marriage with a d—d *Bodkin* out of
the twelve tribes of Galway, about a hundred and
eighty years ago. We never got over that!"

" For Heaven's sake, sir," said Doctor T——,
" do come to the point."

" Pardon me," said Sir John, " I am on the
point itself."

" As how?" inquired the other.

" Come here," said Sir John, " and I will soon
satisfy you on that head:" and as he spoke he led
him to the window, where three china cups full
of the baronet's gore lay in regular order. " See!
that's the genuine crimson stuff for you, doctor!
eighteen ounces at least of it; the richest in Europe! and as to colour—what's carmine to it?"

The doctor was bewildered ; but so passive, he
stood quite motionless.

" Now," continued Sir John, " we are bringing
the matter to the point. You can *gaurantee* this
gore to be genuine Glinsk blood : it gushed beautifully after your lancet, doctor, eh! didn't it?"

" What of that, sir?" said Doctor T—: " really,
Sir John, I can stay no longer."

" You have much ordinary professional practice," said the baronet—" I mean exclusive of your
noble patients in Rue Rivoli, &c.—visits, for instance, to the Boulevard St. Martin, St. Antoine,
Place de Bastile, De Bourse, &c., which you
know are principally peopled by brokers with

aspiring families; rich *négocians*, with ambitious daughters, &c., who, if they were to give five hundred thousand francs, can't get into one fashionable *soirée* for want of a touch of gentility—not even within smell of sweet little Berry's* under nursery-maids. Now," said Sir John, pausing a moment, " we're at the point."

" So much the better," said the man of medicine.

" I understand that there is a member of the faculty in Paris, who undertakes the *transfusion of blood* with miraculous success, and has not only demonstrated its practicability, but insists that it may by improvement be rendered sufficiently operative to harmonise and amalgamate the different qualities of different species of animals. I am told he does not yet despair of seeing, by transfusion of blood, horses becoming the best mousers, cats setting partridges, and the vulgarest fellows upon earth metamorphosed into gentlemen." ·

" Pshaw ! pshaw !" exclaimed Doctor T——.

" Now, I perceive no reason," resumed Sir John, " why any man should perform such an operation better than yourself: and if you advertise in the *Petit Avis* that you have a quantity of genuine Glinsk

* Sir John is the greatest eulogist of the Duchess of Berry, and has got the Legion of Honour for having given up his bed, blankets, and all, to the Duke of Berry, somewhere on the road, when they were both running away from Napoleon Bonaparte.

O'Bourke *gore* always at command, 'to transfuse into persons who wish to acquire the *gentilities* and the feelings of noblesse, without pain, or patent, my blood, fresh from the veins, would bring you at least a *Nap* a spoonful: and in particular proportions, would so refine and purify the vulgar puddle of the *bourgeois*, that they might soon be regarded (in conjunction with their money) as high at least as the half-starved *quatrième* nobility, who hobble down to their sugar and water at *soirées* in the fauxbourg St. Germain, and go to bed in the dark to save candle-light."

The doctor felt hurt beyond all endurance : he blushed up to his very whiskers, sealed his lips hermetically—by a sardonic smile only disclosing one of his dog-teeth, and endeavoured to depart : but the button was still fast between Sir John's fingers, who begged of his victim not to spare his veins, saying, " that he would with pleasure stand as much phlebotomy as would make a fortune for any reasonable practitioner."

This was decisive : the doctor could stand it no longer ; so snatching up the toilet scissors, he cut the button clean off his new surtout, and vanished without waiting ceremoniously to make the third bow, as had always previously been his custom.

However, the baronet, when Joe (who should have been Ulick) afterward sent him over some of the *dross*, made full metallic compensation to the doctor,—and within this last month I met them walking together in great harmony.

This incident, which I had known and noted long before, was then repeated by Sir John in the doctor's presence; and it affords the very strongest proof what a truly valuable liquid genuine Irish gore is considered by the chiefs of County Galway.

There is not a baronet in the United Kingdom who (with the very essence of good-humour) has afforded a greater opportunity for notes and anecdotes than Sir John Burke of Glinsk Castle and tilt-yard;—and no person ever will, or ever can, relate them so well as himself.

Sir John Burke is married to the sister of Mr. Ball, the present proprietor of Oatlands, commonly called the *Golden Ball*. I witnessed the courtship; negotiated with the brother; read over the skeleton of the marriage settlement, and was present at the departure of the baronet and his new lady for Rome, to kiss the pope's toe. I also had the pleasure of hailing them on their return, as *le Marquis* and *la Marquise de Bourke* of the Holy Roman Empire. Sir John had the *promise* of a *principality* from the papal see when he should be prepared to pay his holiness the regulation price for it. At all events, he came back highly freighted with a papal bull, a nobleman's patent, holy relics, mock cameos, real lava, wax tapers, Roman paving-stones, &c. &c.; and after having been over-

set into the Po, and making the fortune of his
courier, he returned in a few months to Paris, to
ascertain what fortune his wife had ;—a circumstance which his anxiety to be married and kiss
the pope's toe had not given him sufficient time
to investigate before: He found it very large, and
calculated to bear, a good deal of cutting and
hacking ere it should quit his service—with no
great probability of his ever coaxing it back again.
Sir John's good temper, however, settles that matter with great facility by quoting Dean Swift's
admirable eulogium upon poverty:—" Money's
the devil, and God keeps it from us," said the
dean. If this be orthodox, there will be more
gentlemen's souls saved in Ireland than in any
other part of his Britannic Majesty's dominions.

Previous to Sir John's marriage, Miss Ball understood, or rather had formed a conception, that
Glinsk Castle was placed in one of the most cultivated, beautiful, and romantic districts of romantic
Ireland, in which happy island she had never been,
and I dare say never will be. Burke, who seldom says any thing without laughing heartily at
his own remark, was questioned by her pretty
closely as to the beauty of the demesne, and the
architecture of the castle. " Now, Sir John,"
said she, " have you much dressed grounds upon
the demesne of Glinsk ?"

" Dressed, my love !" repeated Sir John,
" why, my whole estate has been nearly *dressed up*
these seven years past."

"That's very uncommon," said Miss Ball; "there must have been a great expenditure on it."

"Oh, very great," replied the baronet, "very great."

"The castle," said her future ladyship, "is, I suppose, in good order?"

"It ought to be," answered Sir John; "for (searching his pockets) I got a bill from my brother Joe of, I think, two hundred pounds, only for nails, iron cramps, and holdfasts—for a single winter."

The queries of Miss Ball innocently proceeded, and, I think, the replies were among the pleasantest and most adroit I ever heard. The lady seemed quite delighted, and nearly expressed a wish to go down to the castle as soon as possible. "As Sir John's rents may not come in instantly," said she, "I have, I fancy, a few thousand pounds in the bank just now, and that may take us down and new-furnish, at least, a wing of the castle!"

This took poor Sir John dreadfully aback. Glinsk was, he told me, actually in a tumbling state. Not a gravel walk within twenty miles of it: and as to timber, "How the devil," said he, "could I support both my trees and my establishment at the same time?—Now," he pursued, "Barrington, my good friend, do just tell her what I told you about my aunt Margaret's ghost, that looks out of the castle window on every anni-

versary of her own death and birth-day, and on
other periodical occasions. She'll be so frightened
(for, thank God! she's afraid of ghosts), that she'll
no more think of going to Glinsk than to America."

" Tell her yourself, Sir John," said I :—" nobody understands a romance better ; and I'm
sure, if this be not a *meritorious*, it is certainly an
innocent one."

In fine, he got his groom to tell her maid all
about *the ghost :* the maid told the mistress, with
frightful exaggerations : Sir John, when appealed
to, spoke mysteriously of the matter ; and the
purchase of Glinsk Castle could not have induced
Miss Ball to put her foot in it afterwards. She is
a particularly mild and gentlewomanly lady, and,
I fancy, would scarcely have survived a visit to
Glinsk, even if the ghost of Madam Margaret had
not prevented her making the experiment.

SWEARING NO VICE.

English slang contrasted with Irish imprecation—The chase of
St. Chrysostom, and his rescue—Meet garnish for an Hiber_
nian anecdote—Futile attempts at imitation by English dra_
matists, &c.—Remarks of a puritan on the author and his
book—A caution, and a shrewd way of observing it—
Michael Heney, steward of the author's father—His notions
concerning swearing—Curious dialogue between him and the
author—New mode of teaching children filial respect.

THOUGH I have more than ordinary cause to be
gratified by the reception the first two volumes of
this work so unexpectedly met with, and am extremely grateful for that reception, yet I am well
aware that certain starched moralists may conceive,
and perhaps, *primâ facie*, with reason, that there is
too much "imprecation," and what the fastidious of
Bond-street call *vulgarity* introduced into the Irish
colloquies.   I admit that a person who has never
been in the interior of Ireland, or accustomed to
the Irish people and their peculiarities, might
naturally think so.   I therefore feel it a duty to
such critics, to give them at least one or two rea-

sons why they should not consider Irish oaths immoral, or Irish colloquy vulgar.

The outrageous blasphemy and indecency, so copious in the *slang* of England, with neither wit, point, or national humour, to qualify it, might indeed disgust even the seven hundred imps whom the devil sent into this world to capture St. Chrysostom.* The curses and imprecations of Ireland are of a nature totally different. They have no great variety ; they are neither premeditated, nor acquired through habits of dissipation. They are idiomatic, a part and parcel of the regular language of the country, and repeated in other countries as a necessary appendage to the humour of an Irish story, though they would be utterly unadapted to any other people. Walter Scott's delightful writings, with all the native simplicity and idiomatic dialect of the ancient Celtic, would be totally spoiled, for instance, had he mingled or introduced in them the oaths and idioms indispensable as a seasoning to Irish colloquy ; an observation sufficiently illustrated by the absurd and stupid attempts to imitate Irish phraseology made by English dramatic mimics and grimacers.

* There is a manuscript of great antiquity in the library of the Vatican, which gives a full and circumstantial account of the chase and running down of St. Chrysostom by a legion of devils, and of his recapture by an inconsiderable number of saints, who came from heaven to the rescue.

Here I am quite prepared for the most severe criticism. " Upon my word (the lank-haired puritan will say), this is a most dangerous and sinful writer ; holding out that an anecdote, if it be Irish, would lose its relish if there were neither oaths nor imprecations tacked to it. No man can, in the opinion of that immoral writer, repeat an innocent Irish story, unless he at the same time calls down the wrath of Heaven upon himself; and, moreover, upon such of his auditors as take any pleasure in hearing him."

I know two very young ladies who told me that their mammas directed them to skim over any *im-proper* parts of the Sketches ;—and that they read every word, to *find out* those improper parts. The book, they said, was extremely diverting ; and as to the oaths, they never swore themselves, and never would, and therefore reading *that part* could do them no harm.

My own notions respecting this Irish habit of imprecation were illustrated many years ago by an actual dialogue with a man of low rank in that country ; and as our conversation bore upon a subject of which scarce a day passes without reminding me, I have retained its import as if it had taken place yesterday : and though, after an interval of more than forty-five years, it is not to be expected I should repeat the exact *words* uttered, yet I really think my memory serves as to the precise *sentences*.

We had got accidentally upon the topic; and I expressed my opinion, as I have already stated it here, that these objectionable phrases were merely idiomatic and involuntary—betraying no radical or intentional vice. His notion went further; he apologised for the practice not only statistically, but said, with characteristic fervour, that the genuine Irish people could not " do without it." " Many," said he, " would not mind what was said to them, unless there was a curse tacked on to the direction. For instance, old Ned Doran, of Cherry Hill, ordered all his children, male and female, neither to curse nor swear, as they regarded their father's orders; and the consequence was, the people all said they were going to turn *swadlers,* and not a maid or a labourer would do a farthing's worth of work—for want of being *forced* to do it in the ' owld way.' "

The man I talked with was a character not very general in England, but frequently met with among the Irish commonalty, whose acuteness of intellect, naturally exceeding that of English labourers, is rather increased by the simplicity of their ideas. Self-taught, they turn any thing they learn to all the purposes that their humble and depressed state can give room for.

Fortune had denied him the means of emerging from obscurity; and Michael Heney was for many years the faithful steward of my father, living with him to the period of his death. His station in life had been previously very low ; his education was correspondent ; but he had from Nature a degree of mental strength which operated in possessing him with a smattering of every thing likely or proper to be understood by persons of his grade. He was altogether a singularity, and would not give up one iota of his opinions. To address him as a casuist, was the greatest favour you could confer on Mick Heney ; and the originality of his ideas, and promptitude of his replies, often amused me extremely.

But for the detail of our dialogue :—

" Is it not extraordinary, Michael," said I one day (as a great number of labourers were making up hay in one of the meadows, and Michael and myself were seated on a heap of it), " that those poor fellows can scarcely pronounce a sentence without some oath to confirm, or some deity to garnish it with ?"

" Master Jonah, (he never said ' please your honour' to any body but his master,) sure its their *only* way of talking *English*. They can speak very good *Irish* without either swearing or cursing, because its their own tongue. Besides, all their forefathers used to be cursing the English day and night for many a hundred years ; so that they never used the Sassanagh tongue without mixing curses along with it, and now its grown a custom, and they say that the devil himself could not break them of it—poor crethurs !"

·'" I should-·think the ·devil won't -try, Mick
Heney."

"· Its no joke, Master Jonah."

" But," said I, (desirous of drawing him out,)
" they never fail to take the name of J—s on every
silly occasion. Sure there's no reason in *that*?"

" Yes, but there is, Master Jonah," said Heney :
" in·the owld time, when the English used to be
cutting and hacking, starving and burning the poor
Irish, and taking all their lands, cattle and goods
from them, the crethurs were always praying to
Jesus and his holy Mother to save them from the
Sassanaghs : and so, praying to Jesus grew so *pat*,
that now they can't help it."

" But then, Michael," said I, " the commandments !"

" Poo-o ! what have the crethurs to do with the
commandments? Sure its the Jews, and not the
poor Catholics, that have to do with them : and
sure the parliament men make many a law twice
as strong as any commandments ; and the very
gentlemen that made those said laws don't observe
their own enactments, except it suits their own
purposes—though every 'sizes some of the *crethurs*
are hanged for breaking one or two of them." ·

Heney was now waxing warm on the subject,
and I followed him up as well as I could. "Why,
Mick, I wonder, nevertheless, that your clergy
don't put a stop to the practice : perpetually calling on the name of our Redeemer, without

any substantial reason for so doing, is certainly bad."

" And what better name could they call on, Master Jonah?" said Heney. " Why should the clergy hinder them? Its only putting them in mind of the name they are to be saved by. Sure there's no other name could do them a pennyworth of good or grace. Its well for the crethurs they have that same name to use. As father Doran says, pronouncing the glorified name puts them in mind every minute of the only friend any poor Irish boy can depend upon; and there can be no sin in reminding one of the place we must all go to, and the Holy Judge we'll be all judged by at the latter end. Sure its not Sergeant Towler,* or the likes of him, you'd have the crethurs swearing by, Master Jonah. He makes them remember *him* plentifully when he comes to these parts."

" And even the schoolmasters don't punish young children for the same thing," remarked I.

" Why should they?" rejoined Michael Heney. " Sure Mr. Beal, though he's a Protestant, does not forbid it."

" How so?"·

" Why, because he says if he did, it would encourage disobedience to their parents, which is by

* Toler, now Lord Norbury, of whom the common people had a great dread.

all clergy forbidden as a great sin as well as shame."

" Disobedience !" said I, in wonder.

" Yes ; the fathers and mothers of the *childer* generally curse and swear their own full share every day, at any rate : and if the master told the childer it was a great sin, they would consider their fathers and mothers wicked people, and so despise and fly in their faces !"

" But, surely you are ordered not to take God's name in vain ?"

" And sure," said Heney, " its *not* in vain when it makes people believe the truth ; and many would not believe a word a man said in this country unless he swore to it, Master Jonah."

" But cursing," persisted I, " is ill-natured as well as wicked."

" Sure there's no harm in cursing a *brute beast*," said Heney, " because there's no soul in *it ;* and if one curses a *Christian* for doing a bad act, sure its only telling him what he'll get a taste of on the day of judgment."

" Or, perhaps, *the day after,* Michael Heney," said I, laughing.

" The devil a priest in the county can tell that," said Heney ; " but, (looking at his watch,) you're playing your *pranks* on me, Master Jonah ! the bells should have been rung for the mowers' dinner half an hour ago, and be d—d to them ! The devil sweep them altogether, the idle crethurs !"

" Fie to yourself, Mr. Heney !" cried I : but he waited for no further argument, and I got out, I really think, the reasons which they all believe justify the practice. The French law makes an abatement of fifteen years out of twenty at the gallies, if a man kills another without premeditation : and I think the same principle may apply to the involuntary assemblage of oaths which, it should seem, have been indigenous in Ireland for some centuries past.

A BARRISTER BESIEGED.

Dinner-party at the Rev. Mr. Thomas's—The author among
the guests, in company with John Philpot Curran—General
punctuality of the latter at dinner-time—His mysterious non-
appearance—Speculations and reports—Diver, from Newfoundland—His simultaneous absence—The house searched
—Discovery of a ghost, and its metamorphosis into Curran—
A curious blockade—Its relief, and accompanying circumstances—Comments of the author.

THE late Mr. Curran was certainly one of the
most distinguished of Irishmen, not only in wit
and eloquence, but in eccentricity : of this quality
in him, one or two traits have been presented to
the reader in the former part of this work ; and
the following incident will still further illustrate it.
The Reverend Mr. Thomas, whose *sobriquet* in
his neighbourhood was " Long Thomas," he being
nearly six feet and a half high, resided near Carlow, and once invited Curran and myself to spend
a day and sleep at his house on our return from
the assizes. We accepted the invitation with pleasure, as he was an old college companion of mine—

a joyous, good-natured, hospitable, hard-going divine as any in his county.

The Reverend Jack Read, a three-bottle parson
of Carlow, with several other jolly neighbours,
were invited to meet us, and to be treated with
the wit and pleasantry of the celebrated Counsellor Curran, who was often extremely fond of shin-
ing in that class of society.

We all arrived in due time ;—dinner was appointed for five *precisely*, as Curran always stipu-
lated (wherever he could make so free) for the
punctuality of the dinner-bell to a single minute.
The very best cheer was provided by our host : at
the proper time, the dishes lay basking before the
fire, in readiness to receive the several provisions
all smoking for the counsellor, &c. The clock,
which, to render the cook more punctual, had been
that very noon regulated by the sundial, did not
on its part vary one second. Its hammer and bell
melodiously sounded *five,* and announced the
happy signal for the banquet. All the guests
assembled in the dining-room, which was, in honest
Thomas's house, that apartment which the fine
people of our day would call a drawing-room—the
latter being then by no means regarded as indispensable in the dwelling-house of a moderate gentlemen. The family parlour, in fact, answered its
purpose mighty well.

Every guest of the reverend host having now
decided on his chair, and turned down his plate,

in order to be as near as possible to Counsellor Curran, proceeded to whet his knife against the edge of his neighbour's, to give it a due keenness for the most tempting side of the luscious sirloin, which by anticipation frizzed upon its pewter dish. Veal, mutton, turkey, ham, duck, and partridge, all " piping hot," were ready and willing to leap from their pots and spits into their respective dishes, and to take a warm bath each in its proper gravy. The cork-screw was busily employed: the wine-decanters ornamented the four corners of the well-dressed table, and the punch, jugged, and bubbling hot upon the hearth-stone, perfumed the whole room with its aromatic potsheen odour.

Every thing bespoke a most joyous and protracted banquet;—but, meanwhile, where was the great object of the feast?—the wheedler of the petty juries, and the admonisher of the grand ones? Where was the great orator, in consequence of whose brilliant reputation such a company was collected? The fifth hour had long passed, and impatience became visible on every countenance. Each guest, who had a watch, gave his fob no tranquillity, and never were timekeepers kept on harder duty. The first half-hour surprised the company; the next quarter *astonished*, and the last *alarmed* it. The clock, by *six* solemn notes, set the whole party surmising, and the host appeared nearly in a state of stupefaction. Day had departed, and twilight was rapidly following its

example, yet no tidings of the orator : never had
the like been known with regard to Curran—punctuality at dinner being a portion of his very nature.
There are not more days in a leap year than there
were different conjectures broached as to the cause
of my friend's non-appearance.   The people about
the house were sent out on the several roads to
reconnoitre.   He had been seen, certainly, in the
garden at four o'clock, but never after ; — yet
every now and then a message came in to announce, that " an old man had seen *a counsellor,*
as he verily believed, walking very quick on the
road to Carlow."   Another reported that " a woman who was driving home her cow met one of
the counsellors going leisurely toward Athy, and
that he seemed very *melancholy ;* that she had seen
him at the 'sizes that blessed morning, and the
people towld her it was the great law preacher
that was in it."   Another woman who was bringing home some turf from the bog, declared before
the Virgin and all the Saints that she saw " a
little man in black with a stick in his hand going
toward the Barrow ;" and a collough sitting at her
own cabin door feeding the *childer,* positively saw
a " black gentleman going down to the river, and
soon afterward heard a great splash of water at
the said river ; whereupon, she went *hot-foot* to
her son, Ned Coyle, to send him thither to see if
the gentleman was in the water ; but that Ned
said, sure enuff nothing natural would be after

going at that time of the deep dusk to the place where poor Armstrong's corpse lay the night he was murthered; and he'd see all the gentlemen in the county to the devil (God bless them!) before he'd go to the said place till morning early."

The faithful clock now announced *seven*, and the matter became too serious to admit of any doubt as to poor Curran having met his catastrophe. I was greatly shocked; our only conjectures now being, not *whether*, but *how*, he had lost his life. As Curran was known every day to strip naked and wash himself all over with a sponge and cold water, I conjectured, as most rational, that he had, in lieu of his usual ablution, gone to the Barrow to bathe before dinner, and thus unfortunately perished. All agreed in my hypothesis, and hooks and a draw-net were sent for immediately to Carlow, to scour the river for his body. Nobody, whatever might have been their feelings, *said* a word about dinner. The beef, mutton, and veal, as if in grief, had either turned into broth, or dropped piecemeal from the spit; the poultry fell from their strings, and were seen broiling in the dripping-pan. The cook had forgotten her calling, and gone off to make inquiries. The stable-boy left his horses; indeed, all the domestics, with one accord, dispersed with lanterns to search for Counsellor Curran in the Barrow. The Irish cry was let loose, and the neighbourhood soon collected; and the good-natured parson, our host,

literally wept like an infant. I never saw so much
confusion at any *dinner-table*.   Such of the guests
as were gifted by Nature with keen appetites,
suffered all the tortures of hunger, of which, nevertheless, they could not in humanity complain; but
a stomachic sympathy of woe was very perceptible in their lamentations for the untimely fate of
so great an orator.

It was at length suggested by our reverend host
that his great Newfoundland dog, who was equally
sagacious, if not more so, with many of the parishioners, and rivalled, in canine proportion, the
magnitude of his master, was not unlikely, by
diving in the Barrow, to discover where the body
lay deposited—and thus direct the efforts of the
nets and hookers from Carlow.   This idea met
with universal approbation; and every body took
up his hat, to go down to the river.   Mary, a
young damsel, the only domestic who remained
in the house, was ordered to call Diver, the dog;—
but Diver was absent, and did not obey the sum-
mons.   Every where resounded, " Diver! Diver!"
but in vain.

New and multifarious conjectures now crossed
the minds of the different persons assembled:—the
mystery thickened: all the old speculations went
for nothing; it was clear that Curran and Diver,
had absconded together.

At length, a gentleman in company mentioned
the circumstance of a friend of his having been

drowned while bathing, whose dog never left his clothes, on the bank, till discovered nearly dead with hunger. The conjecture founded hereon was, however, but momentary, since it soon appeared that such *could not* be the case with Curran. I knew that he both feared and hated big dogs ;* and

---

* Curran had told me, with infinite humour, of an adventure between him and a mastiff when he was a boy. He had heard somebody say, that any person throwing the skirts of his coat over his head, stooping low, holding out his arms and creeping along backward, might frighten the fiercest dog and put him to flight. He accordingly made the attempt on a miller's animal in the neighbourhood, who *would never let* the boys *rob the orchard ;* but found to his sorrow that he had a dog to deal with who did not care which end of a boy went foremost, so as he could get a good bite out of it. " I pursued the instructions," said Curran ; " and, as I had no eyes save those in front, fancied the mastiff was in full retreat : but I was confoundedly mistaken ; for at the very moment I thought myself victorious, the enemy attacked my rear, and having got a reasonably good mouthful out of it, was fully prepared to take another before I was rescued. Egad, I thought for a time the beast had devoured my entire *centre of gravity,* and that I never should go on a steady perpendicular again." " Upon my word, Curran," said I, " the mastiff may have left you your *centre,* but he could not have left much *gravity* behind him, among the bystanders."

I had never recollected this story until the affair of Diver at Parson Thomas's, and I told it that night to the country gentlemen before Curran, and for a moment occasioned a hearty laugh against him; but he soon *floored* me, in our social converse, which whiled away as convivial an evening as I ever experienced.

besides, there was no *acquaintance* between him and the one in question. Diver had never seen the counsellor before that day, and therefore could have no personal fondness for him, not to say, that those animals have a sort of instinctive knowledge as to who likes or dislikes them, and it was more probable that Diver, if either, would be an enemy instead of a friend to so great a stranger. But the creature's absence, at any rate, was unaccountable, and the more so, inasmuch as he never before had wandered from his master's residence.

Mary, the maid, was now desired to search *all* the rooms and offices for Diver, while we sat pensive and starving in the parlour. We were speedily alarmed by a loud shriek, immediately after which Mary rushed tottering into the room, just able to articulate :—

" O, holy Virgin ! holy Virgin ! yes, gentlemen ! the counsellor *is* dead, sure enough. And I'll die too, gentlemen ! I'll never recover it !" and she crossed herself twenty times over in the way the priest had taught her.

We all now flocked round, and asked her simultaneously how she *knew* the counsellor was dead ?

Crossing herself again, " I saw his *ghost*, please your reverence !" cried poor Mary, " and a frightful ghost it was ! just out of the river, and not even *decent* itself. I'm willing to take my affidavy that I saw his ghost, quite *indecent*, straight forenent me."

"Where? where?" cried every body, as if with one breath.

"In the double-bedded room next your reverence's," stammered the terrified girl.

We waited for no more to satisfy us either that she was mad, or that robbers were in the house: each person seized something by way of a weapon: one took a poker, another a candlestick, a third a knife or fire-shovel, and up stairs we rushed. Only one could go in, conveniently, abreast; and I was among the first who entered. The candles had been forgotten; but the moon was rising, and we certainly saw what, in the opinion of some present, corroborated the statement of Mary. Two or three instantly drew back in horror, and attempted to retreat, but others pressed behind; and lights being at length produced, an exhibition far more ludicrous than terrific presented itself. In a far corner of the room stood, erect and formal, and *stark naked* (as a *ghost* should be), John Philpot Curran; one of his majesty's counsel, learned in the law,—trembling as if in the ague, and scarce able to utter a syllable, through the combination of cold and terror. Three or four paces in his front lay Diver, from Newfoundland, stretching out his immense shaggy carcase, his long paws extended their full length, and his great head lying on them with his nose pointed toward *the ghost*, as true as the needle to the pole. His hind legs were gathered up like those of a wild

beast ready to spring upon his prey.   He took an
angry notice of the first of us that came near him,
growled, and seemed disposed to resent our intru-
sion ;—but the moment his master appeared, his
temper changed, he jumped up, wagged his tail,
licked the parson's hand, cast a scowling look at
Curran, and then a wistful one at his master,—as
much as to say, " I have done my duty, now do
you yours:" he looked, indeed, as if he only
waited for the word of command, to seize the
counsellor by the throttle.

A blanket was now considerately thrown over
Curran by one of the company, and he was *put to
bed* with half a dozen more blankets heaped upon
him : a tumbler of hot potsheen punch was administered, and a second worked miracles : the natural heat began to circulate, and he was in a
little time enabled to rise and tell us a story
which no hermit even telling his last beads could
avoid laughing at.   Related by *any one*, it would
have been good ; but as told by Curran, with his
powers of description and characteristic humour,
was superexcellent ;—and we had to thank Diver,
the water-dog, for the highest zest of the whole
evening. .

The fact was, that a little while previous to
dinner-time, Curran, who had omitted his customary ablution in the morning, went to our
allotted bed-chamber to perform that ceremony ;
and having stripped, had just begun to apply the

sponge, when Diver, strolling about his master's premises to see if all was right, placed by chance his paw against the door, which not eing fastened, it flew open, he entered unceremoniously, and observing what he conceived to be an. extraordinary and suspicious figure, concluded it was somebody with no very honest intention, and stopped to reconnoitre. Curran, unaccustomed to so strange a valet, retreated, while Diver advanced, and very significantly showed an intention to seize him by the naked throat; which operation, if performed by Diver, whose tusks were a full inch in length, would no doubt have admitted an inconvenient quantity of atmospheric air into his œsophagus. He therefore crept as close into the corner as he could, and had the equivocal satisfaction of seeing his adversary advance and turn the meditated *assault* into a complete *blockade*—stretching himself out, and " maintaining his position " with scarcely the slightest motion, till the counsellor was rescued, and the siege raised.

Curran had been in hopes that when Diver had satisfied his *curiosity* he would retire; and with this impression, spoke kindly to him, but was answered only by a growl. If Curran repeated his blandishments, Diver showed his long white tusks; —if he moved his foot, the dog's hind legs were in motion. Once or twice Curran raised his hand : but Diver, considering that as a sort of challenge,

rose instantly, and with a low growl looked significantly at Curran's windpipe. Curran, therefore,
stood like a *model*, if not much like a marble divinity. In truth, though somewhat less comely, his
features were more expressive than those of the
Apollo Belvidere. Had the circumstance occurred
at Athens to Demosthenes, or in the days of Phi-
dias, it is probable my friend Curran, and Diver,
would have been at this moment exhibited in virgin marble at Florence or at the Vatican ;—and I
am quite sure the *subject* would have been better
and more amusing than that of " the dying gla-
diator."

GEORGE ROBERT FITZGERALD.

George Robert Fitzgerald and Mr. Richard Martin, M. P. for Galway—The " Prime Sergeant," Lord Altamont's wolf-dog—Shot by Fitzgerald—The circumstance resented by Mr. Martin—The latter insulted by his antagonist in the Dublin Theatre—Mission of Mr. Lyster to George Robert, and its disastrous consequences— A legal inquiry and strange decision—Meeting between the principals—Fitzgerald receives two shots without injury—Explanation of that enigma.

A very illustrative anecdote of the habits of former times is afforded by the celebrated rencontre between George Robert Fitzgerald of Turlow, member for Mayo, and Mr. Richard Martin of Connemara, member for Galway county, which occurred nearly half a century ago. Both were gentlemen of great public notoriety : both men of family and of fortune. But of all the *contrasts* that ever existed in human nature, theirs was in the superlative degree ; for modern biography does not present a character more eminently vindictive and sanguinary than the one, or an individual more signalised by active humanity and benevolence than the other.

With the chief of Connemara I have now been nearly forty years in a state of uninterrupted friendship:—failings he has—"let him who is fault-less throw the first stone!" The character I should give of him may be summed up in a single sentence. " Urbanity toward women; benevolence toward men; and humanity toward the brute creation." I must observe, however, that he is one of those good fellows who would rather do any body's business than his own; and durst look any thing in the face rather than his own situation. As to his *charity*, I cannot say too much; as to his *politics*, I cannot say too little.

His unfortunate antagonist, Mr Fitzgerald, has long since met his miserable fate. Mr. Martin still lives; and seems to defy, from the strength of his constitution, both time and the destroyer. If *ever* he should become defunct, there is not a bul-lock, calf, goose, or hack, but ought to *go into deep mourning* for him.

The virulent animosity and unfinished conflicts between these celebrated personages once formed a subject of very general conversation. When the bullets of holster pistols flatten against the ribs of a gentleman, there can be no great use in fighting any more with *him:* it is better to break fresh ground with some more vulnerable amateur; and as " fire eating" was at the period I allude to

in full taste and fashion, no person who felt a
penchant for chivalry need wait a single hour for a
thrust. Every gentleman then wore his sword or
couteau de chasse, which there could be no trouble
in drawing.

I was quite unacquainted with the true state
of the quarrel between these parties, or the facts
of their rencontres ; and have begged my friend
Martin to give me a circumstantial detail, lest I
might mistake and be called a " bouncer :" he
was so obliging as to comply ; and I conceive that
his Ms. statement is so perspicuous and fair,
almost amounting to perfect impartiality—in.that
conversational style, too, best calculated for narrative,—that I determine to give it in nearly the
same words ; and when it is combined with a few
facts which I learned from another friend, I venture to think that a better outline of Mayo and
Galway lords, commoners, judges, country gentlemen, and *fire eaters,* cannot be found. As, however, there is nothing in it chivalrous in the *ladies'*
way—the whole being about *hate* with not one
particle respecting *love,* I fear it will not be a
favourite sketch with the gentler part of the creation. To make them amends, I'll search my old
trunks, and find if possible some pretty sketch that
has *nothing but love* or *marriage* in it, which they
shall have as well dressed and garnished as they
can reasonably expect from so old a *cuisinier ;*

and now, with their kind permission, we will proceed to County Mayo.

" George Robert Fitzgerald, having a deadly hate to all the Brown family, but hating most Lord Altamont, rode up one morning from Turlow to Westport House, and asked to see the big wolf-dog called the ' Prime Sergeant.' When the animal appeared, he instantly shot it, and desired the servants to tell their master that ' until the noble peer became charitable to the wandering poor whose broken meat was devoured by hungry wolf-dogs, *he* would not allow any such to be kept.' He, however, left a note to say that he *permitted* Lady Anne, Lady Elizabeth, and Lady Charlotte Brown, each to keep one *lap-dog*.

" Proud of this exploit, he rode into Lord Sligo's town of Westport, and proclaimed in the marketplace that he had just shot the *Prime Sergeant* dead. The whole town was alarmed; an uproar arose : but after some debate among the wisest or rather the *stoutest* people in the town, whether George Robert Fitzgerald ought not to be arrested if possible for this deliberate murder of Counsellor Brown; he quieted all by saying, ' I have shot a much worthier *animal*, the big watch-dog.' *

* The Prime Sergeant of the Irish bar was then Lord Sligo's brother—a huge, fat, dull fellow; but the great *lawyer* of the family. Prime Sergeant Brown was considered as an oracle by the whole county of Mayo: yet there could scarcely be found

" I was at this time much attached to the family ; and debating in my own mind how best to conduct myself toward my friends, I determined not to tell George Robert my opinion, as it would be in effect to declare that Lord Altamont wanted courage to defend his own honour. I therefore resolved on seeking some more plausible ground of quarrel, which soon presented itself ; for at the summer assizes of Mayo, holden at Castlebar, Charles Lionel Fitzgerald prosecuted his elder brother George Robert for false imprisonment and savage conduct toward their father, upon whom George Robert had fastened a chain and dray ! .

" The affair came on before Lord Carleton, and I volunteered in the only cause I ever pleaded.*

. " An affidavit was produced, stating that the father was *not* confined. I observed, ' that Robert Fitzgerald had long notice of this cause coming on ; and that the best answer would be the *attendance* of the father when he was called as one of the magistrates in the commission for the county of Mayo.'

a man less calculated to *tell fortunes.* The watch-dog was named after him.

* Mr. Richard Martin had been called to the Irish bar, as the elde t sons of the most respectable families of Ireland then were, not, as might be supposed, to practise for others, but with a supposition that they would thereby be better enabled to defend their own *territories* from judgments, mortgagees, custodiums, &c. &c., and to " stave off" vulgar demands, which if too speedily conceded, might beget very serious inconveniences.

" Remesius Lennon, a battered old counsellor, on the other side, observed that the father was one of the worst men living, and that it would be unjust to censure any son for confining such a public nuisance.

" I opposed putting off the trial of George Robert, and concluded to this effect :—' Though believing that, in course of a long life, this wretched father had committed many crimes, yet the greatest crime against society and the greatest sin against Heaven that he ever perpetrated, was the having *begotten the traverser.*'

" On this, George Robert said, smiling, ' Martin, you look very healthy—you take good care of your *constitution ;* but I tell you, that you have this day taken very bad care of your *life.*'

" The trial went on ; and it was *proved*, among a great number of other barbarities, that the father *was* chained by his son George Robert to a dray, and at times to a muzzled bear : a respectable jury found the traverser guilty ; and Lord Carleton sentenced him to three years' imprisonment, and to pay a fine to the king of five hundred pounds.

" ' Kissing' at this time went ' by favour ;' and Mr. Conally, the brother-in-law of George Robert, obtained from the late Duke of Buckingham, then Lord Lieutenant, the pardon and release of Fitzgerald.

" Some months after, I happened to pass through Castlebar, and learned that Mr. Fitzgerald was in

the town. I had heard of his denunciations, but my
determination was, neither to *avoid* nor *seek* my
antagonist.   Desirous of ascertaining what I had
to expect, I requested a friend to call on him, and,
after conversation on some ordinary subject, to say
that *I* had been in the town.

- " This was done, and George Robert answered,
' that he hoped, whenever we met, it would not
be as *enemies*.'

" My friend reported this : but, on the whole, I
thought it as well not to seek any occasion of meeting a person who, I apprehended, might, so soon
after our dispute, be induced to depart from his
pacific resolution; I therefore proceeded on my
journey to Dublin.

" Mrs. Crawford, I found, had been engaged to
play for a few nights at Crow Street theatre, and
I determined to see her *Belvidera*.   I had not long
taken my seat in the front row of the stage-box,
when I heard a noisy, precipitate step, and an
order given in a commanding tone for the box to
be opened. I turned, and saw Mr. Fitzgerald,
who took his place on the next row. His look in-
dicated rage, and I therefore left my place in front,
and took my seat on the same row with him. He
stared for a moment or two directly into my face,
then turned away and laughed, on which I asked,
' Have you any thing particular to say to *me*, Mr.
Fitzgerald ?'

" He answered, with a stern look of defiance—

' Only to tell you that I followed you from Cas-tlebar, to proclaim you the *bully* of the Alta-monts.'

" ' You have said enough, Mr. Fitzgerald ; you no doubt expect to hear from me, and it shall be early in the morning.'

" ' *I* shall hear from *you* to-morrow !' he repeat-ed, contemptuously, making, as he spoke, a blow at me, and adding, ' this will refresh your memo-ry.' He then pulled back his body from behind the curtain of the box, and instantly retreated toward the lobby.

" My feet got entangled in the curtain when I rushed out to follow my antagonist, and I fell upon the floor. The present Lord Howden, then Major Craddock, kindly lifted me up. When on my feet, I sprang into the lobby, which was crowded almost to an overflow. I uttered all that rage could dictate, accused Fitzgerald of cowardice, and told him he had created the present *scene* in order that we should be both bound over to the peace.

" ' You have got a blow,' replied he : ' I desire to disgrace you, and when you are punished to my liking *that* way (and not before) you shall have the *satisfaction* of being shot, or run through the body.'

" Next day, I met the late Lord Donoughmore, and he most kindly said, if I required it, he would deliver a message to Fitzgerald. I said, ' No, I could not think of embroiling any friend of mine with such a fellow ; that I would wear my sword, and trust to my opportunities of meeting Fitzgerald.'

. " I watched his house closely for several days, but he did not appear. At this critical moment, a Mr. George Lyster called upon me, and said he would take my message to Fitzgerald. .

- " I answered, ' that of all things I most desired to meet him; that I found I could not unkennel the fox; and that I would thank whomsoever should succeed in putting us face to face.' I was, however, cautious of employing Lyster, knowing him to be Fitzgerald's cousin, and supposing it possible he might have been employed by Fitzgerald himself: this induced me to try him and to say, ' As you have *offered* to go to this gentleman, I will thank you to appoint the *earliest moment* for a meeting.'

" Mr. Lyster drew not back, but went to his cousin's house, and was ushered by one of the servants into the drawing-room. Mr. Fitzgerald shortly entered, and as soon as Mr. Lyster hinted his business, our hero desired the footman to send one of the valets : when the latter entered, Fitzgerald said, ' Francis, bring my cudgel with the green riband.' When Fitzgerald got this weapon, he addressed his relative thus—' How dare you bring a *message* to me ? Hold out your finger with the diamond-ring upon it !' Poor Lyster obeyed, ignorant of his design, and with one blow Fitzgerald broke the finger, and the band of the ring, which fell on the floor. ' Now,' proceeded he, ' I order you to take up the ring, and present it to me.' As if thunderstruck, Lyster obeyed. When Fitzgerald got possession of the ring, he put it into paper, and returned it to Lyster, saying, ' Young fellow, take care of the ring! put it up very safe, and don't swear I robbed you of a present from some fair one.'

" This dialogue (recounted to me by Lyster himself) was followed by several blows, which cut and battered the young man severely. At last, he rushed to the window, drove his head through a pane of glass, and cried out for assistance. The police, hearing the cry, soon assembled; and not finding any of the city magistrates, they having seized both parties, conducted them into the presence of Mr. Justice Robinson.

" The judge first heard Lyster, and seeing him severely bruised, and supposing his skull might be fractured, declared that the prisoner could not be bailed.

" Fitzgerald now, on the other hand, asked to have his examination entered against Lyster. He stated, ' that Lyster was his relative, and protected by him, and that I had *influenced* the young man to deliver a message from me. He said, ' that Mr. Lyster *had* delivered such a *message:* that *he* had answered mildly, that he would not fight Mr.

Martin; whereon, (says Fitzgerald,) this young gentleman said, ' Then you must fight *me.*' My answer was, that I would not fight *any man;* on which, continued George Robert, he made several blows of the cudgel I hold in my hand (his own) at me. I happened to be more dexterous than my assailant, and was fortunate enough to take the weapon out of his hands, and in my own defence was obliged to strike in turn, or I should have been murdered.'

" The old judge, believing every word of so plausible a statement, said, ' I have heard enough ; I commit Lyster for trial, and bind over Mr. Fitzgerald to prosecute ; and I do so, expressing my approbation of Mr. Fitzgerald's manly conduct, in refusing to fight Mr. Martin, and thus appealing for redress to the laws of his country.'

" Shortly after this curious scene, I heard that Fitzgerald was at Castlebar, and had it intimated to him that I should be there. I travelled with Mr. H. Flood * in his carriage, and he kindly offered to be my friend, which I declined—fearing to have exposed him to some insult.

" I had sent my duelling pistols by a fellow who got drunk on the road, and forgot his errand ;—so that I remained some hours at Lord Lucan's house,

---

* This was the celebrated Henry Flood, the antagonist of Grattan—certainly the ablest statesman of his day. He had himself fought more than once ; and had killed Mr. Eager, the father of Lord Clifden, of Gowran.

expecting in vain· their arrival, during which period I heard that Mr. Fitzgerald was parading the town with a number of persons from Turlow, his own estate, famous for its mobs trained to every kind of outrage.* I heard, too, that he said, I waited for Lord Altamont's carriage, which, observed he significantly, *would not arrive.* Here I have to remark that I had written a note to Lord Altamont, to say that I would gladly compound for a slight wound in the expected affair, and that I requested his carriage might be in waiting for me at Castlebar, which is only eight miles from Westport. George Robert had heard this, and said to the mob, ' Mr. Martin expects Altamont's carriage, but he may wait long enough; for though the horse is a brave animal, I fancy Altamont's are like the owner, and will not stand the smell of powder.'

" These taunts reached me; and procuring a case of the common holster pistols my servant rode with, I determined to use them : but they were so stiff in the trigger that I could hardly let them off. I fastened on my sword, and putting my hand under Doctor Merlin's arm, walked into the town, and soon saw Fitzgerald, followed by his mob. He too wore his sword, and I instantly told him to draw. He answered that he was lame,

---

* These were the gentry by whom the author was some time subsequently so closely beleaguered at the yarn fair at Castlebar, as hereafter mentioned.

the pavement bad, and that he could not keep his footing; that I had Lord Lucan's mob on my side; and that, in short, he would not fight me.

" I then said, ' You will find me in the barrack-yard, where I shall remain.'

" ' I shall be in no hurry, after having struck you for your pertness,' said he.

" On this I flung a switch into his face, walked to the barrack, and got sentries posted, with orders to keep out all persons but Mr. Fitzgerald and his friend, whilst we should be fighting. He and Mr. Fenton soon appeared : he had a good case of pistols in his hand, while I had the wretched tools I named.

" I stood against a projecting part of the barrack wall, and desired Mr. Fitzgerald to come as close as he pleased. He said a cannon would not carry *so far*. I answered, ' I will soon cure that, for I will now march up until I lay my pistol to your face.' I accordingly advanced, until our pistols touched. We both fired : he missed me, but I hit him full in the breast, and he fell back, supporting himself by a projection of rock, and exclaiming, ' Honour, Martin, honour !'

. " I said,—' If you are not disabled, I will wait as long as you choose !'

" At this moment, he couched treacherously like a cat, presented, fired, and hit me. I returned the fire, and hit him : he again recovered, came up, begged my pardon, asked to shake hands, and said, ' Altamont has caused all this, and now would not send you his carriage;—let us both kick him !'

" Flood met me at the gate, and I leaned on him. I was taken to Doctor Lendser's, to have the wound dressed, but on the way desired my servant to go with my compliments and inquire how Mr. Fitzgerald felt. Mr. Flood said, ' On no account make any inquiry, or, if he lives, you will have a second fight.' I was foolish, as will appear, and sent.

" I had not been many moments in bed when my hero entered the room with a careful, timid step. He said, ' Doctor, how do you find Mr. Martin ?' I was quite surprised, but said, ' I am very well, and hope you are not badly hurt.'

" He then addressed me, and observed, ' Doctor Merlin insulted me, and I consider him a bully, and instrument of yours, and as such I will make *you* accountable.'

" I answered, ' If I account with you, on a mutual understanding that Doctor Merlin is beneath your notice, I shall have to fight him also for such an imputation :—so put your renewed quarrel on some other ground. If you say you did not ask my pardon, I will fight you again ; or if you say you are fond of such an *amusement,* I will fight ' until my eyelids can no longer wag.'

" ' Shall you be at Sligo ?' was Mr. Fitzgerald's *reply.*

" I said, ' It was not my present purpose ; but if he *wished* it, I would be there, and that immediately.'.

" He named the day, to which I assented. It was *reported*, but I cannot vouch for the fact, that a party was sent to intercept and murder me. Shortly after I reached Sligo, my opponent sent Sir M. Crafton to say, that ' Mr. Fitzgerald did not require any further renewal of the quarrel;' and thus the affair ended. My surprise at Fitzgerald's being alive and well, after having received two shots from *horse-pistols* full upon him, was soon cleared up ; he had *plated his body* so as to make it completely bullet proof. On receiving my fire, he fell from the force of the balls striking him direct, and touching his concealed armour.— My wound was in the body.

" The elegant and gentlemanly appearance of this man, as contrasted with the savage treachery of his actions, was extremely curious and without any parallel of which I am aware."

RECRUITING AT CASTLEBAR.

Further particulars respecting George Robert Fitzgerald—His
  band of myrmidons—Proposal made to the author—He ac-
  cedes to it, and commences the " recruiting service "—Hospitality at an Irish inn—Practical joking—The author's success in enlisting George Robert's outlaws—Serjeant Hearn
  and Corporal O'Mealy—Fair-day at Castlebar—A speech,
  succeeded by " beating orders "—Mutiny among the new
  levies—The utility of hanks of yarn—An inglorious retreat,
  and renunciation, by the author, of the honours of a military
  life.

THERE were few men who flourished in my
early days that excited more general or stronger
interest than' Mr. George Robert Fitzgerald, of
Turlow,' the principal object of the preceding
sketch.   He was born to an ample fortune, educated in the best society, had read much, travelled,
and been distinguished at foreign courts : he was
closely allied to one of the most popular and also
to one of the most eminent personages of his own
country ; being brother-in-law to Mr. Thomas
Conolly of Castletown, and nephew to the splen-

did, learned, and ambitious Earl of Bristol, Bishop of Derry :—yet, so powerfully did some demon seize upon his mind, and—let us hope—disorder his intellect, that though its starting was thus brilliant, ·his life presented one continuous series of outrage, and his death was a death of ignominy.

I have neither space nor inclination to become his general biographer ;—in. truth, he has never, to my knowledge, had any true one.* Both his friends and enemies are now all nearly- *hors de combat.* I know but two contemporaries capable of drawing his portrait; and in the words of one of these I have recited an anecdote not unworthy of being recorded.—I always conceive that a writer characterising the nearly exhausted generation of which he has been a contemporary, resembles a general who dates dispatches from the field of battle, wherein he details the actions and merits of his friends or enemies, while the subjects of the bulletin lie gasping or quite dead before him—and

---

* I have read, in biographical books, George Robert Fitzgerald described as a great, coarse, violent Irishman, of ferocious appearance and savage manners. His person and manners were totally the reverse of this: a more polished and elegant gentleman was not to be met with. His person was very slight and juvenile, his countenance extremely mild and insinuating ; and, knowing that he had a *turn* for single combat, I always fancied him too *genteel* to kill any man except with the *small*-sword.

he himself only awaiting the fatal bullet which, even while he writes, may send him to his comrades.   This is my own case!

The singular life, and miserable death of Mr. Fitzgerald form an historic episode which the plan and character of this work will neither admit of my detailing nor altogether passing over.   The consideration of his career and catastrophe arouses in the memory acts and incidents long since erased from ordinary recollection, and thus, like a mirror, reflects the manners of the age wherein he lived.

While George Robert Fitzgerald was undergoing a part of his sentence in Newgate, Dublin,* his brother, Charles Lionel, got possession of the house and demesne of Turlow, near Castlebar, County Mayo—one of the most lawless places then in Ireland.   George Robert, as hinted in the former sketch, had armed and organised a band of desperadoes, who knew no will but his, and had no desire but his pleasure.   All men were in awe of them, and the regular army alone was then held sufficient to curb their outrages.   When their leader was convicted and imprisoned their spirit was somewhat depressed; but idleness and vice were by habit so deeply engrafted in their minds,

* Having been tried and convicted of a most *unparalleled* series of assaults upon, and imprisonment of, his own father, he was sentenced to three years' imprisonment; but, as we have before stated, was pardoned (in six months), to the disgrace of the government.

that peaceable or honest means of livelihood were scouted by them. They were at length proclaimed outlaws; the military chased them; and ultimately, a sort of treaty took place, which, like our modern diplomatic negotiations, exhibited only one party endeavouring to outwit the other. The desperadoes agreed to give up all their wild courses on a promise of pardon; a great proportion declared they would " take on" for a musket; and as the army had no objection to receive robbers and murderers to fight for their king, country, and religion, their offer was accepted.

About this time my military propensities were not totally extinguished, but susceptible of being rekindled by proper stimuli—and Dean Coote, brother to Sir Eyre Coote, then Commander-in-chief in India, sent to my father, and made him what my family considered a magnificent offer—namely, that one of his sons' should forthwith receive a captain's commission in the East India Company's service, on recruiting a hundred men for that service, and for each of which recruits, if the number were completed, twenty guineas should be paid on their being handed over to the depôt in Dublin.

In acknowledgment of this flattering offer my father immediately nominated me. I now almost fancied myself a nabob, or something better, helping to plunder and dethrone a few of the native princes—then quite plentiful, and considered fair

game by the Honourable Company's servants, civil
and military.   I with joy accepted the proposi-
tion—fully expecting, in four or five years, to return loaded with lacks of rupeés, and carats of
diamonds, and enabled to realise all my visions of
ulterior happiness.   The Dean also sent me the
" beating order" and instructions, with a letter of
introduction, and a strong recommendation to Mr.
Lionel Fitzgerald, then residing at Turlow, requesting he would aid me in enlisting his brother's
outlaws for the Company's service, of whom above
eighty had promised to accept the king's money on
terms of pardon.   All now went on prosperously ;
the tenants of Cullenagh brought in every shilling
they could rap or run, to set the young captain
a-spinning ; and in a week I was on my road,
through frost and snow, to the county of Mayo :
my father's old huntsman, Matthew Querns, was
selected to attend me as being most *sensible*, at
least among the domestics of the family.

Matthew was attired in his best field clothing—
namely, a green plush coat, scarlet-laced waistcoat of old times, buckskin breeches, and a black
leather hunting cap.   He carried my portmanteau,
with my volunteer broad-sword buckled to it, behind him, and his own hunting horn was strapped
by a belt about his middle :—this he sounded at
every inn door, as he said, to make us *respectable*.

I was mounted on a large *white* horse called
Friday, after Robinson Crusoe's *black* boy.   A

case of huge holster pistols jogged before me, and my cavalry coat-case behind, containing my toilet, flints, a bullet mould, my flute, my beating order, with—to amuse leisure hours—a song-book, and the Sentimental Journey (then in high vogue, being totally new both in style and subject). Thus caparisoned and equipped, the late Matthew Querns and the present Sir Jonah Barrington, set out, fifty years ago, for the purpose of enlisting robbers and outlaws in Mayo, to plunder gentoos in the Carnatic, and establish the Christian religion on the plains of Hindostan.

At that period of my life, cold or fatigue was nothing when I had an object in view ; and at the end of the third day's trotting we arrived, through deep snow, bog roads, and after some tumbles (miserably tired), at a little cabin at Hallymount, near the plains of Kilcommon, where many a bloody battle had been fought in former times ;— and as the ground was too rocky to dig graves, thousands of human skeletons had been covered up with stones—of which there is no scarcity in any, particularly that part of Ireland. Our reception was curious ; and as affording an excellent idea of the species of inns and innkeepers then prevalent in Ireland, I shall sketch one of the oddest imaginable places of " entertainment for man and horse,"—which notification was written in large letters over the door,—and the house certainly did not belie it.

The landlord was a fat, red-nosed, pot-bellied, jovial fellow, the very emblem of goodnature and hospitality; he greeted me cordially before he knew any thing about me, and said I should have the best his house afforded, together with a hearty welcome (the welcome of an innkeeper, indeed, is generally very sincere). He also told Matthew that he never suffered his bin of oats in the stable to be closed, always leaving it to gentlemen's beasts to eat at their own discretion—as he'd engage they would stop of themselves when they had got enough; and the more they eat at one meal, the less they would eat the next—so he should be no loser.

The inn consisted of cabins on the ground-floor only, and a very good hard dry floor it certainly was. The furniture was in character : but my bed (if I were to judge from its bulk and softness) had the best feathers of five hundred geese at least in it : the curtains had obviously once been the property of some greater personage than an innkeeper, as the marks of embroidery remained (on crimson silk), which had been carefully picked out—I suppose to sell the silver. My host begged I would not trouble myself as to dinner, as he knew what was good for me after so bad a journey. He protested that, so far as poultry, game, and lobsters went, no man in Mayo could beat him ; and that he had a vessel of Powldoody oysters, which was sent him by Squire

Francis Macnamara, of Doolan, for old acquaintance sake.

. I promptly asked for a bottle of his best wine; but he told me he never sold a *single* bottle to a gentleman, and hoped I would have no objection to two. Of course I acquiesced, though intending to dine alone and only to drink the half of one. I was therefore surprised to see shortly a spruce young maid-servant lay out the table for six persons, with every thing in good order:—and on dinner coming in, my landlord introduced his old wife, two smart pretty daughters, and his son, by no means a " promising boy." He uncorked both bottles at once, and no persons ever fared more sumptuously. The wine, he said, was the finest old claret, of the " real smuggling " by Sir Neil O'Donnel's own cutter called Paddy Whack, from the Isle of Man ;—and Sir Neil (a baronet of Newport) never sent a bad hogshead to any of his *customers:* his honour's brandy, likewise, was not a jot worse than his claret, and always tasted best of a cold morning.

We had got deep into our second bottle, of which the ladies took a glass each, while the young gentleman drank a bumper of brandy, when my host, who knew every body and every thing local, gave me the life, adventures, and character, of almost each person of note in that county, including numerous anecdotes of George Robert, which originated in, and were confined to the neighbourhood. He laughed so heartily at his own stories, that it was impossible not to join him. Tea and hot cakes followed; a roast goose, brandy punch, and old ale, made the supper, and I retired to bed hearty and careless.

Next morning I was roused rather early by a very unexpected guest, namely, a hen, which having got into my room, layed a couple of eggs at once on my coat, which lay beside me; and then, as hens accustom themselves to do, (and it is no bad practice,) she gave as loud and protracted a notice of her *accouchement* as her voice could furnish.

I immediately rose, brought out my two eggs to our breakfast-table, and was expressing my surprise at the circumstance, when Miss Betty Jennings winked, and whispered me that it was a standing joke of her father's.—The breakfast was nearly as good as the dinner had been the previous day; and on procuring my bill, I found I was charged eighteen pence for dinner, eighteen pence for claret, tenpence for my horses, sixpence for my breakfast, and nothing for the rest, though Matthew Querns had got dead drunk, my horses were nearly bursting, and I was little better myself. My host told me, when a guest who would drink with him had a bottle of claret, he always indulged in one himself; and that if I had drunk two, he should have thought it mighty uncivil if he had not done the same. I left his house with an impression that he was the most extraordinary inn-keeper I had ever met with, and really bade adieu to himself and his daughters with regret.*

Arriving in the course of the day at Turlow, I found that the whole family were at Castle Ma-garret; but Mr. Fitzgerald had got a letter about me, and all was ready for my reception. I found I was left to the care of one Hughy Hearn, who had been a serjeant of the band, but had changed sides and come over to Mr. Lionel at Turlow, after losing one of his arms in some skirmish for George Robert. I did not know who Hughy was at the time, or I should have kept aloof from him.

" Mr. Hearn," said I, next day, " have you a gun in the house ? I should like to go out."

" I have, captain," said he.

" Have you powder and shot ?" said I.

" No powder," said Hughy. " I fired all I had left of it last night at a man whom I saw skulking about the road after nightfall."

---

* Both Mr. Jenning's daughters were pretty and pleasant girls. I observed Miss Betty mending silk stockings, which was rather odd at the plains of Kilcommon. I told her I fan-cied she was kind-hearted, and had an uncommon degree of sense for her years, and she firmly believed me. I made her a present of the " Sentimental Journey," which I had in my coat-case. I construed the French for her (except two words): and on my return she told me it had taught her what *sentiment* was ; that she found she had a great deal of sentiment herself, but did not know the name of it before; and that she would always keep the book in kind remembrance of the donor.

" Did you hit him?" asked I, rather alarmed.

" I can't say," replied Hughy: " there was only one bullet *in it*, and its not so easy to shoot a man with a single bullet when the night is very dark—and I'm hard set to aim with one arm, though I dare say I all as one as *scratcht* him, for he cried out, ' Oh! bad luck to you, Hughy!' and ran down the cross lane before I could get the other double to slap after him."

I immediately set about recruiting the outlaws with the utmost activity and success. I appointed Hughy Hearn, who had but one arm, my drill-serjeant, and a monstrous athletic ruffian of the name of O'Mealy, my corporal, major, and inspector of recruits. I found no difficulty whatsoever in prevailing on them to take my money, clap up my cockade, get drunk, beat the towns-people, and swear " true allegiance to King George, Sir Eyre Coote, and myself." This was the oath I administered to them, as they all seemed zealous to come with me; but I took care not to tell them *where*.

The kindness and hospitality I meanwhile received at Turlow, from Mr. and Mrs. Fitzgerald, was extremely gratifying : nobody could be more interesting than the latter. There I met two remarkable persons of that country—George Lyster, whose finger was broken by George Robert Fitzgerald, as previously mentioned, and a little, decrepid sharp-witted dog, called George Elliston;

who afterward challenged me, and threatened Counsellor Saurin, because we did not succeed in a bad cause of his in the King's Bench, wherein we had taken his briefs without fees, as a matter of kindness to a pretended sufferer.

In less than a fortnight I had enlisted between fifty and sixty able, good-looking outlaws; and as my money was running low, I determined to march off my first batch of fifty men, three serjeants, and three corporals, for Dublin, and having placed them in depôt there, to return and make up my number with a replenished purse.

To give my march the greater eclat, I chose a market-day of Castlebar whereon to parade and address my company. There happened to be also a fair of linen yarn, and the street was crowded with cars laden with hanks of yarn of different sizes and colours. Having drawn up my men, I ordered each one to get a bumper of whisky; after which, taking off their hats, they gave three cheers for King George, Sir Eyre Coote, and Captain Barrington. I then made them a speech from the top of a car. I told them we were going to a place where the halfpennys were made of gold; where plunder was permitted by the Honourable Company, and the officers taught their men how to avail themselves of this permission; where robbery and murder were not hanging matters, as in Ireland.; where women were married at nine years' old, and every soldier had as many wives as he could keep from starving, with a right to rob the rich, in order to support a barrack full of them.

In short, I expatiated on all the pleasures and comforts I purposed for them ; and received in return three more cheers—though neither so·long or loud as I could have wished ; and I perceived a good deal of whispering among my soldiers which I could not account for, save by the pain they might feel in taking leave of their fellow-robbers, as was natural enough. I was, however, soon undeceived, when, on ordering them to march, one said aloud, as if he spoke for the rest, " March *is it?* march, then, *for fat?*"

Observing their reluctance to quit Castlebar, I felt my young, slight, and giddy self swell with all the pride and importance of a martinet ; I almost fancied myself a giant, and my big recruits mere pigmies. " Here, serjeant," said I arrogantly to Hughy Hearn, " draw up those *mutineers* : fall in— fall in !" but nobody fell in, and Serjeant Hearn himself fell *back*. " Serjeant," pursued I, " this moment arrest Corporal O'Mealy, he's the ring-leader."

" He won't *let* me, captain," replied Serjeant Hearn.

" 'Tis your captain's command !" exclaimed I.

" He says your honour's no captain at all," said Hughy Hearn ; " only a slip of a *crimp*, nothing else but a gaoler's son, that wants to sell the boys like *negers*, all as one as Hart and the green linnets in Dublin city."

My choler could no longer be restrained :—I drew my broadsword, and vowed I would divide the head of the first man that refused to march. " I'll teach these mutineers to obey his majesty's commission and officer," said I.

Corporal O'Mealy and two others then took off their hats, and coming up to me, said with great good-humour and civility; " Well, captain dear, you'll forgive and forget a joke from your own boys, so you will. Sure 'twas nothin else but a parting joke for the fair, your honour! Arrah! put up that sliver of yours : sure it looks nasty in the fair, to be drawing your falchion on your own recruits, captain."

I had no suspicion ; and the hanger was scarce secure in its scabbard, when some of my soldiers came behind me, and others in front, and I was completely surrounded. " I'll show you all that I am a captain, and a true captain," continued I. " Here, serjeant! bring me my beating orders."

" *Beating*—Ough! is *that* what you'd be at ?" said Corporal O'Mealy, who now assumed the command. " Ough! if its ' beating ' you want, by my sowl you'll be easily satisfied without Hughy Hearn's orders." ·

. I could stand it no longer : I could not run away if I wished ; a crowd was collecting around me, and so I sprang at the smallest of the recruits, whom I thought I could master, and seized him by the throat; but a smart crack given with a hank of linen yarn by some hand behind soon made me quit my prey; another crack from another quarter quickly followed. I turned round to see my executioners, when I was suddenly wheeled back by the application of a third hank. This *cracking*, like a *feu de joie*, increased every moment, and was accompanied with vociferous laughs. In short, they pounded me almost to a jelly with hanks of linen yarn, which lay ready to their hands on all the cars around us. At length, stooping down between two cars, I had the pleasure of seeing the whole of my recruits, drawn up by O'Mealy—for it appeared he was their *real captain*—march regularly by me, every fellow in turn saluting any part of me he thought proper with a hank of yarn;—and with a shout I still remember of "A George! a George! long life to our colonel!" they quitted the fair—as I learned, to take forcible possession of a house and farm from which one of them had been ejected—which feat I afterward heard they regularly performed that very night, with the addition of *roasting* the new proprietor in his own kitchen.

Though I had no bones broken, some of my flesh took pretty much the colour and consistence of what cooks call aspic jelly.—I was placed on a low garron, and returned to Turlow at night, sick, sore, and sorry. There I pretended I was only *fatigued*, and had taken cold ; and after experiencing the kind hospitality of Mrs. Fitzgerald— then a most interesting young lady—on the fourth day, at an early hour of a frosty morning, old Matthew Querns and I mounted our horses, without my having obtained any thing more for my trouble, and money spent in the recruiting service, than a sound beating. A return carriage of Lord Altamont's having overtaken me on the road, I entered it, and was set down at the little inn at Hallymount, where, I remained some days with Mr. Jennings and family, recovering from my bruises, and sighing over the wreck of my fondly anticipated glories as a renowned colonel at the head of my regiment, plundering a pagoda and picking precious stones out of an idol. But, alas ! having lost all the remaining cash out of my pocket during the scuffle at Castlebar, instead of a *lac* of *rupees,* I found myself labouring under a complete *lack* of *guineas,* and was compelled to borrow sufficient from Candy, the innkeeper at Ballynasloe, to carry me home by easy stages. Thus did my military ardour receive its definitive cooling : no ice-house ever chilled champaign more effectually. I, however, got quite enough of hospitality at Turlow, and quite enough of thrashing at Castlebar, to engraft the whole circumstances on my memory.

This journey gave me an opportunity of inspecting all the scenes of Mr. George Robert Fitzge-

rald's exploits. The cave in which he confined
his father, showed to me by Hughy Hearn, was
concealed by bushes, and wrought under one of
the old Danish moats, peculiar, I believe, to Ireland. Yet, in the perpetration of that act of bru-
tality, almost of parricide, he kept up the singular
inconsistency of his character. Over the entrance
to the subterraneous prison of his parent a specimen of classic elegance is exhibited by this in-
scription graven on a stone :

> Intus ager dulces——vivoque
> Sedilia Saxo——Nympharumque domus.

A NIGHT JOURNEY.

Mr. Fitzgerald's agent and attorney—Capriciousness of courage—Jack tar, his intrepidity—New lights—Sailors and
saints—Description of Mr. T——— —His temerity in court
and timorousness out of it—Regularly retained by Fitzgerald
—Starts with him on a journey to Turlow—Travelling companions—The eloquent *snore*—Mr. T——'s apprehensions—
A daylight discovery—Double escape of the solicitor—His
return to Dublin—Mr. Brecknock, his successor—Fate of
that individual—The " murderer murdered."

Mr. T——, a solicitor of repute in Dublin, had
been selected by George Robert Fitzgerald to
transact all his law and other business, as his
attorney and agent.

The choice was extremely judicious :—Fitzgerald had made a secret vow, that while he
existed, he never would encourage such a nest of
tricksters and *extortioners* as attorneys, by paying
any bill of cost, right or wrong, long or short; and
to carry this pious vow into full execution, so far
as regarded *one* attorney, he could not have made
a better selection than that above stated.

There are few qualities of the human mind more capricious than courage ; and I have known many instances in my passage through life, wherein men have been as courageous as a lion on one occasion, and as timorous as a little girl on others. I knew an English general who had never failed to signalise himself by intrepidity and contempt for death or fracture when engaged with the enemy, and was yet the most fearful being in the world lest he should be overset in a mail-coach. I have known men ready to fight any thing by daylight, run like hares in the night-time from the very same object. The capriciousness of courage is, indeed, so unaccountable, that it has ever been to me a source of amusing reflection. Not being myself of a very timorous disposition, and though I cannot say I ever experienced great fear of actual death in any proper reasonable way by the hands of a Christian—nay, even should it be a doctor— I always felt the greatest dread of getting a bite from the teeth of a mastiff, and never passed the heels of a horse without experiencing strong symptoms of cowardice. I always felt much stouter by daylight too than in the night-time.

. I have ever observed that the courage of *sailors* is, of all other species, the most perfect. I scarce ever met a common sailor that had *any* sense of danger ; the two most tremendous elements, fire and water, they totally disregard, and defy hurricanes and cannon, as if they were no more than

Zephyrs or *Catherine-wheels*. They have not the
same chance of getting away with soldiers from
their combats :—a sailor cannot rest one second
from fighting till the battle is ended ; and a few
years' experience of burning, sinking, bombarding,
blasting, and blowing up,—of thunder, lightning,
and shipwreck,—ossifies the *nerves*, or rather
changes them into *muscles*, and renders habit second nature. The sailor, therefore, acquires, a
constitutional contempt for danger in all its ramifi-
cations, while the soldiers' battles are *comparatively*
quiet, regular transactions, and their generals take
themselves carefully out of the fray if they imagine
they are getting the worst of it.

I have always, in fact, conceived that the
noblest fighting ever invented was a sea battle,
and the most intrepid animal in the creation, a
British sailor. How far the new lights, in changing their natural *rum* into *hot water*, their *grog* into
bohea tea, and their *naval dialect* into *methodistical
canting*, may increase their courage (which was
already ample), is for the projectors to determine.
Our naval victories over the whole world proved
that no change of liquids was necessary : when any
thing cannot be *improved*, alteration is injurious;
and I cannot help thinking that one sailor sending
his compliments by a cabin-boy to a brother tar,
requesting the " honour of his company to take
a dish of *tea* with him after *prayers*," is perfectly
ridiculous. God send it may not be worse than

ridiculous !—You may man your fleet with *saints :* but remember, it was the old *sinners* that gained your victories.

But to recover from one of my usual digressions : I must now advert, though in a very different point of view, to the bravery of *attorneys,* and exemplify the species of capriciousness I allude to in the person of Mr..T——. There was not another solicitor or practitioner in the four courts of Dublin, who showed more fortitude or downright bravery on all *law* proceedings. He never was known to flinch at any thing of the kind ; would contest a *nisi prius* from morning till night without sense of danger; and even after a defeat, would sit down at his desk to draw out his bill of costs, with as much *sang froid* as a French general, in Napoleon's time, would write despatches upon a drum-head in the midst of action.

Yet, with all this fortitude, he presented a singular example of the anomaly I have alluded to. Nature had given him a set of nerves as strong as chain cables, when used in mooring his clients' concerns ; and it seemed as if he had another and totally different set (of the nature of packthread) for his own purposes. His first set would have answered a sailor, his last a *young lady ;* in plain English, he would sooner lose a good bill of costs, than run a risk of provoking any irritable country gentleman to *action.* In such cases he was the most mild, bland, and humble antagonist that a debtor could look for. Such (and, I repeat, most judiciously chosen) was the attorney of George Robert Fitzgerald. In person he was under the middle proportion;—and generally buttoned up in a black single-breasted coat, with what was then called a flaxen Beresford bob-wig, and every thing to match. I remember him well, and a neat, smug, sharp, *half-century* man he was.

This gentleman had been newly engaged by Mr. Fitzgerald to prepare numerous leases for his desperadoes; to serve ejectments on half his reputable tenantry; to do various other acts according to law, with a high hand in the county of Galway; and to go down with him to Turlow, to see that all was duly executed. The several preparations for these things were of a very expensive description, and therefore the attorney would fain have had a little *advance* toward stamps, office-fees, &c. : but on remotely hinting this, Mr. Fitzgerald replied (with one of those mild, engaging modes of muzzling people in which he was so great a proficient), " Surely, Mr. T——, you don't doubt my honour and punctuality,"—which kind expression he accompanied by such a look as that wherewith the serpent is said to fascinate its prey.

This expressive glance brought down Mr. T—— to the exclamation—" O Lord, Mr. Fitzgerald, doubt your honour! O not at all, sir. I only, Mr. Fitzgerald, only—"

Here George Robert, with a bland smile, and

graceful motion of the hand, told him, " that he need say *no more*," and desired him to make out his bill of costs in full, to have it ready receipted, and so soon as they arrived among Mr. Fitzgerald's tenantry at Turlow, Mr. T—— might be assured he'd pay him off entirely *without taxing*.

Mr. T—— was quite charmed, expressed his satisfaction, and declared his readiness to accompany his client to Turlow, after a few days' preparation in engrossing leases, having one thousand five hundred ejectments filled up, and other preliminaries. " And be so good," said Mr. Fitzgerald, " to include in your bill, this time, all the expenses of your former journey to Turlow (where I fear you were badly accommodated), as well as what may be due upon every other account. I intend to settle all at once."

Mr. T—— was still more delighted :—all matters were prepared, the bills of costs reckoned, with a full acquittance and discharge for the whole (except the date) at the conclusion, to prevent delay or cavil; all the leases, ejectments, &c. were duly packed in a trunk, and the day fixed for setting out for Turlow; when Mr. Fitzgerald sent for the attorney, and told him, that if his going down was previously known, there were several of the tenants and others, under the adverse influence of his father and brother, who would probably abscond; and that therefore, since spies were watching him perpetually, to give notice in the county of his every movement, it was expedient that he should set out two or three hours before day-break, so as to have the start of them. That his own travelling carriage should be ready near the gate of the Phœnix Park, to take up Mr. T———, who might bring his trunk of papers with him thither in a hack carriage, so that there may be no suspicion.

All this was both reasonable and proper, and accordingly done. Mr. Fitzgerald's carriage was on the spot named, near the wall of the Phœnix Park. The attorney was punctual; the night pitch-dark ; and the trunk of papers put into the boot ; the windows were all drawn up ; Mr. T— stepped into the carriage with as great satisfaction as ever he had felt in his whole lifetime, and away they drove cheerily, at a good round pace, for the county of Galway.

Mr. T——— had no idea that any body else was coming with them—Mr. Fitzgerald not having at all mentioned such a thing. He found, however, a third gentleman in a travelling cloak sitting between himself and his client, who was dozing in the far corner. This stranger, too, he found not over-courteous; for though the carriage was not very roomy, and the gentleman was bulky, he showed no disposition whatever to accommodate the attorney, who begged him, with great suavity and politeness, to " move a little." To this he received no reply, but a snoring both from the strange tra-

veller and Mr. Fitzgerald. Mr. T—— now felt
himself much crowded and pressed, and again
earnestly requested " the gentleman " to allow
him, if possible, a little more room : but he still
only received a snore in return. He now concluded that his companion was a low, vulgar fellow. His nerves became rather lax : he got
alarmed, without well knowing why ; he began to
twitter—the twitter turned into a shake ; and, as is
generally the case, the shake ended with a cold
sweat, and Mr. T—— found himself in a state of
mind and body far more disagreeable than he had
ever before experienced. The closeness and pressure had elicited a hot perspiration on the one
side ; while his fears produced a cold perspiration
on the other : so that (quite unlike the ague he
had not long recovered from) he had hot and
cold fits at the same moment. All his apprehensions were now awakened : his memory opened
her stores ; and he began to recollect dreadful
anecdotes of Mr. Fitzgerald, which he never before
had credited, or indeed had any occasion to remember. The ruffians of Turlow passed as the ghosts in
Macbeth before his imagination. Mr. Fitzgerald he
supposed was in a fox's sleep, and his *bravo* in
another,—who, instead of receding at all, on the
contrary squeezed the attorney closer and closer.
His respiration now grew impeded, and every fresh
idea exaggerated his horror; his surmises were of
the most frightful description ; his *untaxed costs*, he

anticipated, would prove his certain death, and that a cruel one! neither of his companions would answer him a single question, the one replying only by a rude snore, and the other by a still ruder.

"Now," thought Mr. T——, "my fate is consummated. I have often heard how Mr. Fitzgerald cut a Jew's throat in Italy, and slaughtered numerous creditors while on the grand tour of Europe. God help me! unfortunate solicitor that I am! my last day, or rather night, is come!"

He thought to let down the window, and admit a little fresh air, but it was quite fast. The whole situation was insupportable; and at length he addressed Mr. Fitzgerald, most pathetically, thus: "Mr. Fitzgerald, I'll *date the receipt* the moment you choose; and whenever its your *convenience*, I have no doubt you'll pay it most honourably; no doubt, no doubt, Mr. Fitzgerald! but not necessary at all till perfectly *convenient*—or *never*, if more agreeable to you, and *this other gentleman*."

Fitzgerald could now contain himself no longer, but said, quite in good-humour, "Oh, very well, Mr. T——, very well: quite time enough; make yourself easy on that head."

The carriage now arrived at Maynooth, where the horses were instantly changed, and they proceeded rapidly on their journey—Mr. Fitzgerald

declaring he would not alight till he reached Turlow, for fear of pursuit.

The attorney now took courage, and very truly
surmising that the other gentleman was a *foreigner,*
ventured to beg of Mr. Fitzgerald to ask " his
friend " to sit *over* a little, as he was quite
crushed.

Mr. Fitzgerald replied, " That the party in
question did not speak English ;—but when they
arrived at Killcock, the matter should be better
arranged."

The attorney was now compelled, for some time
longer, to suffer the *hot-press,* inflicted with as little compunction as if he were only a sheet of paper ; but on arriving at the inn at Killcock, dawn
just appeared ; and Mr. Fitzgerald, letting down a
window, desired his servant, who was riding with
a pair of large horse-pistols before him, to rouse
the people at the inn, and get some cold provisions
and a bottle of wine brought to the carriage :
" And, Thomas," said he, " get five or six pounds
of raw meat, if you can—no matter of what kind—
for this *foreign gentleman.*"

The attorney was now petrified :—a little twilight glanced into the carriage, and nearly turned
him into stone. The stranger was wrapped up in
a blue travelling cloak with a scarlet cape, and
had a great white cloth tied round his head and
under his chin ;—but when Mr. Solicitor saw the

face of his companion, he uttered a piteous cry, and involuntarily ejaculated, " Murder ! murder !" On hearing this cry, the servant rode back to the carriage-window and pointed to his pistols. Mr. T—— now offered his soul up to God, the stranger grumbled, and Mr. Fitzgerald, leaning across, put his hand to the attorney's mouth, and said, he should direct his servant to give him *reason* for that cry, if he attempted to alarm the people in the house. Thomas went into the inn, and immediately returned with a bottle of wine and some bread, but reported that there was no raw meat to be had—on hearing which, Mr. Fitzgerald ordered him to seek some at another house. The attorney now exclaimed again, " God protect me!"— Streaming with perspiration, his eye every now and then glancing, toward his mysterious companion, and then starting aside with horror, he at length shook as if he were relapsing into his old ague ; and the stranger, finding so much unusual motion beside him, turned his countenance upon the attorney. Their cheeks came in contact, and the reader must imagine—because it is impossible adequately to describe—the scene that followed. The stranger's profile was of uncommon prominence ; his mouth stretched from ear to ear ; he had enormous grinders, with a small twinkling eye; and his visage was all bewhiskered and mustachoed, more even than Count Platoff's of the Cossacks.

Mr. T——'s optic nerves were paralysed, as he gazed instinctively at his horrid companion; in whom, when he recovered his sense of vision sufficiently to scrutinise him, he could trace no similitude to any being on earth save a *bear!*

And the attorney was quite correct in this comparison; it was actually a Russian bear, which Mr. Fitzgerald had *educated* from a cub, and which generally accompanied his master on his travels. He now gave bruin a rap upon the nose with a stick which he carried, and desired him to hold up his head. The brute obeyed: Fitzgerald then ordered him to *kiss* his *neighbour;* and the beast did as he was told, but accompanied his salute with such a tremendous roar, as roused the attorney (then almost swooning) to a full sense of his danger. Self-preservation is the first law of Nature, and at once gives courage, and suggests devices. On this occasion, every other kind of law—civil, criminal, or equitable—was set aside by the attorney. All his ideas, if any he had, were centred in one word—" escape ;" and as a weasel, it is said, will attack a man if driven to desperation, so did the attorney spurn the menaces of Mr. Fitzgerald, who endeavoured to hold and detain him. The struggle was violent, but brief; bruin roared loud, but interfered not. Horror strengthened the solicitor; dashing against the carriage-door, he burst it open; and tumbling out, reeled into the public-house,—then rushing through a back door, and up a narrow lane that led to the village of Summer-hill (Mr. Roly's demesne), about two miles distant, he stumbled over hillocks, tore through hedges and ditches, and never stopped till he came breathless to the little alehouse, completely covered with mud, and his clothes in rags. He there told so incoherent a story, that the people all took him for a man either bitten by a mad-dog or broken loose from his keepers; and considered it their duty to *tie* him, to prevent his *biting* or other mischief. In that manner they led him to Squire Roly's, at the great house, where the hapless attorney was pinioned and confined in a stable for some hours till the squire got up. They put plenty of milk, bread, butter, and cheese into the *manger*, from the cock-loft above, to prevent accidents as they said.

Thus situated, Mr. T—— had leisure to come somewhat to his recollection, so as to be able to tell the story rather rationally to Mr. Roly, when he came to examine him—being held fast by four men while under interrogation; the result of which nearly killed old Roly with laughter. The attorney was now released, invited into the house to clean himself, and supplied with a surtout coat and hat; and after offering as many thanksgivings as could be expected from a solicitor of those days, for his providential escape, he had a comfortable breakfast provided; and at his earnest desire, Mr. Roly sent one of his carriages, and two armed servants, with him to his own house in Dublin, where he safely arrived in due season.

This adventure was circulated throughout Dublin with rapidity (as every thing comical then was), but with many variations and additions ; and I remember it a standing story in every company that relished a joke.

It was some months before Mr. T—— wholly recovered from his terror ; and several clients, who lost their causes, attributed their failures to the bear having turned the brain and injured the legal capacity and intellect of their lawyer.   However, as a proof of the old adage, that " whatever is, is right," this very adventure in all probability saved Mr. T—— from being hanged and quartered (as will immediately appear).   So terrific did the very idea of George Robert Fitzgerald appear to him afterward, that he never ventured to ask him for the amount of his bill of costs, and *gave* him (in a negative way) all the leases, ejectments, and papers—together with his wardrobe, and a trifle of cash contained in his trunk which was left in the carriage.

Mr. Fitzgerald, having long had a design to put one Mr. M'Donnell, of his county, *hors du combat*, for some old grudge, determined to seek an opportunity of doing it under the colour of M'Donnell's illegal resistance to a law process, which process Mr. T—— had (innocently) executed ; in which

case the attorney would, of course, as sportsmen
say, " be in at the death."

After the affair of the bear, no attorney or
other legal man would entrust himself at Turlow ;—
it was, therefore, some time before Mr. Fitzgerald
could carry the above purpose into execution;—
when, at length, he found an old lawyer, who,
with the aid of Mr. T——'s said ejectments,
leases, &c. struck out a legal pretence for *shooting*
Mr. M'Donnell, which would probably have been
fathered upon poor Mr. T—— if the bear had not
stood his friend and packed him off to Summer-
hill instead of Turlow. As it was, this man (whose
name was Brecknock), who acted for Fitzgerald
as agent, adviser, attorney, &c. was hanged for
his pains, as an accessory before the fact, in giving
Mr. Fitzgerald a *legal* opinion ; and Mr. Fitzgerald
himself was hanged for the murder, solely on the
evidence of his own groom, Scotch Andrew, the
man who really *committed* it, by firing the fatal
blunderbuss.

There can be no doubt he deserved the death
he met; but there is also no doubt he was not
legally convicted ; and old Judge Robinson, then
accounted the best lawyer on the bench, sarcas-
tically remarked, that " the murderer was murdered."

This incident had escaped both my notes and
memory, when it was fully revived by the affair

between my good old friend, Richard Martin of Connemara, and Mr. Fitzgerald, described in a preceding sketch, and originating in the latter yoking his own father in a dray by the side of that very bear.

MARTIAL LAW.

Law in Ireland half a century ago —Its delay remedied, but not
its uncertainty—Principal and Interest—Eustace Stowell
and Richard Martin — Valuable *precedents*—A bloodless
duel—High sheriffs and their *Subs*—Irish method of serving
a writ — Cases of warranty — Messrs. Reddy Long and
Charley White—The latter guarantees an unsound horse to
the author—Zeal of a *second*—Mr. Reddy Long's valuable
legacy to Sir Jonah Barrington.

THE administration of the law among gentlemen
in Ireland fifty years back, is curiously illustrated
by the following little narrative, the circumstances
whereof have been communicated to me from such
a quarter as not to admit of their being doubted.

Our laws, in their most regular course (as every
body knows, who has had the honour and happiness of being much involved in them), are neither
so fleet as a race-horse, nor so cheap as water-
cresses. They indisputably require eloquent ad-
vocates and keen attorneys;—who expound, com-
plicate, unriddle, or confuse, the respective sta-
tutes, points, precedents, and practice, of that

simple science, which too frequently, like a burning-glass, consumes both sides of what it shines upon.

Some prudent and sensible gentlemen, therefore, principally in the country parts of Ireland (who probably had bit upon the bridle), began to conceive that justice ought to be neither so dear nor so tardy ; and when they reflected that what were called their " barking irons " brought all ordinary disputes to a speedy termination—why, thought they, should not these be equally applicable to matters of law, property, and so forth, as to matters of honour ? At all events, such an application would be incalculably *cheaper*, than any taxed bill of costs, even of the most conscientious solicitor.

This idea became very popular in some counties, and, indeed, it had sundry old precedents in its favour,—the writ of right and trial by battle having been originally the law of the land, and traditionally considered as far the most honourable way of terminating a suit. They considered, therefore, that what was lawful one day, could not be justly deemed unlawful another, and that by shortening the process of distributing justice, they should assist in extending it. The old jokers said, and said truly, that many a cause had been decided to a *dead* certainty in a few minutes, by simply touching a trigger, upon which attorneys, barristers, judges, jurors, witnesses, and sometimes all the peers of the realm, spiritual and temporal, had been working and fumbling for a series of years without bringing it even to an *un*satisfactory issue.

My old and worthy friend, " Squire Martin," afforded a most excellent illustration of this practice ; and as all the parties were " gentlemen to the backbone," the anecdote may be deemed a *respectable* one. I have often heard the case quoted in different companies, as a beneficial mode of ensuring a compromise. But the report of my friend makes it any thing but a *compromise* on his part. The retrograding was no doubt on the part of *the enemy*, and equally unequivocal as Moreau's through the Black Forest, or that of the ten thousand Greeks, though neither so brave nor so bloody as either of them.

I name place, parties, cause, proceedings, and final judgment—just as I received these particulars from the defendant himself; and I consider the case as forming a very *valuable precedent* for corresponding ones.

Eustace Stowell, Esq. challenger.

Richard Martin, Esq. acceptor.

Operator for the challenger, D. Blake, Esq.

Operator for the acceptor, Right Honourable St. George Daly, late judge of the King's Bench, Ireland.

Case as reported by Defendant.

Eustace Stowell lent me a sum of money on interest, which interest I had not paid *very* regularly. Mistaking my means, I promised to pay him at a certain time, but failed. He then called on me, and said I had broken my word. I answered, " Yes, I have, but I could not help it. I am very sorry, but in a few days will satisfy the demand." Accordingly, my worthy friend the late Earl of Mountjoy accepted my bills at three and six months for the whole amount.

Having arranged the business thus, I enclosed the bills to Mr. Eustace Stowell, who immediately returned them, saying, that as I had broken my word, he would accept of no payment but hard money.

I replied that I had no hard money, nor was there much of it afloat in my part of the country; upon which Mr. Eustace Stowell immediately sent his friend to me, requiring me either to give him cash or *personal satisfaction ;* and in the latter event, to appoint time and place. My answer was, that I did not want to shoot him unless he *insisted* upon it; but that as to *cash,* though Solomon was a wise man, and Sampson a strong one, neither of them could pay ready money if they had it not. So I prepared to engage him : my friend, the Right Honourable St. George Daly, since judge of the King's Bench, assisted in arranging pre-

liminaries to our mutual satisfaction, and pretty
early next morning we met to *fight out* the debt in
that part of the Phœnix Park called the Fifteen
Acres.

Every thing proceeded regularly, as usual. Our
pistols were loaded, and the distance measured,
eight yards from muzzle to muzzle. I stepped on
my ground, he on his. I was just presenting my
pistol at his body, when, having, I suppose, a pre-
sentiment that he should go somewhere out of this
world if I let fly at him, he instantly dropped his
weapon, crying out, " Mr. Martin ! Mr. Martin !
a pretty sort of *payment* this ! You'd shoot me for
my interest money, would you ?"

" If it's your *pleasure*, Mr. Eustace Stowell,"
said I, " I certainly will; but it was not my desire to come here, or to shoot you. You insisted
on it yourself : so go on, if you please, now we
are here."

" What security will you give me, Mr. Martin,"
said he, " for my interest money ?"

" What I have offered you already," said I.

" And what's that ?" demanded Mr. Stowell.

" I offered you Lord Mountjoy's bills at three
and six months," said I. Before I had time to
finish the last words Mr. Stowell cried out,
" Nothing can be better or more reasonable, Mr.
Martin ; I accept the offer with pleasure. No
better payment can be. It is singular you did not
make this offer *before*."

" I think," said I, " you had better take your

ground again, Mr. Eustace Stowell, for I tell you I *did* make this offer before, and may be you don't like so plump a contradiction. If not, I'm at your service. Here is a letter under your own hand, returning the bills and declining to receive them. See, read that!" continued I, handing it him.

" Bless me!" said he, " there must be some great misunderstanding in this business. All's right and honourable. I hope the whole will be forgotten, Mr. Martin."

" Certainly, Mr. Stowell," replied I : " but I trust you'll not be so hard to please about your interest money in future, when its not convenient to a gentleman to pay it."

He laughed, and we all four stepped into the same carriage, returned the best friends possible, and I never heard any thing irritating about his interest money afterward.

This case, however, was only a simple one on the *money counts*—a mere matter of *assumpsit*, in which all the gross and ungentlemanly legal expressions used in law declarations on *assumpsits* were totally avoided—such as " intending thereby to deceive and defraud :"—language which, though *legal*, a Galway gentleman would as soon eat his horse as put up with from his equal—though he would bear it from a shopkeeper with sovereign indifference. When such a one, therefore, was sued in *assumpsit* for a horse or so by a

gentleman, the attorney never let his client read
the law declaration—the result of which would
be injurious to two of the parties at least, as one
of the litigants would probably lose his life, and
the attorney the litigation. The foregoing cause
was conducted with as much politeness and de-
corum as could possibly be expected between four
high well-bred persons, who, not having " the
fear of God before their eyes," but, as law in-
dictments very properly set forth, " being moved
and seduced by the instigation of the devil," had
congregated for the avowed purpose of committing
or aiding in one or more wilful and deliberate
murders.

I must here observe that, in addition to the other
advantages this mode of proceeding between gentlemen had over that of courts of justice, a certain
principle of equity was understood to be connected
with it.' After a gentleman was regularly called
out, and had duly fought the challenger respecting
any sum of money, whether the trial ended in
death or not, after a single shot the demand was
extinguished and annulled for ever : no man can
be sued twice for the same debt. Thus, the challenger in a money case stood in rather an unpleasant situation—as, exclusive of the chance of getting
a *crack*, the money was for ever gone, whether
his adversary lived or died—unless, indeed, the
acceptor, being a " gentleman *every inch of him*,"
might feel disposed to wave his " privilege."

But this short, cheap, and decisive mode of terminating causes was not confined to simple money counts; it extended to all actions at law and proceedings in equity. The grand old procrastinators of Irish courts—*demurrers* and *injunctions*—were thus dissolved or obviated by a *trigger*, in a shorter time than the judges took to put on their wigs and robes. Actions also of trover, assault, trespass, detenu, replevin, covenant, &c. &c. were occasionally referred to this laudable branch of jurisprudence with great success, seldom failing of being finally decided by seven o'clock in the morning.

The system was also resorted to by betters at cock-fights, horse-races, or hurlings; as well as on account of breaches of marriage-contracts with sisters, nieces, or cousins; or of distraining cattle, beating other gentlemen's servants, &c. &c.: but none were more subject to the *trigger process* than high sheriffs when their year was over, if they had permitted their *subs* to *lay on* (as they called it) such things as executions, *fieri facias*, or *scire facias*, *haberes*, &c.; or to molest the person, property, or blood relations, of any *real* and spirited gentleman in his own bailiwick, or *out of it*.

The high sheriff being thus, by the laws of custom, honour, and the country gentlemen of Ireland, subject to be either shot or horsewhipped, or forced to commit a breach of public duty, very

fortunately discovered an antidote to this poison
in the person of his sub-sheriff—an officer generally selected from the breed of country attorneys.
Now, it was an invariable engagement of the *sub*
that he should keep, guarantee, and preserve his
high from all manner of injury and annoyances.
But as it was by common accord decided, that a
sub-sheriff could not possibly be considered a
gentleman, none such would do him the honour of
fighting him. Yet, being necessitated to adopt
some mode of keeping the *high* out of the fangs of
fire-eaters, and himself from a fracture by the *butt-
end* of a loaded whip, or the welts of a cutting one,
or of having his " seat of honour " treated as if it
were a foot-ball, the *sub* struck out a plan of pre-
venting any catastrophe of the kind—which plan,
by aid of a little smart affidavit, generally succeeded extremely well in the superior courts.

When the sub-sheriff received a writ or process
calculated to annoy any gentleman (*every inch of
him*, or *to the backbone*), he generally sent his
bailiff at night to inform the gentleman that he had
such a writ or process, hoping the squire would
have no objection to send him the little fees on it
with a small *douceur*, and he would pledge his
word and honour that the squire should hear no
more about the matter for that year. If the
gentleman had not by him the amount of the
fees (as was generally the case), he faithfully
promised them, which being considered a debt of

honour, was always, like a gambling debt, entitled to be earliest paid. Upon this, the sub, as soon as he was forced to make a return to such writs, did make a very sweeping one—namely, that the defendant had neither " body nor goods." This was, if required, confirmed by the little smart affidavit ; and if still doubted by the court, the *sub* never wanted plenty of *respectable* corroborating bailiffs to kiss *their thumbs*, and rescue the *high* out of any trifling dilemma that " his honour might get into through the Dublin people, bad luck to them all! root and branch, dead or alive," as the country *bums* usually expressed themselves.

Of the general application of this decisive mode of adjudicating cases of warranty and guarantee, I can give a tolerably clear example in my own proper person. When very young, I was spending a day at a cottage belonging to Mr. Reddy Long, of Moat, near Ballyragget, a fire-eater, when one Mr. Charley White sold me a horse for ten guineas, which he warranted sound, and which seemed well worth the money. Next day, when the seller had departed, the beast appeared to my host (not to me) to limp somewhat, and the dealing had thereby the appearance of jockeyship and false warranty—which occurring in the house of a fire-eater, rendered the *injury* an *insult,* and was accounted totally unpardonable. I knew, that if the beast were really lame, I could oblige the seller to return the money ; and accordingly told my host that if it turned out unsound, I'd get John Humphreys, the attorney, to write to Charley White to *refund.*

" An *attorney* write to a *gentleman !*" said Reddy Long, starting and staring at me with a frown. " Are you out of your wits, my neat lad? Why, if you sent an attorney in an affair of horse-flesh, you'd be damned in all society—you'd be out of our list, by—"

" Certainly," said I, " its rather a small matter to go to law about " (mistaking his meaning).

" Law ! Law !" exclaimed Reddy, " Why, thunder and oones ! *jockeying* one is a personal insult all the world over, when its a *gentleman* that resorts to it, and in the house of another gentleman. No, no ; you must make him give up the *shiners,* and *no questions asked,* or I'll have him out ready for you to shoot at in the meadows of Ahaboe by seven in the morning. See here !" said he, opening his ornamented mahogany pistol-case, " see, the boys are as bright as silver ; and I'm sure if the poor things could speak, they'd thank you for getting them their liberty: they have not been out of their own house these three months."

" Why, Reddy Long," said I, " I vow to God I do not want to *fight ;* there's no reason for my quarrelling about it. Charley White will return my money when I ask him for it."

" That won't do," said Reddy: " if the horse limps, the insult is complete ; we must have no bad precedents in this county. One gentleman warranting a *limper* to another in *private* is a gross affront, and a hole in his skin will be indispensable. At fairs, hunts, and horse-races, indeed, its ' catch as catch can;' there's no great dishonour as to beasts in the open air. That's the rule all the world over. Law, indeed! no, no, my boy, ten guineas or death—no sort of alternative! Tom Nolan," continued he, looking out of the window, " saddle the pony;—I'll be with Charley White of Ballybrophy before he gets home, as sure as Ben Burton!"

" I tell you, Mr. Long," said I, rather displeased, " I tell you I don't want to fight, and I won't fight. I feel no insult yet at least, and I desire you not to deliver any such message from me."

" You do!" said Reddy Long, " you do!" strutting up and looking me fiercely in the face. " Then, if you won't fight *him*, you'll fight *me*, I suppose?"

" Why so?" said I.

" What's that to you?" said he; but in a moment he softened and added, taking me by the hand, " My good lad, I know you are a mere boy, and not up to *the ways* yet; but your father would be angry if I did not make you do yourself justice; so come, get ready, my buck, to canter off to Denny Cuff's, where we'll be more handy for to-morrow."

I persisted in desiring him not to deliver any hostile message ; but in vain. ·" If," said he, as he mounted his pony, " you won't fight, I must fight him myself, as the thing occurred in my house. I'll engage that, if you did not call out Charley, all the bullock-feeders from Ossory, and that double-tongued dog from Ballybrophy at the head of them, would *post* you at the races at Roscrea."

Before I could expostulate further Mr. Reddy Long galloped off with a *view holloa*, to deliver a challenge for me against my will * to Mr. Charley White, who had given me no provocation. I felt very uneasy ; however, off I rode to Cuffsborough, where I made my complaint to old Denny Cuff, whose daughter was married to Reddy Long, and whose son afterward married my sister.

Old Cuff laughed heartily at me, and said, " You know Charley White ?"

" To be sure I do," said I ; " a civil and inoffensive man as any in Ossory."

" That's the very reason Reddy will deliver a challenge to him," said Cuff.

" 'Tis an odd reason enough," answered I.

" But a right good one too," rejoined old Cuff.—" Reddy knew that Charley would rather give *fifty* yellow boys than stand *half* a shot,

---

* I had made an unbending rule, for which I was dreadfully teased in the country, never to fight or quarrel about horse-flesh.

let alone a *couple*.   I'll answer for it Reddy knows
what he is about :" and so it proved.

My self-elected second returned that evening
with Charley White's groom, to take back the
horse ; and he brought me my ten guineas.   On
my thanking him, and holding out my hand to
receive them, after a moment's hesitation, he said,
" You don't want them for a day or two, do
you ?"

Taken completely by surprise, I answered involuntarily, " No."

" Well, then," said my friend Reddy, " I am
going to the races of Roscrea, and I won't give
you *the ten* till I come back.   It's all one to
you, you know?" added he, begging the question.

It was *not* all one to me : however, I was too
proud or rather silly to gainsay him, and he put
the pieces into his purse with a number of similar
companions, and went to the races of Roscrea,
where he was soon disburdened of them all, and contracted sundry obligations into the bargain.   I was
necessitated to go home, and never saw him after.
He died very soon, and bequeathed me an excellent chestnut hunter, called Spred, with Otter,
a water-dog of singular talents.   I was well
pleased when I heard of this ; but, on inquiry,
found they were *lapsed legacies*, as the horse had
died of the glanders a year before, and the dog
had run mad, and was hanged long ere the de-

parture of his master. I suppose, when death was torturing poor Reddy, (for he died of the gout in his head,) he forgot that the horse had been then skinned more than a twelvemonth.

BULLETIN EXTRAORDINARY.

The author and Counsellor Moore laid by the heels at Rock
House—Dismal apprehensions—A recipe and recovery—
The *races* of Castlebar—The author forms a party to visit the
spot—Members of the party described—Serjeant Butler and
the doctor—Differences of *opinion*—The serjeant's bulletin
of the famous battle of Castlebar.

AFTER fifteen days of one of the hottest election
contests I had ever witnessed, I accompanied my
friend, Counsellor Moore, to his aunt's, (Mrs,
Burke of Rock House, Castlebar,) where plenty,
hospitality, and the kindest attentions would have
soon made amends for our past misfortunes.—
But ill luck would not remit so suddenly :—we
had both got a Mayo *chill* on us, from the effects
whereof, not even abundance of good claret and
hot punch could protect us.

We had retired to rest after a most joyous festivity, when Moore (who had not been two hours in
bed) was roused by the excruciating tortures of an
inflammation of the stomach ; and in less than half

an hour after I heard his first groan, I found my own breath rapidly forsaking me; pins and needles seemed to be darting across my chest in all directions, and it was quite clear that another *inflammation* had taken a fancy to *my lungs* without giving the slightest notice. I could scarcely articulate, though my pains were not so very great as those of my poor friend : but I lost half the power of respiring, and had not even the consolation of being able to moan so loud as he. This was truly mortifying; but I contrived to thump strongly against the wainscot, which being hollow, proved an excellent *conductor*. The family took for granted that the house was on fire, or that some thief or ghost had appeared ; and, roused up by different conjectures, its members of each sex, age, and rank, quickly rushed into our room screeching, and jostling each other, as they followed the old man-servant, who, with a hatchet in his hand, came on most valiantly. None waited for the ceremony of the toilet; but approached just as they had quitted their couches—not even a " blanket " being " in the alarm of fear caught up."

The first follower of the old footman was a fat cook of Mrs. Burke's, Honor O'Maily, who, on learning the cause of the uproar, immediately commenced clearing herself from any suspicion of *poisoning ;* and cursing herself, without any reservation as to saints and devils, if the victuals, as she

dressed them, were not sweet, good, and right
wholesome : her pepper and salt, she vowed, had
been in the house a fortnight before, and both
the fritters and pancakes were fried in *her own
drippings !*

. Honor's exculpatory harangue being with some
difficulty silenced, a hundred antidotes were immediately suggested : Mrs. Burke, an excellent
woman, soon found a receipt at the end of her
cookery book for. curing all manner of poisons (for
they actually deemed us poisoned), either in man
or beast; and the administration of this recipe
was approved by one Mr. Dennis Shee, another
family domestic, who said " he had been *pysoned*
himself with some love-powders by a young woman who wanted to marry him, and was cured
by the very same stuff the mistress was going
to make up for the counsellors ; but that any how
he would run off for the doctor, who to be sure
knew best about the matter."

It was now fully agreed, that some of Denis
Brown's voters had got the poison from a witch at
Braefield,* out of spite, and all the servants cried

---

* In old times, Braefield near Turlow had been noted for
witches, several of whom had been burned or drowned for poisoning cattle, giving love-powders to people's *childer* ere they
came to years of maturity, and bestowing the shaking ague on
every body who was not kind to them. When I was at Turlow, they showed me near Braefield five high granite stones
stuck up in the midst of a green field, which they called " the

out that there was no luck or grace for any real gentleman in that quarter from the time George Robert was hanged.

Poor Mrs. Burke was miserable on every account, since the story of " two counsellors being poisoned at Rock House" would be such a stain on the family.

Being raised up in my bed against pillows, I began to think my complaint rather *spasmodic* than *inflammatory*, as I breathed better apace, and felt myself almost amused by the strange scenes going on around. Mrs. Burke had now prepared her antidote. Oil, salt, soapsuds, honey, vinegar, and whisky, were the principal ingredients. Of these, well shaken up in a quart bottle, she poured part down her nephew's throat (he not being able to drink it out of a bowl), much as farriers drench a horse; and as soon as the first gulp was down, she asked poor Moore if he felt any easier. He answered her question only by pushing back the antidote, another drop of which he absolutely refused to touch. She made a second effort to *drench* him, lest it might be *too late ;* but ere any thing more could be done, the doctor, or rather apothecary and man-midwife, arrived, when bleeding, blistering, &c. &c. were had recourse to, and on the third day I was totally recovered ; my poor

Witches of Braefield." They said there was a witch under every one of these, buried a hundred feet deep " at any rate." ,

friend got better but slowly, and after two dangerous relapses.

The incidents which had taken place in Castlebar during the French invasion, three years before,
were .too entertaining not· to be pried into (now I
was upon the spot) with all my zeal and perseverance. The most curious of battles, which was
fought there, had always excited my curiosity ; I
was anxious to discover what really caused so
whimsical a defeat. But so extremely did the
several narratives I heard vary—from the official
bulletin to the tale of the private soldier, that I
found no possible means of deciding on the truth
but by hearing every story, and *striking an average*
respecting their veracity, which plan, together with
the estimate of *probabilities,* might, perhaps,. bring
me pretty near the true state of the affair. There
had certainly been a battle and flight more humorous in their nature and result than any that had
ever before been fought or accomplished by a
British army ; neither powder, ball, nor bayonet
had fair claim to the victory ; but to a single true
blunder was attributable that curious defeat of our
pampered army—horse, foot, and artillery,—in half
an hour, by a handful of half-starved Frenchmen.
So promptly (as I heard) was it effected, that the
occurrence was immediately named—and I suppose
it still retains the appellation—" The *races* of
Castlebar." I cannot vouch for any single piece
of information I acquired ; but I can repeat some

of the best of it ; and my readers may strike the average as I do, and form their own conclusions on the subject. At all events, the relation may amuse them ; and, as far as the detail of such an event can possibly do, afford a glance at French and Irish, civil and military, high and low, aristocracy and plebeians :—undoubtedly proving that, after a battle is over, it suggests the simile of a lady after her baby is born—what was a cause of great uneasiness soon becomes a source of great amusement.

To attain this, my laudable object, the first thing I had to do was, as far as practicable, to fancy myself a general ; and in that capacity, to ascertain the errors by which the battle was lost, and the conduct of the enemy after their victory. *Experientia docet ;* and by these means I might obviate the same disaster on any future occasion. In pursuance of this fanciful hypothesis, my primary step was, of course, to reconnoitre the position occupied by our troops and those of the enemy on that engagement ; and in order to do this with effect, I took with me a *very clever* man, a serjeant of the Kilkenny militia, who had been trampled over by Chapman's heavy horse in their hurry to get off, and left with half his bones broken, to recover as well as he could. He afterward returned to Castlebar, where he married, and continued to reside. An old surgeon was likewise of our party, who had been with the army, and had (as he informed me) made a most deliberate retreat when he saw the rout begin. He described the whole affair to me, being, now and then, interrupted and " *put in*," as the corporal called it, when he was running out of the course, or drawing the long-bow. Three or four country fellows (who, it proved, had been rebels), wondering what brought us three together, joined the group; and, on the whole, I was extremely amused.

The position shown me, as originally held by the defeated, seemed, to my poor *civil* understanding, one of the most difficult in the world to be routed out of. Our army was drawn up on a declivity of steep, rugged ground, with a narrow lake at its foot, at the right whereof was a sort of sludge-bog, too thick to swim in, and too thin to walk upon—snipes alone, as they said, having any fixed residence in, or lawful claim to it. On the other side of the lake, in front of our position, was a hill covered with underwood, and having a winding road down its side. In our rear was the town of Castlebar, and divers stone walls terminated and covered our left. None of my informants could agree either as to the number of our troops or cannon; they all differed even to the extent of thousands of men, and from four to twenty pieces of cannon. Every one of the parties, too, gave his own account in his own way. One of the rebels swore, that " though he had nothing but ' this same little switch ' (a thick cud-

gel) in his fist, he knocked four or five troopers
off their beasts, as they were galloping over himself, till the French gentlemen came up and *skiver-
ed* them; and when they were once down, the
' devil a much life' was long left in them."

" Were you frightened, Mr. O'Donnell?" said
I (he told me that was his name).

" By my sowl!" replied O'Donnell, who seemed
a decent sort of farmer, " if you had been in it
that same day, your honour would have had no
great objections to be out of it agin."

" Now," said I, " pray, Serjeant Butler, how
came the Kilkenny to run away that day so soon
and with so little reason?"

" Becaize we were *ordered* to run away," answered the serjeant.

" How can you say that, serjeant?" said the
doctor. " I was myself standing bolt upright at
the left of the Kilkenny when they ran without
any order."

" O yes, indeed! to be sure, doctor!" said Serjeant Butler; " but were you where I was when
Captain Millar the *aidycam* ordered us off in no
time?"

" He did not," replied the doctor.

" Why, then, since you make me curse, by J—s
he *did;* becaize the officers afterward all said, that
when he ordered us off, he forgot half what he
had to say to us."

" And pray, what was the other half, serjeant?" inquired I.

" Ah, then, I'll tell you that, counsellor," replied Butler. " That same *aidycam* was a fat, bloated gentleman, and they said he was rather thick-winded like a beast, when his mind was not easy : so he comes up (my lord was looking at the fight, and did not mind him), and he kept puffing and blowing away while he was ordering us, till he came to the words, ' you'll get off,' or ' you'll advance backwards,' or some words of the same kind, I can't exactly say what;—but it seems, when he desired us to make off, he forgot to say ' thirty yards,' as the officers told us at Tuam was the general's word of command :—and as he desired us to *make off*, but didn't order us when to *stop*, by my sowl some of us never stopped or stayed for thirty good *miles*, and long miles too, only to get a drink of water or half a noggin of whisky, if there was any in the alehouse. And sorry enough we were, and sore likewise !—Then there was that Chapman and his heavy horse ; troth I believe every horse in the place cantered over us as if we were sods of turf. Bad luck to their sowls ! many a poor Kilkenny lad couldn't get out of their way while *they* were making off, and so they tumbled over the Kilkenny themselves, and all were tumbling and rolling together, and the French were coming on to stick us ; and

we were trampled and flattened in the dust, so
that you'd hardly know a corpse from a sheet of
brown paper, only for the red coat upon it."

The doctor now attempted to tell the story in
his way, when the Kilkenny serjeant, being at
length a little provoked at the other's numerous in-
terruptions and contradictions, exclaimed, " Arrah!
doctor, be *asy;* it's I can tell the counsellor, for
it's I that was *in it,* and almost *kilt* too ; and
that's more than you were, barring with the
fright!"

The doctor gave him a look of sovereign contempt, and me a significant wink, as much as to
say, " the fellow is mad, and drunk into the
bargain."

However, the serjeant conquered all opposition,
and proceeded to give me the full narrative, in
his own dialect. " Counsellor," said he, " do
you know that Chapman—so I think they called
him—is as tall as any May-pole ?"

" Very well," said I.

" Well," said the serjeant, " on the spot near
the bog, where the devil could not get at us
without drying it first and foremost—there we
were drawn up at first, all so neat and tight on
the ridge there, one would think us like iron rails,
every lad of us. Very well; being firm and fast
as aforesaid on the ridge, with the shaking bog by
the side of *the Chapman's*—bad cess to them,
man and beast!—Oh! it was not most agreeable

when the French let fly at us without giving us the least notice in life; and by my sowl, they hit some of the boys of our regiment, and that same set them a roaring and calling for a drink of water and the doctor! but the devil a doctor was *in it;* (can you deny that same?) and his honour, Lord Ormond, our colonel, grew red in the face with anger, or something or other, when he heard the boys bawling for *water*, and good reason they had, for by my sowl they were *kilt* sure enuff. So we leathered at the French across the water, and the French leathered at us likewise. Devil such a *cracking* ever you heard, counsellor, as on that day; and by the same token it would make a dog laugh to see how Captain Shortall with his cannons let fly at the French out of the bushes; and by my sowl, *they* were not idle either! So, we were all fighting mighty well, as I heard General Lake say in the rear of us; and as I looked round and took off my cap to hurra, I heard the devils roar at my elbow, and saw my poor comrade, Ned Dougherty, staggering back for all the world just as if he was drunk, and the devil a nose on his face any more than on the back of my hand, counsellor, the present minute: and on a second glance at poor Ned, I saw one of his eyes not a whit better off than his nose;—so I called as loud as I could for a doctor, but the devil a one showed."

The doctor could stand the imputation no longer,

and immediately gave the retort not courteous to the serjeant.

"Why, then, do you hear that?" said the serjeant, quite coolly. "Arrah! now, how can you say you were *in it?* When Ned Dougherty was *kilt,* you know you were sitting *behind* the cannon; and the devil a bit of you would have been seen while the powder was going, if the nose was off the *general,* let alone Ned Dougherty."

I feared much that my whole inquiries would be frustrated by the increase of this dispute, when one of the country fellows who was by, said, "You're right enuff, serjeant. It was myself and two boys more, after yees all ran away, that pulled the doctor from under a cart; but we let him go, becaize he towld us he had ten *childer* and a wife, who would crack her heart if she thought he was slaughtered;—and that's the truth, and nothing else—though the devil a wife or child ever ye had, doctor."

I now winked at the doctor not to mind the fellows, and requested the serjeant to go on with *the battle.*

"And welcome, counsellor," said he: "stay, where did I leave off? O! ay, at Ned Dougherty's nose:—very well, poor Ned wasn't kilt *dead;* only lost his nose and eye, and is very comfortable now, as he says, in Kilmainham. Very well, as I was saying, we went on slashing away like devils across the water, when, by my sowl, I heard some

cracks up at the left of us, and the balls began
to whiz all across us, lengthways. ‘ What the
deuce is this job?’ says I. ‘ D—mme if I know,’
said the serjeant-major;—when Captain Millar,
the general’s *aidycam*, comes up full pelt, and
orders us to *get off* as aforesaid. When we
heard that same order, we thought we were fairly
beat; and so, losing no time, set off as hard as
we could to get into Castlebar town again ere the
French could take it before us. And then, Chapman’s people, bad chance to them, cried out, ‘ Get
on! get on!’ and galloped away as if the devil was
under their tails, and no more minded *the' Kilkenny*
than if we were Norway rats, trampling us up and
down, and some of them tumbling over our carcases. You’d think it was a race-course : my ribs
were all knocked in, and my collar-bone broken ;
and—and—that’s all I know, counsellor.”

“ Is that *all*, serjeant ?” asked I.

“ O no, counsellor,” replied he. “ I have
more to tell, now I think of it. Every boy in our
regiment declared, if it had been Hutchinson that
commanded us, the devil a one would run away if
he stayed till this time, or go to the French either ;
but all the lads used to say afterward, ‘ Why should
we fight under Lake, (whom we neither knew nor
cared to know,) when we had our own brave country general to the fore, that we’d stick by till
death ?’ and I forgot to tell you, counsellor — a
hundred or so of our boys who could not run fast,

thought it better to stay quiet and easy with the French than be murdered without the least reason imaginable; and so they stayed and were treated very handsome: only owld Corney hanged a good many of the poor boys at Ballynamuck; and the devil a bit better is Ireland made by hanging any body — and that's the truth, and nothing else! Faith, if they hanged a quarter of us all, another quarter would be wanting it against the next assizes. So, what use is hanging the boys? Little good will it ever do the remainder!"

BREAKFASTS AT BALLINROBE.

Election for County Mayo—Author and Counsellor Moore at
Ballinrobe—Mr. Dan Martin's " little paved parlour "—
Preparations for a festive breakfast—A formidable incursion
—Counsellor Moore laid prostrate—Advance of the foe—
The two barristers take up an elevated position—Disappear-
ance of the various eatables—General alarm—Dislodgment
of the enemy—Mr. Dan Martin's comments upon the " af-
fair "— *Secrets* worth Knowing — All's Well that Ends
Well.

THE following is almost too trifling an anecdote
to be recorded; but, as it characterises place,
time, and people, and is besides of a novel description, I cannot deny myself the pleasure of
relating it. The period at which it occurred was
that of the Mayo election alluded to in the last
sketch.

After some days of hard labour, bad food,
worse wine, and no tranquillity, Mr. Martin (I
think that was his name), the owner of an alehouse in our interest, told us with great glee, he
had got in a few loaves of good white bread and a

paper of tea from Castlebar, fit for the chancellor
—together with fresh eggs and new milk ; and
that if we would vouchsafe to put up with his own
" little paved parlour," we should have a roaring
fire, capital buttered toast, and, in short, every
thing to our satisfaction, one meal *any how ;* it was
God's curse and a thousand pities he had nothing
better for the "dear counsellors ;" but there was to
be a fine slip of a pig killed in the town that night
by a friend of his own, and we might have a beautiful griskin next morning broiled to our liking.

My friend Moore and I were delighted at the
announcement of a comfortable breakfast (for
some time a stranger to us), and immediately went
into the little paved parlour, where every thing
was soon in full array according to Mr. Daniel
Martin's promises. The turf fire glowed fit to
roast an ox ; abundance of hot buttered toast was
quickly placed before it ; plenty of new-laid eggs
appeared—some boiled, some poached ; a large
saucepan with hot water was bubbling on the
ashes ; our tea was made (as the tea-pot leaked)
in a potsheen-jug ; and every thing appeared in
the most proper state to *feast* two lately *half-fed*
Dublin barristers (as they called us). My mouth
watered, Moore licked his lips, and we never sat
down to the sensual enjoyment of the palate with
more *goût* or satisfaction than in Mr. Martin's
" little paved parlour."

It seemed as if nothing short of an earthquake

.(perhaps not even that) could have disappointed us. But I do not recollect any incident during a long life so completely verifying the old aphorism of " Many a slip between the cup and the lip." During our happy state of anticipation, rather a loud rap was heard:—I was just in the act of cracking the shell of an egg, with my back to the door, and cried out, " Come in! come in!" Nobody entered; but another and still louder rap succeeded. My friend, not being at that instant so busily occupied as I, stepped to the door, with the purpose of telling whoever it might be to " call again " in half an hour. I meanwhile proceeded with my egg; when I heard Moore, who was not in the habit of using imprecations, cry out piteously, " Oh! blood and oons!" 'and his exclamation was accompanied by a crash that alarmed me. On turning rapidly round, to aid him in any possible emergency, I saw my companion extended on the floor, his heels kicked up in the air, and eight or ten young *pigs* making the best of their way over the counsellor's prostrate body with great vivacity. Their *mother*, with divers deep and savage grunts, snorting, and catching the air through her enormous proboscis, took her way round the other side of the room, and effectually cut us off both from the door and our weapons on the breakfast-table. This manœuvre certainly would have daunted much greater heroes than either of us pretended to be; and I doubt if there is a field-marshal in the service either of his Britannic or Most Christian Majesty who would have felt himself quite at ease under similar circumstances.

We had no retreat: the foe had anticipated us, and appeared both able and willing to slaughter us for the sake of her progeny. "Mount, Moore," said I. He limped, for his leg was hurt, to a high old-fashioned chest of drawers, which fortunately stood in a corner. Upon these drawers each of us got, and thence watched ulterior operations, but by no means considering ourselves *out of danger* from so *frightful* an enemy.

That the reader who has not been accustomed to associate with swine at Ballinrobe may form a just idea of our situation, he shall be made accurately acquainted with the species of lady visitor we had to deal with. The eight or ten *childer* were what we call " piggin riggins," too old for a dainty and too young for bacon—the " *hobble-de-hoys*" of swinehood. Their mother literally " towered above her sex," and was the lankiest and most bristly sow I ever beheld. Her high arched back, taller than a donkey's, springing from the abutments of her loins and shoulders, resembled a coarse rustic bridge; her dangling teats swept the ground ; long loose flabby ears nearly concealed a pair of small fiery blood-shot sunken eyes, and their ends just covered one half of a mouth which, dividing her head as it were into an upper and under story, clearly showed that she had the means of taking what bite she pleased out of any thing. Her tusks, indeed, like a boar's, peeped under her broad and undulating nostrils, which were decorated with an iron ring and hook, that appeared to afford the double power of defending the wearer against assaults and hooking in an enemy.

Of such a description was the family that paid us this unwelcome visit, demonstrating thereby the uncertainty of all sublunary expectations. The fact was, that the lady, with ten of her *childer*, had been wallowing in the quagmire by the side of our parlour-window, which we had opened to give a part of the captive smoke an opportunity of escaping—but which at the same time let out the savoury perfume of our repast; this entering piggy's sensitive nostrils, she was roused to action, and, grunting to her family as a trumpeter sounds " to horse," they made their way to the well-known door of the little paved parlour, which finding closed (a very unusual circumstance), madam's temper was somewhat ruffled; and the catastrophe ensued. Ceremony from a sow, under such circumstances, could not be reasonably looked for, and any delay in disposing of our luxuries was still less to be expected. In her haste to accomplish that achievement, she had on gaining admittance run between the legs of Counsellor Thomas Moore, and, as on an inclined plane, she first raised, then deposited him upon the pavement; and leaving him to the discretion of her *piggin riggins*, changed her own course to our breakfast-table, which having duly overset, the whole was at her mercy—of which, however, she showed none;—the toast, the bread, the eggs—in short, *every thing*, disappearing in marvellous quick time.

The two counsellors, from their elevated position, beheld the destruction of all these comforts, and congratulated themselves on the good luck of being personally out of danger : but here also we " reckoned without our host:" we entertained no doubt of madam sow's peaceable departure, and did not wish to expose ourselves to the ridicule of being discovered perched upon a chest of drawers. One of the *piggins*, however, not content with the prey he had already got, in roaming about for more, and unaccustomed to boiling water, happened to overset the large saucepan which was steaming upon the hob, and which descended full on his unseasoned hide. Hereupon, feeling his tender bristles getting loose, and at the first scratch coming away with a due quantity of scarf-skin to keep them together, he set up the most dreadful cries I ever heard, even from the most obstinate of his race when the butcher was taking the preliminary steps towards manufacturing corned pork—that comrade of pease-pudding, and glory of the British navy!

The *mamma* of course attributed the cries of her darling to some torture inflicted by the *Christians* upon the drawers; to the foot of which she there-fore trotted, and with deep and loud grunts looked up at us, opening her wide jaws, and seeming to say, "I wish I had you both down here, and my dear little *piggin riggins* should soon be revenged for your cruelty!" I thought that, once or twice, she appeared disposed to try if she could balance her body on her hind-legs and rear up against the chest of drawers; in which case, even if her jaws did not clearly take hold of us, the strong iron hook in her nose would be sure to catch and hawl down one or other by the leg—as, if once hooked, it would only be a trial of strength between the sow's snout and the tendon Achilles of either counsellor. We could not kick at her for fear of the same hook; so we kept dancing and stamp-ing, to try if that would deter her. But she was too much bent on mischief to care for our defen-sive operations; and we were ultimately obliged to resort to that step generally taken by people when they find themselves failing in point of fortitude, and manfully cried out—"Murder! murder!" But as no one came, Moore said they were so used to *that* cry in Ballinrobe (and par-ticularly in the "little paved parlour"), that the people never minded it; so we changed our tone, and roared " Fire! fire!"

In a second the entire population of the house was in the room, when an *éclaircissement* took place. Still, however, the *lady* would not beat a retreat: —sticks, flails, handles of rakes, and pitchforks, belaboured her in vain; she minded them no more than straws. At length, they seized hold of her *tail:*—this action seemed to make her imagine that it was desired to *detain* her *in* the room; upon which, that spirit of contradiction inherent in more animals than one, determined her to *go out.* She accordingly rushed off, followed by the whole brood, and we saw no more of her or her hopeful family.

After they were gone, it took Mr. Martin above five minutes to lavish on the sow and *piggin riggins* every imprecation his vocabulary could furnish; and he concluded thus:—" Ough! May the curse of Crummell light on yee, for a greedy owld sow as you are! yee need not have taken such trouble to cater for your *childer.* If they had just peeped up the chimney, they'd have seen their *father* as well dried and smoked as any boar that ever was *kilt* in Ballinrobe these two years, any how; and by my sowl I expect to have six of the *childer* along with him by next Michaelmas, at latest."

All being now arranged, we begged Mr. Martin to replenish our board as quickly as possible. Daniel, however, looked grave and chop-fallen, and in two monosyllables apprised us of the extent of our misfortunes. " I can't," said he.

" Why ?" we both asked in a breath.

" Oh, holy poker !" exclaimed Mr. Dan Martin, " what shall I do to feed yee, counsellors dear ! By my sowl, Sir Neil will *skiver* me ! Devil a bit or sup more I have in this same house. Arrah ! Mary ! Mary !"

" What's that, avourneen ?" said Mary, entering.

" What have you in the house, Mary ?" demanded the landlord.

" Ough! the devil a taste was left from the Newport voters, barring what we kept for the counsellors."

" And have you literally *nothing*, Mr. Martin ?" demanded we.

" All as one," was the reply. " Sir Neil's men got the last of the meat ; and a minute or two ago, who should come in—devil's cure to him ! but Denis Brown Sallough's body-sarvant, and pretended, the villain, that he was Sir Neil's man ; and he bought all the rest of the bread and tay for ready money. If I had thought, counsellors, of the incivility my sow put on yees—bad luck to her sowl, egg and bird !—I'd have seen Denis Brown Sallough's body-sarvant *carded* like a tithe proctor* before I'd have sold him as much as would fill a hollow tooth—and by my sowl he has plenty of *them,* counsellors dear!"

" Have you no eggs, Mr. Martin?"

" Why, plase your honour, it's not two hours since the high sheriff's cook (as he called himself) came and took every cock and hen I had in the world (he paid like a gentleman, to be sure), for he has a great dinner to-day, and being disappointed

* *Carding* the tithe proctors (who certainly were the genuine tyrants of Ireland) was occasionally resorted to by the White Boys, and was performed in the following manner.

The tithe proctor was generally waked out of his first sleep by his door being smashed in ; and the *boys* in white shirts desired him " never to fear," as they only intended to *card* him this bout for taking a quarter instead of a tenth from every poor man in the parish. They then turned him on his face upon the bed ; and taking a lively ram cat out of a bag which they brought with them, they set the cat between the proctor's shoulders. The beast, being nearly as much terrified as the proctor, would endeavour to get off ; but being held fast by the tail, he intrenched every claw deep in the proctor's back, in order to keep up a firm resistance to the White Boys. The more the tail was pulled *back,* the more the ram cat tried to go *forward ;* at length, when he had, as he conceived, made his possession quite secure, main force convinced him to the contrary, and that if he kept his hold he must lose his tail. So, he was dragged backward to the proctor's loins, grappling at every pull, and bringing away here and there strips of the proctor's skin, to prove the pertinacity of his defence.

When the ram cat had got down to the loins he was once more placed at the shoulders, and again *carded* the proctor (*toties quoties*) according to his sentence.

of poultry, he *kilt* every mother's babe of mine, gentlemen."

" You have milk ?"

" I'd have plenty of that stuff, counsellors, only (oh my poor cow, and the three heifers!) Sir Neil's voters are generally so *dry,* and by my sowl, I believe not far from *hungry* either, that they, five or six times a day if they can, get a drink out of the poor animals. They have been milked, indeed, till their teats are raw, gentlemen, and that's the truth, and nothing else but the *true truth.*" Recollecting himself, however, he added—" But, counsellors, dear, if your honours can put up with *our own* little breakfast, you'll be more welcome nor the flowers of May, and there will be plenty of that, gentlemen, such as it is, and I'll tell you *what* it is. First and foremost, there's no better than the apple pratees, and they are ready hot and smothering for ourselves and that d——'d sow and her *childer,* and be cursed to them! but the devil a one they will get this day, for affronting yees, gentlemen!—And next to the pratees, there's the potsheen. I *still'd* it myself a year ago, and hid it under ground when the elections came on; but I get a bottle or two out always. And then, gentlemen, I can broil for you (but that's a secret, plase your honours,) a few beautiful rashers out of the two flitches I have hid on a little shelf up the chimney for fear of the two-guinea freeholders;—it's more like clear horn nor bacon, counsellors dear," pursued he, hauling down a side of it as he spoke, and cutting out several large rashers.

" I suppose," said I, " this is some of your good sow's family ;—if so, I shall have great pleasure in paying her off in her own style ?"

" Why, then, counsellor," said Mr. Martin, laughing and rubbing his hands—" you are the very devil at finding out things!—ha! ha!—By my sowl, it is a *sister* of the said sow's, sure enuff— bad luck to the whole breed for eating the buttered toast this blessed morning!"

The result was, that we got rashers, potatoes, and potsheen, for our breakfast; at the end of which Mr. Martin brought in a jug of capital home-brewed ale ;—and the possession of this, also, he said was a secret, or the gauger would play the deuce with him. We fared, in a word, very well ; I much doubt, to speak truth, if it were not a more appropriate meal for a desperate bad day and much hard work than a lady's teapot would afford ; and, in pursuance of this notion, I had a rasher, potatoe, and draught of good ale, every day afterward during my stay at that abominable election.

English people would hardly credit the circumstances attending an electioneering contest in Ireland, so late as twenty-three years ago. Little attention was then paid by the country gentlemen to their several assize towns ; and there was not a single respectable inn at Ballinrobe. Somebody indeed had built the shell of an hotel; but it had not been plastered either within or without, or honoured by any species of furniture: it had not indeed even banisters to the stairs.

Perhaps the time of year and desperate state of the weather (uncheckered by one ray of sunshine) tended to disgust me with the place: but I certainly never in my lifetime was so annoyed as at the election of Ballinrobe, though every thing that could possibly be done for our comfort *was* done by Sir John Brown—than whom I never met any gentleman more friendly or liberal.

NEW MODE OF SERVING A PROCESS.

The author at Rock House—Galway election—*Searching* for voters—Mr. Ned Bodkin—Interesting conversation between him and the author—Process-serving at Connemara—Burke, the bailiff—His hard treatment—Irish method of discussing a chancery bill—Ned Bodkin's " Lament "—False oaths, and their disastrous consequences—Country magistrates in Ireland.

THE election for County Galway was proceeding whilst I was refreshing myself at Rock House, Castlebar, after various adventures at Ballinrobe— as already mentioned.   I met at Rock House an old fellow who told me his name was Ned Bodkin, a Connemara boy ; and that he had come with two or three other lads only to *search* for voters to take to Galway for Squire Martin's poll.   Bodkin came to Mrs. Burke's house to consult Counsellor Moore, and I determined to have a full conversation with him as to the peninsula of Connemara and its statistics.   He sent off eight or nine freeholders (such as they were) in eight-and-forty hours ; they were soon polled for the squire, and came back as happy as possible.

I asked Mr. Bodkin where he lived.

"Ah! then where should it be but at Conne-mara?" said he.

"And what's your trade or calling, when you're at home, Mr. Bodkin?" inquired I.

"Why, plase your honour, no poor man could live upon one calling now-a-days as we did in owld times, or no calling at all, as when the squire was *in it*. Now I butchers a trifle, your honour! and burns the kelp when I'm entirely idle. Then I take a touch now and then at the still, and smuggle a few in Sir Neil's cutter when the coast is clear."

"Any thing else, Mr. Bodkin?"

"Ough yes, your honour; 'tis me that tans the brogue leather for the colonel's yeomen: (God bless them!) besides, I'm bailiff-bum of the town lands, and make out our election registries; and when I've nothing else to do, I keep the squire's accounts: and by my sowl that same is no asy matter, plase your honour, till one's used to it! but, God bless him, up and down, wherever he goes, here or hereafter! he's nothing else but a good master to us all."

"Mr. Ned Bodkin," continued I, "every body says the king's writ does not *run* in Connemara?"

"Ough! then whoever towld your honour that is a big liar. By my sowl, when the King George's writ (crossing himself) comes within smell of the big house, the boys soon make him run as if the seven red devils was under his tail, saving your presence. It's King George's writ that *does run* at Connemara, plase your worship, all as one as a black greyhound. O the devil a stop he stays till he gets into the courthouse of Galway again!"

Mr. Bodkin talked allegorically, so I continued in the same vein:—" And pray if you catch the king's writ, what do you do then?"

" Plase your honour, that story is asy towld. *Do,* is it? I'll tell your honour that. Why, if the *prossy-sarver* is *cotched* in the territories of Ballynahinch, by my sowl if the squire's not *in it,* he'll either eat his parchments every taste, or go down into the owld coal-pit sure enuff, whichever is most *agreeable* to the said prossy-sarver."

" And I suppose he generally prefers eating his parchments?" said I.

" Your honour's right enuff," replied Mr. Bodkin. " The *varment* generally gulps it down mighty glib; and, by the same token, he is seldom or ever obstrepulous enuff to go down into the said coal-pit."

" *Dry* food, Mr. Bodkin," said I.

" Ough! by no manner of manes, your honour. We always give the prossy-sarver, poor crethur! plenty to moisten his said food with and wash it down well, any how; and he goes back to the 'sizes as merry as a water-dog, and swears (God forgive him!) that he was *kilt* at Connemara by people unknown; becaize if he didn't do that, he

knows well enuff he'd soon be kilt dead by people he did know, and that's the truth, plase your
honour, and nothing else."

" Does it often happen, Mr. Bodkin ?" said I.

" Ough! plase your honour, only that our own
bailiffs and yeomen soldiers keep the sheriffs'
officers out of Connemara, we'd have a rookery
of them afore every 'sizes and sessions, when
the master's amongst the Sassanachs in London
city. We made one lad, when the master was
in said foreign parts, eat every taste of what
he towld us was a chancellor's bill, that he
brought from Dublin town to sarve in our quarter.
We laid in ambush, your honour, and cotched him
on the bridge ; but we did not throw him over
that, though we made believe that we would.
' We have you, you villain!' said I. ' Spare
my life !' says he. ' What for ?' said I. ' Oh!
give me marcy !' says the sarver. ' The devil a
taste,' said I. ' I've nothing but a chancellor's
bill,' said he. ' Out with it,' says I. So he
ups, and outs with his parchment, plase your
honour :—by my sowl, then, there was plenty of
that same !

" ' And pray, what name do you go by when
you are at home ?' said I. ' Oh then, don't you
know Burke the *bum* ?' said he. ' Are you satisfied to *eat* it, Mr. Burke ?' said I. ' If I was as
hungry as twenty hawks, I could not eat it all in
less than a fortnight any how,' said the sarver,
' it's so long and crisp.' ' Never fear,' said I.

" ' Why shu'dn't I fear?' said he.

" ' What's that to you?' said I.   ' Open your mouth, and take a bite, if you plase.'   ' Spare my life!' said he.   ' Take a bite, if you plase, Mr. Burke,' again said I.

"So he took a bite, plase your honour; but I saw fairly it was too dry and tough for common eating, so I and the rest of *the boys* brought the bum to my little cabin, and we soaked *the chancellor* in potsheen in my little keg, and I towld him he should stay his own time till he eat it all as soon as it was *tinder*, and at three meals a day, with every other little nourishment we could give the crethur.   So he stayed very agreeable till he had finished the chancellor's bill every taste, and was drunk with it every day twice, at any rate; and then I towld him he might go back to Galway town and welcome.   But he said he'd got kinder treatment and better liquor nor ever the villain of a sub-sheriff gave any poor fellow, and if I'd let him, he'd fain stay another day or two to bid us good bye.   ' So, Mary,' said I to the woman my wife, ' 'commodate the poor officer a day or two more to bid us good bye.'—' He's kindly welcome,' says she.   So Burke stayed till the 'sizes was over, and then swore he lay for dead on the road-side, and did not know what became of the chancellor's bill, or where it was deposited at said time.   I had towld him, your honour, I'd make good his oath for him; and, accordingly, we made him so drunk, that he lay all as one as a dead man in the ditch till we brought him home, and then he said he could kiss the holy 'pistle and gospel safe in the court-house, that he lay for dead in a ditch by reason of the treatment he got at Connemara; and Mr. Burke turned out a good fellow; and the devil a prossy-sarver ever came into Connemara for a year after, but he sent a gossoon aforehand to tell us where we'd cotch the sarver afore sarvice. Oh! God rest your sowl, Bum Burke, and deliver it safe! it's us that were sorry enuff when we heard the horse kilt you dead—oh bad cess to him! the likes of ye didn't come since to our quarter."

This mode of making process-servers *eat* the process was not at all confined to Connemara. I have myself known it practised often at the colliery of Doonan, the estate of my friend Hartpole, when his father Squire Robert was alive. It was quite the custom; and if a person in those times took his residence in the purlieus of that colliery, serving him with any legal process was entirely out of the question; for if a bailiff attempted it, he was sure to have either a meal of sheepskin or a dive in a coal-pit, for his trouble.

This species of outrage was, however, productive of greater evil than merely making the process-server eat his bill. Those whose business it was to serve processes in time against the assizes, being afraid to fulfil their missions, took a short cut, and swore they *had* actually served them, though they had never been on the spot;—

whereby many a judgment was obtained surreptitiously, and executed on default upon parties who had never heard one word of the business :—and thus whole families were ruined by the perjury of one process-server.

The magistrates were all country gentlemen, very few of whom had the least idea of law proceedings further than when they happened to be directed against themselves ; and the· common fellows, when sworn on the holy Evangelists, conceived they could outwit the magistrates by kissing their own thumb, which held the book, instead of the cover of it; or by swearing, " By the vartue of my oath it's through (true), your worship !" (putting a finger through a button-hole.)

So numerous were the curious acts and anecdotes of the Irish magistrates of those days, that were I to recite many of them, the matter-of-fact English (who have no idea of Irish freaks of this nature) would, I have no doubt, set me down as a complete romancer.

I conceived it would much facilitate the gratification of my desire to learn the customs of the Irish magisterial justices by becoming one myself. I therefore took out my *didimus* at once for *every* county in Ireland ; and being thus a magistrate for thirty-two counties, I of course, wherever I went, learned all their doings ; and I believe no body of men ever united more *authority* and less *law* than did the Irish justices of thirty years since.

DONNYBROOK FAIR.

Donnybrook contrasted with St. Bartholomew's —Characteris-
tics of the company resorting to each fair—Site upon which
the former is held—Description and materials of a Donnybrook tent—Various humours of the scene—The horse fair
—Visit of the author and Counsellor Byrne in 1790—Barter
and exchange — The " gentle Coadjutor" —The " master
cobbler"—A head in chancery—Disastrous mishap of Counsellor Byrne—Sympathy therewith of the author and his
steed—The cobbler and his companion—An extrication—
Unexpected intruders—Counsellor Byrne and his doctor—
A glance at the country fairs of Ireland—Sir Hercules Langreish and Mr. Dundas—Dysart fair—The fighting factions
—Various receipts for picking a quarrel—Recent *civilization*
of the lower classes of Emeralders.

THE fair of Donnybrook, near Dublin, has been
long identified with the name and character of the
lower classes of Irish people ; and so far as the
population of its metropolis may fairly stand for
that of a whole country, the identification is just.
This remark applies, it is true, to several years
back; as that entire revolution in the natural Irish
character, which has taken place within my time,
must have extended to all their sports and places

of amusement; and Donnybrook fair, of course, has had its full share in the metamorphosis.

The *old* Donnybrook fair, however, is on record; and so long as the name exists, will be duly appreciated. Mr. Lysight's popular song of " The Sprig of Shillelah and Shamrock so Green,"* gives a most lively sketch of that celebrated meeting—

* Two lines of Mr. Lysight's song describe, quaintly, yet veritably, the practical *point* of the scenes which occurred at that place of licensed eccentricities. He speaks of the real Irish Paddy, who

" Steps into a tent, just to spend half-a-crown,
Slips out, meets a *friend*, and for *joy* knocks him down!
With his sprig of shillelah and shamrock so green."

It is a literal fact that the blow is as instantly forgiven, and the twain set a-drinking together in great harmony, as if nothing had happened.

A priest constantly attended in former times at an alehouse near Kilmainham, to marry any couples who may have agreed upon that ceremony when they were *drunk*, and made up their minds for its immediate celebration so soon as they should be sober: and after the ceremony he sent them back to the fair for one more drink; and the lady then went home an *honest* woman, and as happy as possible. Many hundred similar matches used, in old times, to be effected during this carnival. Mr. Lysight also describes the happy consequences of such weddings with infinite humour. He says of the ulterior increase of each family

" and nine months after that
A fine boy cries out, ' How do ye do, Father Pat?
With your sprig of shillelah and shamrock so green.' "

This system may somewhat account for the " alarming population of Ireland," as statesmen now call it.

some of the varieties and peculiarities of which may be amusing, and will certainly give a tolerable idea of the Dublin commonalty in the eighteenth century.

All Ireland is acquainted with the sort of sports and recreations which characterise Donnybrook. But the English, in general, are as ignorant of an Irish fair as they are of every other matter respecting the " sister kingdom," and that is saying a great deal. John Bull, being the most egotistical animal of the creation, measures every man's coat according to his own cloth, and fancying an Irish mob to be like a London rabble, thinks that Donnybrook fair is composed of all the vice, robbery, swindling, and spectacle—together with still rougher manners of· its own — of his dear St. Bartholomew.

Never was John more mistaken. I do not know any one trait of character conspicuous alike in himself and brother Pat, save that which is their common disgrace and incentive to all other vices, *drinking ;* and even in drunkenness the English far surpass Pat—though perhaps their superiority in this respect may be attributable merely to their being better able to purchase the poison ; and if they have *not* the means ready, they are far more expert at picking of pockets, burglary, or murder, to procure them—as Mr. *John Ketch* (operative at his majesty's gaol of Newgate in London) can bear ample testimony.

There is no doubt but all mobs are tumultuous, violent, and more or less savage (no matter what they meet about): it is the nature of democratic congregations so to be. Those of England are thoroughly wicked, and, when roused, most ferocious; but they show little genuine courage, and a few soldiers by a shot or two generally send thousands of fellows scampering, to adjourn *sine die*. Formerly, I never saw an Irish mob that could not easily be rendered tractable and complacent by persons who, as they conceived, intended them fairly and meant to act kindly by them. So much waggery and fun ever mingled with their most riotous adventures, that they were not unfrequently dispersed by a good-humoured joke, when it would probably have required a regiment and the reading of a dozen riot acts to do it by compulsion.

A long, erroneous system of ruling that people seems to have gradually, and at length definitively, changed the nature of the Irish character in every class and branch of the natives, and turned into political agitation what I remember only a taste for simple hubbub. The Irish have an indigenous *goût* for fighting, (of which they never can be divested,) quite incomprehensible to a sober English farmer, whose food and *handiwork* are as regular as his clock. At Donnybrook, the scene had formerly no reservation as to the full exhibition of genuine Hibernian character; and a descrip-

tion of one of the *tents* of that celebrated sporting
fair will answer nearly for all of them, and likewise give a tolerable idea of most other fairs in the
Emerald island at the same period. Having twice*
run a narrow risk of losing my life at Donnybrook, (the last time at its fair in 1790,) I am entitled to remember its localities at least as well as
any gentleman who never was in danger of ending
his days there.

The site of the fair is a green flat of no great
extent, about a mile from Dublin city, and on the
banks of a very shallow stream that runs dribbling
under a high bridge :—fancy irregular houses on
one side, and a highroad through the middle, and
you will have a pretty good idea of that plain of
festivity.

Many and of various proportions were the tents
which, in time past, composed the encampment
upon the plains of Donnybrook ; and if persevering
turbulence on the part of the Emeralders should
ever put it into the heads of the members of his
majesty's government to hire a few bands of
Cossacks to keep them in order, (and I really believe they are the only folks upon earth who
could frighten my countrymen,) the model of a
Donnybrook tent will be of great service to the
Don-Russian auxiliaries—the materials being so

* For the first of these occurrences see (Vol. ii.) my adventure with Counsellor Daly and Balloon Crosby.

handy and the erection so *facile*. I shall therefore describe one accurately, that the Emperor Nicholas and his brother Michael, who has seen something of Ireland already, may, upon any such treaty being signed, perceive how extremely well his Imperial Majesty's Tartars will be accommodated.

Receipt for a Donnybrook Tent.

Take eight or ten long wattles, or any indefinite number, according to the length you wish your tent to be (whether two yards, or half a mile, makes no difference as regards the architecture or construction). Wattles need not be provided by purchase and sale, but may be readily procured any dark night by cutting down a sufficient number of young trees in the demesne or plantation of any gentleman in the neighbourhood—a prescriptive *privilege* or rather *practice*, time immemorial, throughout all Ireland. .

Having procured the said wattles *one way or other*, it is only necessary to stick them down in the sod in two rows, turning round the tops like a woodbine arbour in a lady's flower-garden, tying the two ends together with neat ropes of hay, which any gentleman's farm-yard can (during the night time, as aforesaid) readily supply,—then fastening long wattles in like manner lengthways at top from one end to the other to keep all tight

together; and thus the " wooden walls " of Donnybrook are ready for roofing in; and as the
building materials cost nothing but *danger*, the
expense is very trivial.

A tent fifty feet long may be easily built in
about five minutes, unless the builders should
adopt the old mode of *peeling* the wattles; and
when once a wattle is stripped to its *buff*, he must
be a wise landlord indeed who could swear to the
identity of the timber—a species of evidence nevertheless that the Irish wood-rangers are extremely
expert at.*   This precaution will not however be
necessary for the Don Cossacks, who being educated as highway robbers by the Emperor of all
the Russias, and acting in that capacity in every
country, cannot of course be called to account for
a due exercise of their vocation.

The covering of the tents is now only requisite;
this is usually done according to fancy; and being
unacquainted with the taste of the Russian gentlemen on that head, I shall only mention the
general mode of *clothing* the wattles used in my
time—a mode that, from its singularity, had a far
more imposing appearance than any encampment

---

* I recollect a man at the assizes of Maryborough swearing
to the leg of his own goose, which was stolen—having found it in
some *giblet broth* at the robber's cabin.   The witness was obviously right; the web between the goose's toes being, he said,
snipped and cut in a way he could perfectly identify.

ever pitched by his majesty's regular forces, horse, foot, or artillery. Every cabin, alehouse, and other habitation wherein quilts or bedclothes were used, or could be procured by *civility* or *otherwise* (except *money*, which was not current for such purposes), was ransacked for *apparel* wherewith to cover the wattles. The favourite covering was *quilts*, as long as such were forthcoming; and when not, old winnowing sheets, sacks ripped open, rugs, blankets, &c. &c.—Every thing, in fact, was expended in the *bed* line (few neighbours using that accommodation during the fair)—and recourse often had to women's apparel, as old petticoats, praskeens, &c. &c.

The covering being spread over the wattles as tightly and snugly as the materials would admit, all was secured by hay ropes and pegs. When completed, a very tall wattle with a dirty birch-broom, the hairy end of an old sweeping brush, a cast-off lantern of some watchman, rags of all colours made into streamers, and fixed at the top by way of sign, formed the invitation to *drinking;* —and when *eating* was likewise to be had, a rusty tin saucepan, or piece of a broken iron pot, was hung dangling in front, to crown the entrance and announce good cheer.

The most amusing part of the coverings were the quilts, which were generally of patchwork, comprising scraps of all the hues in the rainbow—

cut into every shape and size, patched on each
other, and quilted together.

As to furniture, down the centre doors, old or
new, (whichever were most handy to be *lifted*,)
were stretched from one end to the other, resting
on hillocks of clay dug from underneath, and so
forming a capital table with an agreeable variety
both as to breadth and elevation. Similar con-
structions for benches were placed along the sides,
but not so steady as the table; so that when the
liquor got the mastery of one convivial fellow, he
would fall off, and the whole row generally following his example, perhaps ten or even twenty gallant *shamrocks* were seen on their backs, kicking
up their heels, some able to get up again, some
lying quiet and easy, singing, roaring, laughing, or
cursing; while others, still on their legs, were
drinking and dancing, and setting the whole tent
in motion, till all began to long for the open air,
and a little wrestling, leaping, cudgelling, or fighting upon the green grass. The tent was then
cleaned out and prepared for a new company of
the shillelah boys.

The best tents, that supplied " neat victuals,"
had a pot boiling outside on a turf fire, with good
fat lumps of salt beef and cabbage, called " spoo-
leens," always ready simmering for such customers
as should like a *sliver*. The potatoes were plentiful,
and salt Dublin-bay herrings also in abundance.

There was, besides, a cold round or rump of beef at double price for the *quality* who came to see the *curiosities*.

Except toys and trinkets for children, merchandise of any sort they seemed to have a contempt for; but these were bought up with great avidity; and in the evening, when the parents had given the *childer* a glass each of the *cratur* (as they called whisky), " to keep the cowld out of their little stomachs," every trumpet or drum, fiddle, whistle, or pop-gun, which the fond mothers had bestowed, was set sounding (all together) over the green, and chimed in with a dozen fiddlers and as many pipers jigging away for the dance,—an amalgamation of sounds among the most extraordinary that ever *tickled* the ear of a musician. Every body, drunk or sober, took a share in the *long* dance, and I have seen a row of a hundred couple labouring at their jig steps till they fell off actually breathless, and rather *wetter* than if they had been river deities of the Donnybrook.

This however must be remarked as constituting a grand distinction between the beloved St. Bartholomew of the cockneys and the Emeralders' glory;—that at the former, robbers, cheats, gamblers, and villains of every description collect, and are most active in their respective occupations; whilst at the latter, no gambling of any sort existed;—nor were thieves, pickpockets or swindlers often there: for a good reason—because there was no money worth stealing, and *plenty* of *emptiness* in the pockets of the amateurs. However, love reigned in all its glory, and Cupid expended every arrow his mother could make for him : but with this difference, that love is in general represented as discharging his shafts into people's hearts, whereas, at Donnybrook, he always aimed at their *heads ;* and before it became quite dusk he never failed to be very successful in his archery. It was after sunset, indeed, that sweethearts made up their matches ; and a priest (Father Kearny of Liffy Street, a good *clergy*) told me that more marriages were celebrated in Dublin the week *after* Donnybrook fair, than in any two months during the rest of the year : the month of June being warm and *snug* (as he termed it), smiled on every thing that was good, and helped the *liquor* in making arrangements ; and with great animation he added, that it was a gratifying sight to see his young parishioners who had made up their matches at Donnybrook coming there in a couple of years again, to buy whistles for their children.

The *horse* part of the fair was not destitute of amusement—as there was a large ditch with a drain, and a piece of a wall, which the sellers were always called upon to " leather their horses over" before any body would bid for them ; and the tumbles which those venturous jockies constantly received, with the indifference wherewith

they mounted and began again, were truly entertaining.

,. The common Irish are the . most heroic horse-
men . I ever saw :—it was always one of their attributes. They ride on the horse's bare back with
rapidity and resolution; and coming from fairs, I
have often seen a couple or sometimes three fellows
riding one bare-backed horse as hard as he could
go, and safely—not one of whom, if they were on
their own legs, could stand perpendicular half a
minute. ,

It is a mistake to suppose that Donnybrook was
a remarkable place for *fighting*, or that much· *blood*
was ever drawn there. On the contrary,'it was
a place of good-humour. · Men, to be sure, were
knocked down now and then, but, there was no
malice in it.‾ A head was often cut, but quickly
tied up again. , The women first parted the combatants and then became mediators; and every
fray which commenced with a knock-down, gene-´
rally ended by shaking hands, and the parties
getting dead drunk together. _ . ·

That, brutal species of combat, *boxing*, was
never· practised at our fairs; and that savage nest
and hot-bed of ruffians called the " Ring," so
shamefully tolerated in England, was unknown
among the Emeralders.* , With the shillelah, in-

* I remember one man of tremendous strength from Carlow
County (Corcoran by name)‾: he fancied he could knock down
any man or beast on earth with his fist, and by downright mus-

deed, they had great skill; but it was only like sword exercise, and did not appear savage. Nobody was disfigured thereby, or rendered fit for a doctor. I never saw a bone broken or any dangerous contusion from what they called "*whacks*" of the shillelah (which was never too heavy): it was like fencing: a cut on the skull they thought no more of than we should of the prick of a needle: of course, such accidents frequently occurred, and (I believe very well for them) let out a little of their blood, but did not for a single moment interrupt the song, the dance, the frolicking and good-humour.

I have said, that the danger I underwent at Donnybrook sank deep into my memory. The main cause of it was not connected with my rencounter with Counsellor Daly, recited in the second volume of the present work, but with one which was to the full as hazardous, though it involved none of those points of honour. or "fire-eating" which forced me to the other conflict.

In the year 1790, Counsellor John Byrne, (afterward one of his majesty's counsel-at-law,) a very worthy man, and intimate friend of mine, called on me to ride with him and aid him in the pur-

cular vigour, bear down the guards of all science or resistance. He went over to England to fight any "man, woman, or child," in the whole nation; and when I was at temple, made sad examples of some of the scientific fancy. He could knock down the ablest horse with one blow of his fist. I never saw near so strong a person.

chase of a horse at the fair of Donnybrook. I
agreed, and away we rode, little anticipating the
sad discomfiture we should experience. We found
the fair rich in all its glories of drinking, fighting,
kissing, making friends, knocking down, women
dragging their husbands out of frays, and wounded
men joining as merrily in the dance as if the clout
tied round their heads were a Turkish turban.
Whatever happened *in* the fair, neither revenge
nor animosity went *out* of it with any of the
parties; to be sure, on the road to town, there
were always seen plenty of pulling, hauling, and
dragging about, in which the ladies were to the
full as busily employed as the gentlemen; but for
which the latter offered, next day, one general
excuse to their wives, who would be mending
their torn coats and washing their stockings and
cravats.

"Sure, Moll, it wasn't *myself* that was *in it*
when I knocked Tom Sweeny down in the tent;
it was the *drink*, and nothing else."

"True for you, Pat, my jewel!" would the wife
cry, (scrubbing away as hard as she could,) "true
for you, my darling: by my sowl, the whisky and
water was all *spirits*. Myself would as soon strike
my owld mother, God forgive me for the word!
as have struck Mary Casey, only for that last
noggin that put the devil into me just when I
was aggravated at your *head*, Pat, my jewel. So
I hit Mary Casey a wipe; and by my sowl it's I

that am sorry for that same, becaize Mary had neither act nor part in cutting your head, Pat; but I was aggravated, and did not think of the *differ*."

This dialogue, with variations, I have heard a hundred times; and it will serve as a true specimen of the species of quarrels at Donnybrook in former times, and their general conclusion;—and such were the scenes that the visitors of the fair were making full preparation for, when Counsellor John Byrne, myself, and a servant lad of mine (not a very good horseman), entered it in the year 1790. The boy was mounted on a fiery horse, which Byrne wanted to exchange; and as I never liked *any thing* that was too tame, the horse I rode always had spirit enough, particularly for a gentleman who was not very remarkable for *sticking over-fast* to those animals. .

Into the fair we went, and riding up and down, got here a curse, and there a blessing; sometimes a fellow who knew one of us, starting out of a tent to offer us a glass of the " cratur." When we had satisfied our reasonable curiosity, and laughed plentifully at the grotesque scenes interspersed through every part, we went to the horse-fair on the · green outside. There the jockies were in abundance; and certainly no fair ever exhibited a stranger *mélange* of the halt and blind, the sound and rotten, rough and. smooth—all galloping; leaping, kicking, or. tumbling—some in. clusters,

some singly; now and then a lash of the long
whip, and now and then a crack of the loaded
butt of it! At length, a horse was produced (which
we conceived fit for any counsellor) by Mr. Irvin
the jockey, and engaged, upon his *honour*, to be
as sound as a *roach*, and as steady as any beast
between Donnybrook and *Loughrea*, where he had.
been the favourite gelding of Father Lynch, the
parish priest, who called him " Coadjutor"—(he
had broken the holy father's neck, by the bye,
about a year before). " Do just try him, Counsellor Byrne," said Mr. Irvin; " just mount him
a bit, and if ever you get off him again till you
grease my fist, I'll forgive you the luck-penny.
He'll want neither whip nor spur; he'll know
your humour, counsellor, before you're five minutes
on his body, and act accordingly."

" You're sure he's *gentle?*" said Byrne.

" Gentle, is it ? I'll give you leave to skin both
himself and me if you won't soon like him as well
as if he was (begging your pardon) your own
cousin-german. If he wasn't the thing from
muzzle to tail that would suit you, I'd hang him
before I'd give him to a counsellor—the like of
yees at any rate."

A provisional bargain and exchange was soon
struck, and Byrne mounted for trial on the
favourite gelding of the late Father Lynch of
Loughrea, called Coadjutor;— and in truth he
appeared fully to answer all Mr. Irvin's eulogiums :

we rode through the fair, much amused—I trotting carelessly close by the side of Byrne, and our servant on the fiery mare behind us; when, on a sudden, a drunken shoemaker, or *master cobbler*, as he called himself, whom my family had employed in heeling, soling, &c. seeing me pass by, rushed out of his tent with a bottle of whisky in one hand and a glass in the other, and roared, "Ough! by J—s, Barnton, you go no further till you take a drop with me, like your father's son, that I've been these many a long year tapping and foxing for: here, my darling, open your gob!"

Byrne being nearest, the cobbler stepped under the neck of my friend's horse, and his sconce getting entangled in the loose reins, the horse (not understanding that species of interruption) began to caper—which at the same time rather shaking Counsellor Byrne in his seat, and further entangling the shoemaker's head, I leant across to get Byrne's rein fair; but being unable to do so, from the fury of the son of Crispin, who was hitting Bucephalus on the skull as hard as he could with the bottle, to make him *stand easy* and to get his own head clear, my leg got entangled in the reins; and Byrne's *gentle* gelding making one or two simultaneous leaps forward and kicks behind, I had the horror of seeing my poor friend fly far over his horse's head, alight rather heavily upon his own, and having done so, lie quite flat and still, seeming to take no further notice either of the fair, the horses, myself, or any earthly matter whatsoever.

. My steed now began to follow so bright a precedent;—the cobbler, meanwhile, still cracking away with his bottle at both beasts. My seat of course became less firm; and at length I yielded to imperative circumstances, and being detached from my saddle (and also, fortunately, from the stirrups), I came easily down—but not clear of either horse; for I reluctantly fell just between the two, one of my legs being fast in Byrne's bridle and the other in my own. Both animals were prepared to set off with the utmost expedition; but I believe without the least idea as to whither they were going. The cobbler fought hard to get his head loose; but in vain; so with me he must come, go wherever I might. The two geldings now wheeled us off, plunging, kicking, and giving me to understand (so far as I could understand any thing) that I had little further to do than commend my soul to Heaven, which, to tell truth, I had neither leisure nor presence of mind to attempt. It was lucky that the horses' heads were pulled together by the bridles; by holding which, I defeated the attempt of " Coadjutor " to kick me to pieces—a compliment that, with might and main, he strove to pay me; and while dragged on my back through a short space of the fair of Donnybrook in company with the shoemaker (who was obliged to run obliquely or be strangled by the bridles), I had the additional pleasure of feeling the wind of " Coadjutor's " heels every second dashing about my head, and also of looking up at the bellies of both steeds; for I could see nothing else, except the cobbler, who roared in a voice that brought every man, woman and child out of the tents. Some men, at the risk of their own lives, closed on " the mad horses," and with their knives cut the bridles of both, and then away went the two geldings, quite disencumbered, as hard as their legs could carry them,—upsetting tables, forms, pots of hot water, and in fact every thing that came in their way—till they reached the spot where Mr. Irvin stood, and sundry members of their own species were disporting under their master. When they were caught, and the *death* of the two counsellors announced by the Dublin horse-jockies, who were jealous of Mr. Irvin, news was instantly sent to town that Galway Irvin, a horse-jockey, had sold a vicious animal to Counsellor Byrne, which had killed both him and Counsellor Barrington on the green of Donnybrook.

The mare my servant rode, though she did not know what all this row was about, thought proper to emulate so good an example. But being fonder of *galloping* than *rearing*, she fairly ran away; and the lad being unable to hold her in, they upset every thing in their course, till having come in contact with the cord of a tent, and being entangled therein, down went horse and rider plump against the wattles, which (together with the quilts) yielding to their pressure, Byrne's mare and my groom instantly made an unexpected portion of the company inside.

'My readers must picture to themselves a runaway horse and his rider tumbling head foremost into a tent among from ten to twenty Irishmen, who had got *the drink in them.* Many were the bruises and slight scarifications of the company before they could get clear of what they thought nothing but the devil or a whirlwind could possibly have sent thus, without the least notice, to destroy them. In fact Byrne had, a few months after, a considerable sum to advance to satisfy all parties for broken ware, &c. : but the poor fellows would charge nothing for broken heads or damaged carcases.

The shoemaker, who had certainly stood a narrow risk of being choked, was the first to tell every body his sad adventure; and to the end of my days, I never shall forget the figure he cut. His waistcoat was quite torn off his back while on the ground ; he lost both shoes ; and the lower part of his shirt acting as *locum tenens* for the back of his small-clothes, which had likewise been rent aside, nothing (with the conjunction of his horrified countenance) ever presented a more ludicrous appearance. He continued to roar " Murder ! murder !" much in the yelping tone of a poor dog run

over by a carriage, or of a little cur, when, having
got a shrewd bite from a big one, he is galloping
off with his tail between his legs, to claim the
protection of his mistress.   On being disengaged,
the son of Crispin limped off to the next tent,
where (every body flocking round him) he held up
the bottle, of which he loudly swore he had never
quitted his gripe,—" Not," he said, " for the lucre
of a glass bottle—the bottle be d—'d! but for the
sake of the *cratur* that was in it, though that was
all spilt."

As for myself, I really know not how I escaped
so well : my hat stuck fast, which saved my
head ; I held as tightly as I could by both reins ;
and in the short distance we were dragged, received very few hard bumps upon the ground,
which, fortunately for all parties, was grassy, and
had neither stones nor gravel.   My coat was torn,
my hands a little cut by the reins, and my ankle
by the stirrup, as my foot got disentangled therefrom ;—but I received no injury of any consequence.

The most melancholy part of the story relates to
my friend Byrne, who (though by far the simplest
process) was the only material sufferer.   So soon
as I could set myself to rights in the next tent,
and had taken a large tumbler of hot punch—as
they said, to *drive the fright* out of me—I hastened
to my companion, who, when last I saw him, lay
motionless on the ground.   I was told he had

been brought into a tent, and there laid out upon a table as if dead ; and had he not exhibited signs of life pretty soon, the folks would have proceeded to *wake* and *stretch* him, and when he was *decent*, to cover him with a quilt, and carry him home *next morning* on a door to his family.

On my arrival, I found him greatly confused, and quite helpless : there was, however, no bone broken, or any wound or bruise that I could see. He merely complained of a pain in his neck and shoulders, and I considered that the general shock he had received was his only injury. While he lay nearly insensible, but had shown signs of life, the women forced burnt whisky down his throat out of a bottle, which certainly revived him. He was then bled by a farrier, and we got him home in a carriage, though in considerable pain. The surgeon employed (I don't name him) said nothing was injured ; but in less than a week, to the horrible torture of poor Byrne, and the discomfiture of the *doctor*, it turned out that his right shoulder had been dislocated, and the use of his arm entirely destroyed. After the lapse of such an interval, of course extreme inflammation took place, and for many months he could scarcely move.

I fancy *horse jockeying* and the *fair of Donnybrook* never subsequently escaped Byrne's memory. In fact, the circumstance proved nearly fatal to him several years after. His shoulder having remained so long unset, the muscles became rigid, and he never had the power of raising his right arm upon a level again. This deprivation, as mentioned in Vol. ii., he felt acutely on his duel with the Earl of Kilkenny, who hit him before he could bring up his arm to any position.

I have thus given a true sketch of Donnybrook fair forty years ago. I, however, remember it twenty years earlier—as I used to be taken thither when a child by the maid-servants, under pretence of diverting " little master ;" and they.and their sweethearts always crammed me with cakes to a surfeit, that I might not tell my grandmother what I saw of them.

The *country* fairs of Ireland, though of the same genus, were of a different species ; and there were great varieties among that species—according to the habits, customs, and manners of the several provinces, counties, or parishes, wherein they were held. The southern, eastern, and western fairs had considerable similitude to each other ; but the northern, if I may apply exaggerated epithets, could boast more *rogues,* while at the former the preponderance was of *madmen.* The *southerns* certainly loved fighting vastly better, and after they had done were vastly less vindictive than the northern descendants of the Caledonians.*

* I do not think that the southern and western Irish have, or ever will have, any ardent brotherly affection for their northern fellow-countrymen (exclusive of differences in religion). The

At country fairs, the feasting and drinking were still more boisterous—what they call *obstropulous* in Ireland ; but being generally held in towns, there was less character exhibited, and consequently less food for observation to spectators. The fighting, too, was of a different nature, and far more serious than at Donnybrook. I will cite a fair that I seldom missed attending for several years, solely in order to see the fight which was sure to conclude it. It was called the fair of Dysart, held in a beautiful country in the valley below the green Timahoe hills, and close to one of the most interesting and beautiful of Irish ruins, the rock of Donnamase, where, in ancient times, sword-duels were fought, as I have heretofore mentioned. Cromwell battered it, and slaugh-

former descended direct from the aboriginals of the land ; the latter are deduced from Scotch colonists, and those not of the very best occupations or character either.

An anecdote told of Sir Hercules Langreish and Mr. Dundas is illustrative of this observation, and was one of our standing jokes, when Ireland existed as a nation.

Mr. Dundas, himself a keen sarcastic man, who loved his bottle nearly as well as Sir Hercules, invited the baronet to a grand dinner in London, where the wine circulated freely, and wit kept pace with it. Mr. Dundas, wishing to procure a laugh at Sir Hercules, said :—

" Why, Sir Hercules, is it true that we Scotch formerly *transported* all our criminals and felons to Ireland ?"

" I dare say," replied Sir Hercules; " but did you ever hear, Mr. Dundas, of any of your countrymen *returning* to Scotland from transportation ?"

tered the warders of the O'Moores, who held their hereditary fortress while they had an arm to defend it.

To this fair resorted sundry factions—as they were termed; a *faction* consisting of one of two parishes, baronies, or town-lands, that were very good friends in small parties or individually, but had a prescriptive deadly hatred to each other at all great meetings, fairs, returns from alehouses, &c. At races or hurlings, where gentlemen presided, no symptoms of animosity were apparent.

But a tacit compact was always understood to exist that the *factions* should fight at the fair of Dysart once a year; and accordingly, none of them ever failed to attend the field of battle with their wives, and generally a reasonable number of infant children, whose cries and shrieks during their *daddies'* conflict formed a substitute for martial music—mingled, indeed, with the incessant rattle of the ladies' tongues, as they fought and struggled, like the Sabine women, to separate combatants, who would come on purpose to fight again.

The fair went on quietly enough at first as to buying, selling, and *trucking* of cows, pigs, frieze and other merchandise: but when trade grew slack, the whisky got in vigour, and the time came when the same little " whacking, plase your honour, that our fathers before us always did at Dysart," could no longer be deferred.

There being however no personal or ostensible cause of dispute, one or two *boys* were always sent out to *pick* a quarrel and give just reason for the respective *factions* to come to the rescue.

Their weapon was almost exclusively an oaken cudgel :—neither iron, steel, nor indeed any deadlier substance, so far as I ever saw, was in use among them ; and " boxing matches," as before observed, were considered altogether too gross and vulgar for the direct descendants of Irish *princes,* as in fact many of them were. The friends and neighbours of the pugnacious factions, always in bodies, joined more or less warmly in the fray. In truth, it would be totally impossible to keep an Irish peasant, man or woman (if *the drop* was in), from joining in any battle going merrily on. Before the fray had ended, therefore, the entire assemblage was engaged in some degree ; and it was commonly a drawn battle, seldom concluding till all parties and each sex, fairly out of breath, were unable to fight any more. Two hours or thereabouts was considered as a decent period for a beating match, and some priest generally put an end to it when the *factions* were themselves tired.

. These battles commenced in the most extraordinary manner ; the different modes of picking a quarrel being truly comical. One fellow generally took off his long frieze coat, and flourishing his shillelah, which he trailed along the ground, vociferated, " Horns ! horns ! ram's horns ! who dares say any thing's crookeder than ram's horns?"

"By J—s, I know *fat* will be twice crookeder nor any ram's horns before the fair's over," another sturdy fellow would reply, leaping, as he spoke, out of a tent, armed with his "walloper" (as they called their cudgel), and spitting in his fist—"By J—s, I'll make your own skull crookeder nor any ram's horn in the barony." The *blow* of course followed the *word;*—the querist was laid sprawling on the ground;—out rushed the *factious* from every tent, and to work they fell —knocking down right and left, tumbling head over heels, then breaking into small parties, and fighting through and round the tents. If one fellow lost his "walloper," and was pressed by numbers, he sometimes tugged at a wattle till he detached it from a tent, and sweeping it all around him, prostrated men, women, and children :—one, tumbling, tripped up another; and I have seen them lying in hillocks, yet scarcely any body in the least injured. Sometimes one faction had clearly the best of it; then they ran away in their turn, for there was no determined stand made by any party —so that their alternate advancing, retreating, running away, and rallying, were productive of huge diversion. Whoever got his head cut (and that was generally the case with more than half of them), ran into some tent, where the women tied up the hurt, gave the *sufferer* a glass of whisky,

and kept him fair and easy till news arrived that
the priest was come—when the combatants soon
grew more quiet. The priest then told them how
sinful they were. They thanked his reverence,
and said " they'd stop, *becaize* he desired them; but
it wasn't *becaize* they wouldn't like to make *sartain* who'd have the best of it."

The hair being detached from about the cuts on
the head, the cuts themselves dressed, rags applied
to battered shins, &c., the whisky went round
merrily again, and the several *factions* seldom departed till they were totally *unable* to fight any
more. Some were escorted home by the priests
upon garrons (their wives behind them); some on
straw in cars; and some, too drunk to be moved,
remained in the neighbourhood. No animosity
was cherished; and until next fair they would do
each other any kind office. I witnessed many of
these *actions*, and never heard that any man was
" dangerously wounded." But if they fought on
the road home, in very small parties, serious mischief was not unfrequently the consequence.

The *quere* as to ram's horns was only one of
many curious schemes whereby to get up a quarrel. I have seen a fellow going about the fair
dragging his coat, which was always considered
a challenge, like throwing down a glove or gaunt-
let in olden times—and in fact was a relict of that
practice. Another favourite mode was, exclaiming

" black's the white of my eye!—who dares say *black* is *not* the *white* of my eye?"

These scenes certainly took place at a time when Ireland was reputed, and with truth, to be in a very rough state. It has since undergone plenty of civilization. Sunday schools, improved magistracy, and a regular police, have recently been introduced; and the present state of Ireland proves the great advances it has made in consequence. Of late years, therefore, though the factions still fight, as usual, it is with more civilised weapons. Instead of shillelahs and "wallopers," swords, pistols, and guns are the genteel implements resorted to: and (to match the agriculturists) scythes, hatchets, bill-hooks, and pitchforks are used in their little encounters: and surely the increased refinement of the country is not to be relinquished on account of the loss of a few lives.

I fear some of my readers may call the latter observations *ironical;* but the best way for them to avoid that supposition is, to reflect what *savage* Ireland was at the time I allude to, and what *civilised* Ireland is at the moment I am writing;— in the year 1780, when the peasantry fighting at the fair of Dysart was in a savage state, the government were so stingy of their army that they would only spare the Irish five or six thousand soldiers; and no militia, to teach them to behave themselves : but after an interval of forty years, they are now so kind as to allow us five-and-thirty thousand troops to teach the new rudiments of civilization—the old six thousand having had nothing to do amongst these semi-barbarous islanders. Nay, the government finding that Ballinrobe (where, as I have stated, a sow and her ten *piggin riggins* came to breakfast with two counsellors) was making slow progress to this desirable state of refinement, was so considerate as to send certainly the best-bred regiment in the king's service to give lessons of urbanity to the people for three hundred and sixty-five days without intermission.

This boon to so backward a population as County Mayo presented, must ever be remembered with gratitude by the *undressed* gentlemen of that county, though I have not seen any authentic *exposé* of those beneficial effects which no doubt resulted.

THE WALKING GALLOWS.

Brief reflections on the Irish Revolution of 1798—Mutual atro-
cities of the Royalists and Rebels—Irish humour buoyant to
the last—O'Connor, the schoolmaster of County Kildare—
" 'Tis well it's *no worse*"—The Barristers' corps—Its commander—Lieutenant H———— —His zeal for loyalty, and its
probable origin—Indemnities unjustly obtained for cruelty
against the insurgents—Lieutenant H————'s mode of executing a rebel—His *sobriquet*, and its well-earned application.

NEVER was there an era in the history of any
country which, in so short a space of time, gave birth
to such numerous and varied circumstances as did
the memorable year 1798 in Ireland : nor was
there ever yet an event so important as the Irish
insurrection, but has afforded a veracious—or, at
least, a tolerably impartial narrative. But the party rancour and virulent hatred of the religious sects
in the south, the centre and west of Ireland (where
the rebellion principally raged), operated to prevent any fair record of those scenes of bloodshed
and atrocity which, on *both sides,* outraged every
principle of morality and justice, and every feeling

of consanguinity, honour, or humanity. The very
worst qualities were fostered to full maturity, and
the better ones turned adrift like discarded servants. Blood, fire, and famine were the only
umpires resorted to by the contending parties.

Those barbarities were nearly, if not altogether,
unexampled either in ancient or modern Europe :
but it is now thirty years since their termination;
the surviving contemporaries are old enough to
have their blood cooled and their prejudices mo-
derated ;—and they should have grown sufficiently
dispassionate to speak of those scenes (if at all)
with honesty and candour.

I was myself in the midst of the tumult : a zealous loyalist; an officer in the corps of barristers ;
an active partizan ; in a word, a *strong* adherent of
government—but not a *blind* one. I could not shut
my eyes; I could not close my ears ; I would
not pervert my reason ; and the full use of those
faculties at that time, enables me now to state as
an historic fact—which some will deny, and many
may discredit—that the barbarities of that period
(though not precisely) were pretty nearly balanced
between the conflicting parties.* Mercy was alike

* Never did there appear a more extravagant and therefore
mischievous historian than Sir Richard Musgrave proved himself in his " History of Irish Rebellions, and principally that
of Ninety-eight,"—almost every chapter whereof is distinguished
by misconception and fanaticism. Lord Cornwallis disclaim-
ed the baronet's dedication—who, on sinking into the grave,

banished by both; and the instruments employed
of death and torture, though dissimilar, were alike
destructive: the bullet, sabre, bayonet, lash, and
halter, being met by the pike, the scythe, the
blunderbuss, the hatchet, and the firebrand.

Yet while human blood was pouring out in
streams, and human beings consuming in fire, or
writhing either upon rebel pikes or royal bayonets
—will it be believed?—men had grown so fami-
liarised to scenes of horror, that the eccentric humour of the Irish people was insusceptible of de-
crease. In the midst of tortures, either suffered
or inflicted, it frequently broke out into the most
ludicrous actions and expressions, proving to me
that an Irishman's humour is so drilled into his
nature, as to be inexhaustible even to the moment
of his death (if that is not unusually too deliberate).*

left a legacy to his country—having fomented prejudices
against her in Great Britain which another century may not
extinguish. .

* O'Connor, a fat, comely, cheerful-looking schoolmaster of
County Kildare, was the first rebel executed for high treason.
His trial gave rise to one of the most curious dialogues (between
him and Judge Finucane) that ever took place in a court of
justice. It ended, however, by the judge (who was a humane
man) passing the usual sentence on him—" That he should be
hanged by the neck, but not till he was dead: that while still
alive his bowels should be taken out, his body quartered," &c.
&c. The culprit bore all this with firm though mild complacency; and on conclusion of the sentence bowed low, blessed
the judge for his *impartiality*, and turning about, said, " God's

It is not in the nature, or within the comprehension, of the sober English people to form any
judgment of what a true-born Irishman is capable
of saying or doing in his deepest extremities: and
I am sure they will give me little credit for veracity when I mention some instances which, I own,
in any other country might be reasonably considered incredible. In no other place existing
could the cruel and ludicrous be so mingled, as
they were in the transactions of the sanguinary
period in question; nor do I think there can be a
better way to inform and amuse the reader, than
by giving alternate anecdotes of the *royalists* and
the *rebels*, leaving it to his own judgment to draw
conclusions.—This one observation, however, it is
necessary, in justice, to premise;—that the royalists were, generally speaking, of a higher class
than the rebels—and had received the advantages
of education, while the rebels were in a state of
total ignorance and beggary. The wanton barbarities, therefore, of the more enlightened classes
have less ground of palliation than those of a
demi-savage peasantry, urged by fanaticism, and
blinded by ignorance. This observation was

will be done! 'tis well *it's no worse!*" I was surprised. I pitied
the poor fellow, who had committed no atrocity, and asked
him what he meant. " Why, Counsellor," said he, " I was
afraid his lordship would order me to be *flogged!*" Every
rebel preferred death to the cat-o'-nine-tails! . O'Connor's head
remained some years on the top of Naas gaol.

strongly impressed on my mind throughout the
whole of that contest; and it would be acting
unfairly toward the officer who so judiciously
commanded the military corps I was then attached to, not to say, that, though an unqualified
Protestant—an hereditary Huguenot, filled with
that spirit of sectionary zeal which drove his eloquent ancestor from his native country; yet,
during the whole of the rebellion, Captain Saurin
never suffered the corps he led to indulge any
religious distinctions;—scarcely, indeed, could his
own sect be discovered by any particular of his
acts, orders, or conduct; nor did that corps ever
participate in, or even countenance, the violent
proceedings so liberally practised by other military
yeomen.*

. This line of conduct was most exemplary; and
from a thorough knowledge of the constitutional
attributes of the man, I am convinced that neither

---

* I knew at least but of one exception to this remark respecting the lawyers' corps. Very early in the rebellion an
officer took down a detachment of that corps to Rathcool,
about seven miles from Dublin, without the knowledge of the
commandant. They were not aware of his object, which turned
out to be, to set fire to part of the town. He captured one
gentleman, Lieutenant Byrne, who was hanged;—and returned
to Dublin, in my mind *not* triumphant.

. He got several severe lectures, but none so strong as one
from the late Sir John Parnell, then chancellor of the exchequer, whose heir, the present Sir Henry Parnell, was among
those unwittingly taken down.

his philanthropy, toleration, humility, or other good qualities have been much increased by his *schooling*, for the last twenty years, in the Irish Four Courts.

Among the extraordinary characters that turned up in the fatal " ninety-eight," there were few more extraordinary than Lieutenant H——, then denominated the " walking gallows ;"—and such he certainly was, literally and practically.*

Lieutenant H—— was an officer of the line, on half pay. His brother was one of the solicitors to the Crown—a quiet, tremulous, *vino deditus* sort of man, and a leading Orangeman ;—his widow, who afterward married and survived a learned doctor, was a clever, positive, good-looking Englishwoman, and, I think, fixed the doctor's avowed *creed :* as to his genuine *faith,* that was of little consequence.

Lieutenant H—— was about six feet two inches high ;—strong, and broad in proportion. His strength was great, but of the dead kind, un-accompanied by activity. He could lift a ton, but could not leap a rivulet ;—he looked mild, and his

---

* This circumstance is mentioned in my " Historic Anecdotes of the Union," among several others, which were written before the present work was in contemplation. But the incident now before the reader is so remarkable that I have gone into it more particularly. Many will peruse this book who will never see the other, into which have been interwoven, in fact, *numerous* sketches of those days that I now regret I did not retain for the present work, to which they would have been quite appropriate.

address was civil—neither assuming nor at all ferocious. I knew him well, and from his countenance should never have suspected him of cruelty ;
but so cold-blooded and so eccentric an executioner of the human race I believe never yet existed, save among the American Indians.*

His inducement to the strange barbarity he
practised I can scarcely conceive ; unless it proceeded from that natural taint of cruelty which so
often distinguishes man above all other animals
when his power becomes uncontrolled. The propensity was probably strengthened in him from
the indemnities of martial law, and by those
visions of promotion whereby violent partizans
are perpetually urged, and so frequently disappointed.†

At the period alluded to, law being suspended,
and the courts of justice closed, the " question "
by torture was revived and largely practised. The

---

* His mode of execution being perfectly novel, and at the
same time *ingenious,* Curran said, " The lieutenant should
have got a patent for cheap strangulation."

† " We love the treason, but hate the traitor," is an aphorism which those who assume prominent parts in any public
convulsion are sure to find verified. Many instances took
place in Ireland ; and in France exemplifications occurred to a
very considerable extent. A blind *zealot* is of all men most
likely to become a *renegade* if he feel it more convenient : prejudice and interest unite to form *furious* partizans, who are
never guided by *principle*—for principle is founded on judgment.

commercial exchange of Dublin formed a place of execution; even *suspected* rebels were every day immolated as if *convicted* on the clearest evidence; and Lieutenant H———'s *pastime* of hanging *on his own back* persons whose physiognomies he thought characteristic of rebellion was, (I am ashamed to say) the subject of jocularity instead of punishment. What in other times he would himself have died for, as a murderer, was laughed at as the manifestation of loyalty: never yet was martial law so abused, or its enormities so hushed up* as in Ireland. Being a military officer, the lieutenant conceived he had a right to do just what he thought proper, and to make the most of his time while martial law was flourishing.

Once, when high in blood, he happened to meet a *suspicious-looking* peasant from County Kildare, who could not satisfactorily account for himself according to the lieutenant's notion of evidence; and having nobody at hand to vouch for him, the lieutenant of course immediately took for granted that he *must* be a rebel strolling about,

---

* The open indemnification of Mr. Judkin Fitzgerald, of Tipperary, for his cruelties in that county, was one of the worst acts of a vicious government. The prime serjeant, Mr. St. George Daly, though then the first law officer, (a *Union* one, too, as subsequently appeared,) voted against that most flagitious act of Parliament, which nothing but the raging madness of those times could have carried through any assembly. The dread of its recurrence did much to effect the Union.

and imagining the death of his Most Gracious
Majesty.* He therefore, no other *court of justice*
being at hand, considered that he had a right to
try the man by his *own opinion;* accordingly, after
a brief interrogation, he condemned him to die,
and without further ceremony proceeded to put
his own sentence into immediate execution.

However, to do the lieutenant justice, his *mode*
was not near so tedious or painful as that practised by the grand signior, who sometimes causes
the ceremony to be divided into three acts, giving
the culprit a drink of spring water to *refresh* him
between the two first; nor was it so severe as the
burning old women formerly for witchcraft. In
fact, the " walking gallows " was both on a new
and simple plan; and after some kicking and

* The lieutenant's brother being a Crown solicitor, had now
and then got the lieutenant to copy the high treason indict-
ments : and he, seeing there that *imagining* the death of a *king*
was punished capitally, very naturally conceived that *wishing*
it was twice as bad as *supposing* it : having therefore no
doubt that *all* rebels wished it, he consequently decided in the
tribunal of his own mind to hang every man who hypotheti-
cally and traitorously wished his majesty's dissolution, which
wish he also conceived was very easily ascertained by the
wisher's countenance.

A cabinet-maker at Charing Cross some years ago put on
his board " patent coffin-maker to his majesty :" it was considered that though this was not an *ill-intentioned*, yet it was a
very improper mode of *imagining* the king's death, and the
board was taken down accordingly. Lieutenant H———
would surely have hanged him in Ireland.

plunging during the operation, never failed to be completely effectual. The lieutenant being, as before mentioned, of lofty stature, with broad and strong shoulders, saw no reason why they might not answer his majesty's service upon a pinch as well as two posts and a cross-bar (the more legitimate instrument upon such occasions): and he also considered that, when a rope was not at hand, there was no good reason why his own silk cravat (being softer than an ordinary halter, and of course less calculated to *hurt* a man) should not be a more merciful choke-band than that employed by any *Jack Ketch* in the three kingdoms.

In pursuance of these benevolent intentions, the lieutenant, as a preliminary step, first knocked down the suspected rebel from County Kildare, which the weight of mettle in his fist rendered no difficult achievement. His garters then did duty as handcuffs: and with the aid of a brawny aide-de-camp (one such always attended him), he pinioned his victim hand and foot, and then most considerately advised him to pray for King George, observing that any prayers for his *own* d—d *popish soul* would be only time lost, as his fate in every world (should there be even a thousand) was decided to all eternity for having imagined the death of so good a monarch.

During this exhortation, the lieutenant twisted up his long cravat so as to make a firm, handsome rope, and then expertly sliding it over the rebel's neck, secured it there by a double knot, drew the cravat over his own shoulders, and the aide-de-camp holding up the rebel's heels, till he felt him *pretty easy,* the lieutenant with a powerful chuck drew up the poor devil's head as high as his own (cheek by jowl), and began to trot about with his burden like a jolting cart-horse,—the rebel choking and gulping meanwhile, until he had no further solicitude about sublunary affairs—when the lieutenant, giving him a parting chuck, just to make sure that his neck was broken, threw down his load—the personal assets about which the aide-de-camp made a *present* of to *himself.*

Now all this proceeding was very pains-taking and ingenious : and yet the ungrateful government (as Secretary Cook assured me) would have been better pleased had the execution taken place on timber and with hemp, according to old formalities.

To be serious :—this story is scarcely credible—yet it is a notorious fact ; and the lieutenant, a few nights afterward, acquired the *sobriquet* which forms a head to this sketch, and with which he was invested by the upper gallery of Crow Street Theatre—nor did he ever get rid of it to his dying-day.

The above *trotting* execution (which was humorously related to me by an eye-witness) took place in the barrack-yard at Kerry House, Stephen's Green. The *hangee* was, I believe, (*as it happened*) in reality a rebel.

Providence, however, which is said to do " every thing for the best," (though some persons who are half starving, and others who think themselves very unfortunate, will not allow it so much credit,) determined that Lieutenant H————'s loyalty and merits should meet their full reward in another sphere—where, being quite out of the reach of all his enemies, he might enjoy his destiny without envy or interruption. It therefore, very soon after the rebellion had terminated, took the lieutenant into its own especial keeping ; and despatched a raging fever to bring him off to the other world, which commission the said fever duly executed after twenty-one days' combustion ;—and no doubt his ghost is treated according to its deserts ; but nobody having since returned from those regions to inform us what has actually become of the lieutenant, it is still a *dead* secret, and I fancy very few persons in Ireland have any wish for the opportunity of satisfying their curiosity. People however give a shrewd guess, that it is *possible* he may be employed somewhere else in the very same way wherein he entertained himself in Ireland ; and that after being duly furnished with a tail, horns, and cloven foot, no spirit could do infernal business better than the lieutenant

CONVERSION AND INVERSION.

Rebel pranks—Caprice of the insurgents—Puns and piking—
Archdeacon Elgy—His capture by the rebels—Captain
Murphy's harangue and argument—Proposal made to the
Archdeacon—An " Orange parson " converted into a " green
priest "—Father Cahill and Father Pat Elgy—Another exploit of Captain Murphy—Parson Owen of Wexford—His
concealment in a grocer's cockloft—Discovered by the *scat-
tle boys*—Dragged to a window and hung therefrom, by his
heels, over a number of pikes—His delirium, and escape
through Captain Murphy's humanity—Parson Owen's superin-
duced squint, and consequent nuptials—His lady left a widow—Instance of the fatal effects of unpleasant and unexpected news.

WE have, in the foregoing sketch, seen something of the unwarrantable acts whereof loyal zeal
was capable. Let us now take a glance, in fair-
ness and impartiality, at the conduct of the insurgents, — which varied exceedingly in different
instances. Sometimes, almost as the humour of
the moment guided them, they would treat such
as fell in their power with lenity and moderation :

at others, no degree of cruelty was spared toward those unfortunate individuals.

They had at their mercy, during the whole period, a man of high rank, their avowed, zealous, and active enemy, a Protestant and Orangeman. Yet, while numerous persons of inferior classes were piked and butchered, the Earl of Kingston was unmolested, and left at liberty on their evacuation of Wexford. It were to be wished that General Lake had shown similar generosity to Mr. Cornelius Grogan, whose hasty and unmerited execution by martial law savoured of deliberate murder as strongly as the death of most who were slaughtered by the rebels.

On many occasions during that dreadful struggle, jests were so strangely mixed up with murder, that it was not easy to guess which way a scene would terminate—whether in tragedy or comedy; so much depended on the sobriety or intoxication of the insurgents.

One or two anecdotes (out of hundreds worth recording) will serve to show in some degree the spirit of the times; and we will preface them by observing, that the district (the barony of Forth, in County Wexford,) most active in rebellion, most zealous and most sanguinary, was the identical point whereon Strongbow, the first British soldier who set foot in Ireland, had, six hundred and twenty seven years before, begun his colonization. Most of the Wexford rebels, indeed, were lineal descendants of the original Britons who came over there from South Wales and Bristol, and repeopled that district after their countrymen had nearly exterminated the aboriginal natives.

· The rebels had obliged Major Maxwell, with the king's troops, far too precipitately to evacuate Wexford; and that officer, by the rapidity of his movements, gave neither time nor notice to the loyalists to retreat with him. It was therefore considered, that Archdeacon Elgy, a dignitary of the Protestant church, was the most likely subject for the rebels to begin their slaughter with; and the general opinion ran that he would have at least a dozen pikes through his body before dinner-time on the day the insurgents entered.

Of this way of thinking was the divine himself: nor did the numerous corresponding surmises prove erroneous. Sentence of death was promptly passed upon the archdeacon, who was held to aggravate his offences by contumacy.

A certain shrewd fellow, yclept a *captain* among the rebels, however, saw things in a different point of view; and, though without any particularly kind feelings toward the archdeacon, he, by use of a very luminous argument, changed the determination of his comrades.

"What's the good," said he, " of *piking* the old man? Sure, if he'll give in, and worship the Virgin in our chapel, won't it be a better job? They say he's a very good Orange parson, and why shouldn't he make a good *green priest*, if he'll take on with

Father Cahill? Devil the much harm ever he did us!—so, if yees agree to that same, I'll tell him, fair and easy, to *take on* with the Virgin to-morrow in the big chapel, or he'll find himself more *holy* than *godly* before the sun sets."

The concluding joke, however trite, put them all in good humour; and the orator proceeded: "Come a couple of dozen of ye, boys, with wattles on your shoulders; give me the colours and cross, and we'll go to Parson Elgy."

In fact they went to the archdeacon, and Mr. Murphy, the spokesman, told him very quietly and civilly that he came to "offer his reverence life and liberty, and a good parish too, if he would only *do the thing* cleverly in the way Father Cahill would show him."

The reverend doctor, not comprehending the nature of the condition, and conceiving that they probably only required him to stand neuter, re-plied, in a quivering voice, "that he would never forget the obligations: he was well content with the cure he had, but not the less indebted to them for their kind offer to give him a better."

"Ough!" said Captain Murphy, "your reverence happens to be all in the wrong."

The archdeacon of course fell into his nervous fit again, and stood quaking as if both Saint Vitus' dance and the *tic douloureux* had assailed him at once with their utmost rancour.

" I am only come," resumed Murphy, " just to give your reverence two little *choices*."

" Oh, Lord ! Captain Murphy, what are they ?" cried the clerical gentleman.

" Either to take your turn to-morrow in the big *chapel*, with our clergy, and be one of them yourself, or to receive two-and-twenty pikes straight *through* your reverence's carcase, as you will otherwise do, before the sun sets this blessed day— and by my sowl it's not far from that time now ! (Here the doctor groaned most heavily.) One of the things," pursued the rebel, " is quite easy for your reverence to do, and the other is quite easy for *us* to do ; and so there will be no great trouble in it either way. Come on, lads, and just show your *switches* to his reverence."

Above twenty long pikes were instantly flourished in the air with an hurra that nearly shook every nerve of the archdeacon out of its natural situation.

" Ah, gentlemen !" said he, ".spare a poor old man, who never harmed any of you. For the love of God, spare me !"

" Arrah ! be easy, parson," said Captain Murphy : " sure there's but *one* God between us all, and that's plenty, if there were as many more of us. So what are we differing and bothering about ? whether you say your prayers in the *church* or in the *chapel*, in *Latin* or in *English ;* whether you reckon them on your beads, or read

them on your book,—sure it's all one to Him, and
no great *differ*, I should think, to any sensible gentleman,—especially when he cannot help himself!
Boys, handle your switches; though, by my sowl,
I'd be sorry to *skiver* your reverence."

The archdeacon, though an excellent orthodox parson, now began to see his way, and was
too wise to have any thing to do with Captain
Murphy's *switches* if it were avoidable. He recollected that the great bishops and archbishops
who were roasted alive in Queen Mary's time, for
the very same reason, got but little credit from
posterity for their martyrdom; and how could he
expect *any* for being *piked*, which was not half so
dilatory a death as roasting? Then, again, he considered that twenty pikes in a man's body would
not be near as nourishing as one barnacle or lob-
ster (on which he had for many years loved to
feed). He deemed it better to make a merit of
necessity; and accordingly, putting on a civil
face, agreed to all their proposals. He then took
a drink of holy water (which Captain Murphy
always carried in a bottle about with him); made
several crosses upon his forehead with a feather
dipped in some " blessed oil " (tinged with green);
and after every pikeman had shaken him by the
fist, and called him Father Pat Elgy, it was
finally settled he should next day be rechristened
in " the big chapel" by all the Fathers, taught
to celebrate mass as well as the best of them, and

get a *protection* for having *taken on* as a true Catholic.

The gentlemen with their *switches* now retired, uplifting shouts of exultation at having *converted* the archdeacon, while that dignitary tottered back to his family, who had given him up for lost, were bewailing his cruel martyrdom, and triumphed at his return, though at the expense of his orthodoxy. A cold roast leg of mutton was then produced;—and heartily discussing that *creature comfort,* his reverence could not avoid congratulating himself when he observed the mark of the *spit,* and reflected that there would have been two-and-twenty much wider perforations drilled through his own body had not Captain Murphy made a *papist* of him.

Next morning, *Father Elgy* was duly christened *Patrick ;* renounced Martin Luther, in the great chapel of Wexford, as an egregious impostor; and being appointed a *coadjutor,* celebrated mass with considerable dexterity and proper gesticulation. He subsequently set about getting the double manual by heart, that he might be ready to *chaunt,* as soon as Father Cahill should teach him the several tunes.

The archdeacon, though he had no great reason to be ashamed of his second christening, (particularly as he had always prayed against *sudden death* while he was a Protestant,) could yet never bear, in after times, to hear the circumstance alluded to, since it could not be mentioned but a laugh was unavoidable. I often saw Murphy afterward : he had been generally humane, saved many lives, and was not prosecuted. He himself told me the foregoing story, with that exquisite simplicity which belongs almost exclusively to his rank of Irishmen.

Another Protestant clergyman did not fare quite so well as the archdeacon, being never able to look any man *straight* in the face afterward. Parson Owen, brother to Miss Owen of Dublin (heretofore mentioned in the anecdotes of Doctor Achmet Borumborad), had a small living in the neighbourhood of Wexford ; and as he looked for church preferment, was, of course, a violent, indeed an outrageous royalist. Now, as almost every man among his parishioners held a different creed, both in religion and politics, he was not over-popular in *quiet* days ; and when the bustle began, thinking it high time to secure his precious person, he retired for better security into the town of Wexford. He had not, however, consulted an *oracle ;*—that being the first place attacked by the rebels: and Major Maxwell, as has been stated, having with his garrison retreated without beat of drum, the parson found himself necessitated to resort to a cockloft in a grocer's house in the Bull-ring at Wexford ; where, provisions not being quite handy, and an empty stomach good for contemplation, he had ample opportunity to reflect on the species of death he would. most likely meet. The *promotion* of *Father Pat Elgy* had not come to his knowledge.

Previous to this event, the parson had fallen in love with the only daughter of Mr. Brown, a rich trader, who had formerly kept a tan-yard in Enniscorthy; or rather his reverence *fell in love* with a great number of *government debentures*, bearing interest at five per cent per annum, which the young lady informed him would be all her own if she " behaved herself." He had, therefore, three cogent reasons for seeking to prolong his life:— first, the natural love of it; secondly, the debentures; and *lastly*, the damsel.

However, his security was by no means permanent. Early one morning, wishing to get a mouthful of fresh air, his reverence ventured to peep out of his garret-window into the street, and was instantly recognised by one of the *wattle-boys*, as the pikemen were then called.

" Hah! hah! your reverence is there, sure enough," said the man of the wattle. " Ough! by my sowl if you budge out of that peep-hole till I come back again, we'll make a big bonfire of ye and your Orange family altogether. Plaze, now, don't let me *lose sight* of your reverence while I run for my commander: it's he'll know what to do with the likes of ye."

The rebel immediately ran off, but soon returned with the same " Captain Murphy," and a whole company of pikemen, just to " skiver the parson." Owen was a dapper, saucy, pert-looking, little fellow : he had good sharp eyes, an excellent use of his tongue, and was considered keen : and though a high churchman, he was thought at times to be rather more free and easy in his little sensualities than most bishops could reasonably have approved of. On this latter account, indeed, it was said that Mr. Brown, beforementioned, did not relish him for a son-in-law. Ladies, however, are sometimes more charitable in this respect ; Miss Brown conceived that whatever his *piety* might amount to, his *love,* at least, was orthodox ; and in this belief, she privately counselled her swain to affect more holiness before her papa :—to be lavish, for instance, in abuse of the powers of darkness ; to speak slower, and in a more solemn tone ; to get longer skirts made to his coats and waistcoats, let his hair grow lank, and say grace with becoming gravity and deliberation,—not as if he were impatient to rush at the eatables before they were properly blessed. " Eating," added the didactic lady, " may become a vice if too luxuriously gratified ; whereas hunger must be a virtue, or the popes would not so strongly recommend fasting."

At this stage of the treaty, and of the castle-building on the foundation of a tan-yard, his reverence was unfortunately seized in the cockloft by Captain Murphy ; and though the captain was a

neighbour of his, and a decent sort of cattle-deal-
er, yet Parson Owen gave himself up for lost to
an absolute certainty. His love was, therefore,
quite quenched in horror : his throat swelled up
as if he had a quinsy, and he anticipated nothing
short of that which he had prayed against (like
Doctor Elgy) every Sunday since he obtained
holy orders—namely, a sudden death. He thought
repentance was, as the French say, *meilleur tard
que jamais,* and accordingly *began* to repent and
implore as hard as possible,—though without the
most remote idea that his supplications would have
time to reach heaven before he himself was turned
loose on the road thither.

Captain Murphy, who, as we have seen, was,
although coarse, a *good-tempered* fellow, on entering the room with half-a-dozen wattle-boys,
otherwise *executioners,* very civilly told Parson
Owen, " He would be obliged to him just to prepare himself for the other world : whether the
other world was a *better* place or a *worse,* he
would not attempt to divine ;—all he could *assure*
his reverence was, that he should not be very long
going there.—The boys below," continued Captain Murphy, " having a good many more to send
along with you to-day, your reverence will be so
good as to come down to the first floor as soon
as convenient, that you may drop more agreeably from thence out of the window on the
pikes !"

Without much ceremony, the poor parson was handed down one flight of stairs, when .Captain Murphy opening a window as wide as he could, begged Owen would be *kind enough* to take off his coat and waistcoat, and throw them to the boys below; the remainder of his dress they might take from the corpse, after his reverence had *stiffened!*

The parson was nearly petrified; but there was no appeal. The captain's attendants civilly helped him to remove his upper garments, for which he had the pleasure of seeing an amusing scramble under the window, accompanied by a hundred jokes upon the little parson's surtout, which not being large enough for any middle-sized rebel, the smallest fellow among them appropriated it, and strutted about therein, amidst the horse-laughter of his companions.

Captain Murphy now ordered his wattlers to draw up close under the window, in order to welcome his reverence on the points of their weapons as he went out head-foremost. The order was promptly obeyed, with loud huzzas. The parson's legs were tied firmly together with a towel which the captain found in the room; but his arms were left loose, to flourish about (as they said) like a *windmill*, and make the *sight* the more *agreeable!*

"Now, boys," said the captain, "I'll out with his reverence; and when I let him go, do you all *catch him!*"

The parson was in good earnest thrust out of
the window, and hung with his head downward
and his arms at liberty, (a very disagreeable position,) to the great amusement of the gentlemen
of the wattle, as was proved by a due mixture of
grins and shouts. If any of my readers have seen
a pack of hungry spaniels sitting on their haunches
round a sportsman's table, looking up to their
master, and licking their jaws with impatience
for the morsel he holds in his fingers to throw
among them, they may imagine the enviable situation of Parson Owen, dangling out of the grocer's
window at the Bull-ring in Wexford ;—Serjeant
Murphy meanwhile holding his legs, and now and
then giving him a little shake, as if he intended
to let him drop—asking his reverence if he were
ready to *step down* to the croppies.

The condemned Lutheran was, of course, all
this time gazing with straining eyeballs upon
the forest of pikes underneath. His blood (as
if to witness the curiosity) rushed down to his
head ; and he naturally fell into a state of delirium. All he could recollect or relate afterward
was, that " as his eyes met the pikes just under
him, and heard the rebels call on the captain to
' *let go !*' the influx of blood to his brain operated
as, he should imagine, apoplexy might ;"—and
the captain perceiving his prisoner to be senseless,
and actually intending, if possible, to save him,
cried out to the men below that " by J—s the

parson was ' stone dead' of the *fright*, and was
quite *kilt!*"

" Hurrah!" cried the wattle-boys.

" Hurrah!" repeated Captain Murphy : " The
devil any use in dirtying your pikes with a dead
parson! Better not *spoil his clothes,* boys! his
shirt alone is worth a crown, if it's worth a farthing."

Some of the wattlers bespoke one garment—
some another :—and these were thrown out of the
window by Murphy, who left the poor parson in
his " birth-day suit," with five times as much
blood in his head as it was anatomically entitled
to. The attendants in the room all thought he
was absolutely dead, and scampered down to
assist in the *scramble.* But Murphy, as he departed, whispered to the owner of the house,
" The parson has life enough in him, yet! you
don't think I intended to kill my neighbour, if I
could help it, do you ? But if ever he *shows* again,
or any of ye tell a single word of this matter, by
J—s every living sowl shall be burnt into black
cinders!"

The *defunct* was then covered with a quilt, carried up to a back cockloft, and attended there by
the two old women who, in fact, alone occupied the
house. He remained safe and sound till the town
was retaken by General Lake, who immediately
hanged several disaffected gentlemen, cut off their
heads by martial law, and therewith ornamented

the entrance of the court-house, as heretofore described. Parson Owen was now fully liberated, with the only difference of having got a lank body, confused brains, a celestial squint, and an illegitimate sort of St. Vitus's dance, commonly called a *muscular contortion*, which, by occasional twitches and jerks, imparted both to his features and limbs considerable *variety*.

However, by the extraordinary caprice of Dame Fortune, what the parson considered the most dreadful incident of his life turned out, in one respect, the most fortunate one. Mr. Brown, the father of his charmer, was moved to pity by his sufferings and escape, and still further conciliated by the *twist* in his optic nerves, which gave the good clergyman the appearance, whenever he played the orator in his reading-desk or pulpit, of looking steadfastly and devoutly up to heaven. Hence he acquired the reputation of being marvellously increased in godliness ; and Miss Brown, with her debentures, was at length committed to his " holy keeping." I believe, however, the worthy man did not long survive to enjoy his wished-for prosperity. St. Vitus grew too familiar ; and poor Owen became, successively, puny, sickly, and imbecile : the idea of the pikes never quitted his sensorium ; and after a brief union, he left his spouse a dashing young widow, to look out for another helpmate, which I understand she was not long in providing.

Sudden fright and horror, or even agitating news, have often the most extraordinary effect on the human frame, exciting a variety of disorders, and sometimes even death. I have myself seen numerous examples of the overwhelming influence of *surprise*. Not long since, a near relative of mine, a clergyman of ample fortune—a pattern of benevolence and hospitality—healthy, comely, happy, and adored by his parishioners—had been driven into some trifling lawsuit. He had conceived a strange opinion, that a clergyman would be *disgraced* by any cause he contested being given *against* him. With this notion, he attached an *ideal* importance to success; and the thing altogether rendered him anxious and uneasy. The day of decision at the assizes of Carlow came on : he drove in his gig to the court-house door, quite certain of the *justice* of his cause, and confident, therefore, of its issue ;—when the attorney who acted for his opponent, coming out of court, abruptly told him that the decision was adverse to him. The extreme suddenness of this unexpected news, like an electric shock, paralysed his frame, extinguished all his faculties—and, in a word, he instantaneously fell *dead !* The event was even if possible more lamentable, as the intelligence was communicated in sport. The cause had been actually decided in my relation's favour.

REBEL PORTRAITS.

Tendency of the imagination *to embody* character—Its frequent
  errors—Exemplified in the personal traits of several of the
  rebel chiefs of Ireland—The Bretons of La Vendée—Intrepidity of their leaders—The battle of Ross—Gallantry of a
  boy twelve years old—Beauchamp Bagenal Harvey—Description of his person and character—His habit of joking—
  Dangerous puns—His bewilderment as rebel generalissimo—
  His capture and behaviour at execution—Portrait, physical
  and mental, of Captain Keogh—Remarkable suicide of his
  brother, and his own execution—Mr. Grogan, of Johnstown
  Castle, described—His case, sentence, and execution—Unmerited fate of Sir Edward Crosby, Bart.

WHEN we read or hear of public and distinguished characters, whether good or bad, we are
naturally disposed to draw in our mind a figure or
face for each, correspondent to the actions which
rendered the individual conspicuous. We are inclined, for instance, to paint in our imagination a
rebel chieftain as an athletic powerful personage,
with a commanding presence ;—an authoritative
voice to controul ; and impetuous bravery to lead

on a tumultuous army of undisciplined insurgents. Were this always the case, insurrections would, perhaps, stand a better chance of being successful.*

In the Irish Rebellion of 1798, the chief leaders had scarcely any of these attributes. *Numerically*, the rebels were sufficient, and more than sufficient, to effect all their objects; but they had no idea of discipline, and little of subordination. Their intrepidity was great, and their perseverance in the midst of fire and slaughter truly astonishing. Yet on every occasion it was obviously the *cause* and not the *leaders* that spurred them into action : when Irishmen *are* well officered they never yield.†

---

* Such *was* the case with the Bretons in La Vendée. An officer of rank in the French army at that period, commanding a regiment of chasseur republicans, told me very lately, that above 15,000 regular troops (his regiment among the rest) were surprised at noon-day, defeated and dispersed, and their artillery and baggage taken, by a *smaller* number of totally undisciplined Vendeans, with few fire-arms, but led on by officers selected for powerful strength and fiery enthusiasm. Their contempt for life, and impetuosity in close combat, were irresistible ; the latter, indeed, was always a characteristic with them, and the gallantry of their chiefs was quite unparalleled.

† The battle of Ross, in June, 1798, lasted ten hours. The rebel *officers* did nothing, the *men* every thing. While the commander-in-chief, Counsellor Bagenal Harvey, was standing on a hill nearly a mile distant, a boy twelve years old (Lett of Wexford town) called on the insurgents to follow him. He put himself at the head of ten thousand men—approached the

A spirit of uncompromising fortitude or enthusiastic gallantry generally spreads over the countenance some characteristic trait. Undisciplined followers are fascinated by ferocious bravery : they rush blindly any where, after an intrepid leader. But a languid eye, unbraced features, and unsteady movements, palpably betray the absence of that intellectual energy, and contempt of personal danger, which are indispensable qualities for a rebel chief.

To reflect on the great number of respectable and unfortunate gentlemen who lost their lives by the hands of the common executioner in consequence of that insurrection, is particularly sad ;— indeed, as melancholy as any thing connected with the long misrule and consequent wretched state of brave and sensitive Ireland—which is *now*, at the termination of seven hundred years, in a state of more alarming and powerful disquietude than at any period since its first connexion with England.

I had been, as stated in a former volume, in long habits of friendship and intercourse with most of the leading chiefs of that rebellion. Their features and manners rise, as it were in a vision, before my face : indeed, after thirty long years,

town, and stormed it. The town took fire; the rebels got liquor ; and they were killed in sleep and drunkenness. Nothing could have saved our troops had the rebels been well officered : General Johnston, who commanded the royalists, deserved great praise for his judgment on that critical occasion.

of factious struggle and agitation, when nothing remains of Ireland's pride and independence but the memory, every circumstance occasioning and attending that period, and the subsequent *revolution* of 1800, remains in freshest colours in the recollection of a man who *once* prided himself on being born an Irishman.

I made allusion, in a previous part of this work, to a dinner of which I partook in April, 1798, at Bargay Castle, County Wexford, the seat of Beauchamp Bagenal Harvey,—who, I may as well repeat here, was a month afterward general-in-chief over an army of more than thirty thousand men (mostly of his own county), brave and enthusiastic; and, in two months more, died by the hands of the hangman.. He had been my school and class-fellow, and from nine years of age we held uninterrupted intercourse : he was a most singular example of mixed and opposite qualities ; and of all human beings, I should least have predicted for him such a course,. or such a catastrophe.

Harvey was son of: one of the six clerks of chancery, who having amassed a very considerable fortune, purchased the estate and castle of Bargay.

Beauchamp Bagenal, his eldest son, was called to the Irish bar, and succeeded to his father's estates.. It was said that he was nearly related by blood to that most extraordinary of all the country gentlemen of Ireland, Beauchamp Bagenal, of Dunlickry, whose splendour and eccentricities were the admiration of the continent while he was making the grand tour (then reserved as part of the education of the very highest circles). This relationship was the subject of much merriment after a duel which Harvey's reputed kinsman provoked my friend to fight with him, in order to have the satisfaction of ascertaining, " whether or no the lad had metal."*

Harvey's person was extremely unimposing. He was about five feet four inches in height ; and that ancient enemy of all beauty, the small-pox, had shown him no mercy, every feature being sadly crimped thereby. His sharp peaked chin never approached toward a contact with his cravat, but left a thin scraggy throat to give an impoverished hungry cast to the whole contour, by no means adapted to the mien and port of a " commander of the forces." His scanty hair generally hung in straight flakes, and did not even pretend to be an ornament to his visage ; his eye was quick but unmeaning ; his figure thin and ill put together ; his limbs short, slight, and wab-

---

* Mr. Bagenal provoked Harvey to challenge him. They met. Harvey fired, and missed. " D—n you, you young rascal," cried Bagenal, " do you know that you had like to kill your *god-father?* Go back to Dunlickry, you dog, and have a good breakfast got ready for us. ,I only wanted to see if you were *stout.*"

bling; his address cheerful, but tremulous. On the whole, a more unprepossessing or unmartial-like person was never moulded by capricious nature.

Yet Harvey was a very good-tempered friendly man, and a hearty companion. In common life he was extremely well conducted, and in the society of the bar often amusing, and never out of humour.

He was the greatest punster of his profession, and piqued himself on that qualification, in which he often succeeded admirably.* He had, in short, that sort of partial popularity with his bar contemporaries as rendered them always glad to have him in their society; but it was seldom any one inquired what had become of him when he was out of it. He had an ample store of indi-

---

* I cannot omit introducing here one of his puns, because he ran a great risk of being *shot* for making it. A gentleman of the bar, married to a lady who had lost all her front teeth, and squinted so curiously that she appeared nearly blind, happened to be speaking of another lady who had run away from her husband. " Well," said Harvey, " you have some *comfort* as to *your* wife."

" What do you mean, sir?" said the barrister.

" I mean that if once you should lose Mrs. ——, you will never be able to *i-dent-*ify her."

If Mr. —— had cared a farthing for his wife, it would have been impossible to reconcile this joke to him.

The above was an inferior pun, but it was to the *point*, and created great merriment.

vidual courage; feared not single combat, and fought several duels intrepidly, though I do not think he ever *provoked* one. He shot Sir Harding Giffard, late Chief Justice of Ceylon, and obtained a very droll name through that achievement, which never forsook him during his lifetime.

Harvey was a person of the best fortune in his quarter of the county; of a Protestant family; and, being charitable and benevolent to his tenantry, was much beloved by them. Nobody in fact could dislike him: though he was flippant, he did not want sense; and presented an excellent example of those contradictory qualities so often discoverable in the same individual. He was considered by the heads of the United Irishmen to be well adapted—as a man of fortune and local influence in the most disaffected portion of their strongest county—to forward their objects: and he suffered his vanity so far to overcome his judgment, as, without the slightest experience, to assume the command of a great army —for which purpose there were few men in Ireland so utterly unfit.

In his martial office, his head became totally bewildered; the sphere of action was too great— the object struggled for, too comprehensive. Nor did even his *personal* courage follow him to the field. His bravery, as against a single man, was neutralised in a tumult; and a mind naturally intrepid became bewildered, puzzled, and impo-

tent. Amidst the roar of cannon, and the hurly-
burly of the tumultuous and sanguinary battle of
Ross, his presence of mind wholly forsook him,
and he lost the day by want of tact and absence of
spirit. His men fought hand to hand in the
streets of Ross with the regular troops, of whom
they slew a considerable number, including the
Earl of Mountjoy; nor did they at last retire
until they had not a single officer left to continue
the engagement or lead them on to a renewed
attack—which in all probability would have been
effectual. Never did human beings show more
decided bravery than the Irish peasantry in that
bloody engagement. Thrice the town was theirs,
and was finally lost by their inebriety and want
of proper officers. Had Harvey captured New
Ross, all Munster would have risen in his cause;
and then indeed no royalist could have anticipated
without dread the consequences. Officers and
arms would have made the whole country inevi-
tably theirs. When Wexford was retaken, Harvey
concealed himself on an island, but was discovered, brought to that town, and without much ceremony hanged next day upon the bridge, toward
the erection of which he had largely subscribed.

I could not but feel extreme regret at the sad
fate which befell my old friend and school-fellow,
who did not meet his destiny quite so firmly as
his original manly bearing had inclined people to
expect:—poor fellow! he idly strove by entreaty

to avert, or at least retard it; and its infliction was aggravated by every species of indignity. In every thing except his politics, Harvey's character was unimpeachable.

I never knew two persons much more dissimilar than were the commander-in-chief of the insurgents and the rebel governor of Wexford, Captain Keogh. The latter was a retired captain of the British service, who had fought in America, and, like many others, had there received a lesson on *civil liberty* which never escaped his memory. He was married to an aunt of Lady Barrington; and, for many years, when I went the circuit, I lived at his house, and had conceived the greatest friendship for him. He was a very clever man. His housekeeping was characterised by neatness, regularity, and cheerfulness. Every thing was good of its kind; and in that plentiful country, even luxuries were abundant. Calm, determined, moderate, and gentlemanly, Captain Keogh combined good sense with firmness and spirit. But, most unfortunately, ill-treatment sustained from Lord Chancellor Clare perverted half his good qualities, and metamorphosed him into a partizan, which was far from being his natural tendency.

He had a fine soldier-like person, above the middle size; his countenance was excellent; his features regular and engaging; his hair, rather scanty, receded from his forehead; his eyes were penetrating and expressive; and his complexion

exhibited that partial ruddiness which we so frequently see in fine men approaching threescore.
He was appointed rebel governor of Wexford,
but among those savages soon lost his popularity;
and had the insurgents continued much longer
masters of the place, he would surely have been
assassinated. He did what he durst on the side
of humanity, and had supposed that his orders
would be obeyed: but he was deceived; blood,
and blood in torrents, was the object of *both* parties
during that horrid summer. On the surrender
of the town, Keogh was immediately convicted
under martial law. He pleaded for himself; and
I learn that on that occasion every body was affected. He knew his situation to be irretrievable,
and his life forfeit; and he conducted himself at
his execution with the utmost firmness, as became a gentleman and a soldier. He was hanged
and beheaded on the bridge of which he also was
a proprietor; and his head, as mentioned in a
former volume (Vol. i.), was exhibited on a spike
over the court-house door.

A singular circumstance occurred in Keogh's
house while the rebels were in possession of Wexford. His brother, a retired major in the British
army, had also served in America, and lived with
the captain in Wexford, but was a most enthusiastic royalist. Upon the rebels taking the place,
he endeavoured to dissuade his brother from ac-

cepting the office of governor, but failing in the attempt, he retired to his own room and immediately blew his brains out!

The next of my friends and connexions who suffered by the hands of the executioner, was Mr. Cornelius Grogan of Johnstown Castle, a gentleman of large fortune, and great local interest and connexion. He had been twice high-sheriff and representative in Parliament for the county: He resided three miles from Wexford at his castle, where he had a deer-park of one thousand acres of good ground, besides a fine demesne. He lived as a quiet, though hospitable country gentleman. At this unfortunate period he had passed his seventieth year, and was such a martyr to the gout that his hands were wrapped up in flannel; and half carried, half hobbling upon crutches, he proceeded to the place of execution.

Mr. Grogan was in person short and dark-complexioned. His countenance, however, was not disagreeable, and he had in every respect the address and manners of a man of rank. His two brothers commanded yeomanry corps. One of them was killed at the head of his corps (the Castletown cavalry) at the battle of Arklaw; the other was wounded at the head of *his* troop (the Healtford cavalry) during Major Maxwell's retreat from Wexford.

The form of a trial was thought necessary by

General Lake for a gentleman of so much importance in his county. His case was afterward
brought before Parliament, and argued for three
successive days and nearly nights. His *crime*
consisted in having been surrounded by a rebel
army, which placed him under the surveillance of
numerous ruffians. They forced him one day
into the town on horseback ;—a rebel of the appropriate name of Savage always attending him
with a blunderbuss, and orders to shoot him if he
refused their commands. They one day nominated him a *commissary,* knowing that his numerous tenantry would be more willing in consequence to supply them. He used no weapon of
any sort ;—indeed, was too feeble even to *hold* one.
A lady of the name of Seagriff gave evidence that
her family were in want of food, and that she
got Mr. Grogan to give her an *order* for some
bread, which order was obeyed by the insurgents.
She procured some loaves, and supplied her children ; and for that bread (which saved a family
from starvation) Mr. Grogan was, on the lady's
evidence, sentenced to die as a felon—and actually
hanged, when already almost lifeless from pain,
imprisonment, age, and brutal treatment! The
court-martial which tried him was not sworn;
and only mustered seven in number. *His* witness
was shot while on the way to give evidence of
his innocence ; and while General Lake was

making merry with his staff, one of the first gentlemen in the county (in every point his superior) was done to death almost before his windows !   ;

From my intimate knowledge of Mr. Grogan for several years, I can venture to assert most unequivocally (and it is but justice to his memory) that, though a person of independent mind and conduct as well as fortune, and an opposition member of parliament, he was no more a *rebel* than his brothers, who signalised themselves in battle as *loyalists ;* and the survivor of whom was *rewarded* by a posthumous bill of attainder against the unfortunate gentleman in question, by virtue of which estates of many thousands per annum were confiscated to the king. (The survivor's admitted *loyal* brother had been killed in battle only a few days before the other was executed.) This attainder was one of the most flagitious acts ever promoted by any government :—but after ten thousand pounds costs to crown officers, &c. had been extracted from the property, the estates were restored. I spent the summer of 1799 at Johnstown Castle, where I derived much private information as to the most interesting events of that unfortunate era.

It is, of course, most painful to me to recollect those persons whose lives were taken — some fairly—some, as I think, unfairly—at a time when military law had no restraint, 'and enormities were daily committed through it not much inferior to those practised by the rebels.

Sir Edward Crosby, a baronet with whom I was intimately acquainted, and who also lived tranquilly, as a country gentleman, upon a moderate fortune, near Carlow, was another person who always struck me to have been *murdered* by martial law. There was not even a rational *pretence* for *his* execution. His trial, with all its attending documents, has been published, and his innocence, in fact, made manifest. The president of the martial court was one Major Dennis, who some time after quitted the service—I shall not mention why. The sentence on Sir Edward was confirmed by Sir Charles Asgill, I must suppose through gross misrepresentation, as Sir Charles had himself known enough about *hanging* (though personally innocent) in America, to have rendered him more merciful, or at least more cautious in executing the first baronet of Ireland.

The entire innocence of Sir Edward Crosby has since, as I just now mentioned, been acknowledged by all parties. His manners were mild and well-bred : he was tall and genteel in appearance ; and upward of fifty years of age. He had a wife who loved him ; and was every way a happy man till he was borne to execution without the slightest cause. He was the elder brother of my old college friend, Balloon Crosby, whom I have heretofore mentioned in relating my *rencontre* with Mr. Daly. (See Vol. ii.) He did not die with the courage of Keogh, but hoped for mercy to the last minute, relying on the interference of his old friend Judge Downes, who, however, proved but a broken reed.

REMINISCENCES OF WIT.

Wit distinguished from ribaldry—Chief Baron Yelverton and
Mr. Curran—Chief Justice Clonmell—Lord Norbury's comprehensive powers—Sir Hercules Langreish, and his digressions in claret-drinking—Gervoise Parker Bushe,
Chief Baron Burgh, &c.—Peculiar traits of Irish convivial
society in the author's day—Jeremiah Keller—Lord Clare's
funeral—A scanty fee—The Pope and Pretender—Counsellor Norcott's talent of mimickry — Ballinlaw ferry—
Cæsar Colclough, of Duffry Hall, and Julius Cæsar.

There is no intellectual faculty so difficult to
define, or of which there are so many degrees and
gradations, as *wit*. Humour may be termed a
sort of *table d'hôte*, whereat wit and ribaldry sometimes mingle. Certain eminent countrymen of
mine possessed these various conversational qualities in great perfection, and often called them
into action at the same sitting. Among them,
Mr. Curran and Chief Baron Yelverton were most
conspicuous; but the flow of their *bonhomie* was
subject to many contingencies. It is worthy
notice, that all the Irish judges of those days who

could conjure up a single joke, affected *wit*. Lord
Clonmell, chief justice, was but clumsy at repartee, though an efficient humourist. He seldom
rose above *anecdotes*, but these he *acted* whilst he
told them. He had the peculiar advantage of
knowing mankind well, and suiting his speech to
the ears of his company. Lord Norbury had witticisms, puns, *jeux-d'esprit*—in short, jokes of all
kinds, constantly at hand. His impromptus were
sometimes excellent, but occasionally failed;—
he made, however, more *hits* than any one of
his contemporaries. Nobody, it is true, minded
much what he said :—if it was good, they laughed
heartily; if bad, it was only a *Norbury*;—and so,
by an indefatigable practice of *squibbing*, it is not
wonderful that, during a life of eighty years, he
should have uttered many *good things*—though,
oddly enough, few of them are preserved.

Lord Norbury sang extremely well.—On my
first circuit as counsel, in 1787, he went as judge,
and I have often heard him warble " Black-eyed
Susan " and " Admiral Benbow," as well as parts
in divers glees and catches, most agreeably.—
Requiescat in pace !

Sir Hercules Langreish, a commissioner of re-
venue, and one of the most popular *courtiers* of
our society, had an abundance of slow, kind-
hearted, though methodistically pronounced, repartee. (A living friend of mine in high rank has
much more wit than Sir Hercules; but there is

less philanthropy about it). I have heretofore mentioned his *retort courteous* to Mr. Dundas, and will now give another specimen:—He was surprised one evening at his house in Stephen's Green, by Sir John Parnell, Duigenan, and myself, who went to him on an immaterial matter of re-venue business. We found him in his study alone, poring over the national accounts, with two claret bottles empty before him and a third bottle on the wane; it was about eight o'clock in the evening, and the butler, according to general or-ders when gentlemen came in, brought a bottle of claret to each of us. " Why," said Parnell, " Sir Heck, you have emptied *two bottles* already." " True," said Sir Hercules. " And had you nobody to help you?" " *O yes*, I had that bottle of *port* there, and I assure you he afforded me very great assistance !"

Gervoise -Parker Bushe could boast of wit enough for a member of parliament, and more than enough for a commissioner of the revenue. An eminent relative of his,-now living, possesses the finest specimen I know at present of the smooth, classical species.

I never knew two distinguished individuals ap-proach each other so nearly in many respects as the late Chief Baron Hussy Burgh and the per-sonage who now presides over the first law court of Ireland. In some points, it is true, they dif-fered:—the former was proud, the latter affable.

The eloquence of the former was more highly polished, more classical and effective; that of the latter, more simple, more familiar, yet decided. When very young, I was fascinated by the eloquence of the *silver-tongued* orator (as he was then called), and sought every possible opportunity of hearing him both at the bar and in the House of Commons. .His was the purest declamation I have ever listened to; and when he made an instrument of his wit, it was: pointed and acute. He was a miscellaneous poet, and wrote epigrams (several upon Lord Aldborough), which were extremely severe, but at the same time extremely humorous.

It would be almost impossible to enumerate the wits and humourists of Ireland in my early days. Wit was then regularly *cultivated* as an accomplishment, and was, in a greater or less degree, to be found in every society. Those whom nature had not blessed with that faculty (if a blessing it is) still did their very best—as a foreigner sports his broken English.

The convivial circles of the higher orders of Irish society, in fact, down to the year 1800, in point of wit, pleasantry, good temper, and friendly feeling, were pre-eminent; while the plentiful luxuries of the table, and rich furniture of the wine-cellar, were never surpassed, if equalled, among the gentry of any country. But every thing is now changed; that class of society is no more;

neither men nor manners are the same; and even the looking back at those times affords a man who participated in their pleasures higher gratification than do the actual enjoyments of the passing era.

People may say this change is in myself: perhaps so: yet I think that if it were possible for an old man still to preserve unimpaired all the sensations of youth, he would, were he a gentleman, be of my way of thinking. As for those of my contemporaries who survive, and who lived in the same circles with myself, I have no doubt they are unanimously of my opinion. I had very lately an opportunity of seeing this powerfully exemplified by a noble lord at my house. Good fortune had attended him throughout life; always respected and beloved, he had at length become wealthy. When we talked over the days we had spent in our own country, his eyes filled, and he confessed to me his bitter repentance as to *the Union*.

The members of the Irish bar were then collectively the best home-educated persons in Ireland, the elder sons of respectable families being almost uniformly called to that profession. Among them, nevertheless, were some of humbler origin. Jeremiah Keller was such ;—but his talent sufficed to elevate him. He had the rare faculty of dressing up the *severest* satire in the garb of pleasantry —a faculty, by the bye, which makes no friends, and often deepens and fixes animosity.

Keller was a good man, generally liked, and

popular with a considerable portion of his profession. But though not rich, he occasionally exercised an independence of mind and manners
which gave great distaste to the pride and arro-
gance of some of the leading authorities. Lord
Clare could not endure him, and never missed an
opportunity of showing or affecting to show his
contempt for Jerry.

Lord Clare having died *of the Union* and the
Duke of Bedford, it was proposed by his led captains and partizans, that the bar, in a body,
should attend his funeral procession. But as his
Lordship had made so many inveterate foes at the
bar, by taking pains to prove himself *their* foe, it
was thought necessary to *canvass* the profession
individually, and ascertain who among them
would *object* to attend. Very few did;—not that
they cherished any personal respect for Lord
Clare, but wished to compliment the remains of
the first Irish chancellor. As Keller was known to
be obstinate as well as virulent, it was held desirable to conciliate him if possible—though they
anticipated the certainty of a direct refusal.

The deputation accordingly called on him:
" You know, my dear fellow," said Arthur Chi-
chester M‘Courtney, who had been deputed as
spokesman (beating about the bush), " that Lord
Clare is to be buried to-morrow?"

" 'Tis generally the last thing done with dead
chancellors," said Keller coolly.

" He'll be buried in St. Peter's," said the spokesman.

" Then he's going to a friend of the family," said Keller. " His father was a papist."*

This created a laugh disconcerting to the deputation ;—however, for fear of worse, the grand question was then put. " My dear Keller," said the spokesman, " the bar mean to go in procession ; have you any objection to attend Lord Clare's funeral ?"

---

* Old Counsellor Fitzgibbon, Lord Clare's father, was born a Roman Catholic, and educated for a priest. His good sense, however, opened his eyes to his own intellectual abilities; and he determined to get, if possible, to the bar—that sure source of promotion for reasoning talent. But when or where (if ever) he renounced the Romish church, I am ignorant. He acquired great and just eminence as a barrister, and made a large fortune. Lord Clare was born his second son. Mrs. Jeffries (his sister) I knew well, and I cannot pass her by here without saying, that whatever faults she had, her female correctness was unquestioned; and throughout my life I have never met a kinder-hearted being than Mrs. Jeffries, or a fairer though a decided enemy. Old Mr. Fitzgibbon loved to make money, and in his day it was not the habit for lawyers to spend it. They used to tell a story of him respecting a certain client who brought his own brief and fee, that he might personally apologise for the smallness of the latter. Fitzgibbon, on receiving the fee, looked rather discontented. " I assure you, Counsellor," said the client (mournfully), I am ashamed of its smallness; but in fact it is all I have in the world." " Oh! then," said Fitzgibbon, " you can do no more :—as it's ' all you have in the world,'—why—hem !—I must—*take it !*"

"None at all," said Keller, "none at all! I shall certainly attend his *funeral* with the *greatest pleasure imaginable!*"

Examples of Keller's dry species of wit in fact daily occurred; it was always pungent, and generally well-timed. In the year 1798 flourished Sir Judkin Fitzgerald, Bart., a barrister whose loyal cruelties in the county of Tipperary were made the subject of a *post facto* indemnity bill by Lord Castlereagh, to save him from punishment. Among other pastimes, he caused cats-o'-nine-tails to be soaked in *brine*, that the peasantry and every body else at whom he durst have a fling might be better cut, and remember it the longer. Bragging to Keller of his numerous ultra-loyal achievements, this man said, "You must own, Keller, at least, that I preserved the county of Tipperary."

"Ay, and you *pickled* it into the bargain!" said Keller: "you promise to make so good a body confectioner, that I dare say the lord-lieutenant will hire you;" and in fact Sir Judkin was soon afterward put in office at the castle.

The unfortunate Counsellor Norcott, heretofore mentioned in these sketches, was a fat, full-faced, portly-looking person. He had a smirking countenance, and a swaggering air; was an excellent *bon vivant,* a remarkably good mimic, and affected to be witty.

Speaking of the Catholics in the hall of the Four

Courts, Keller seemed to insinuate that Norcott was favourable to their emancipation.

"What!" said Norcott, with a great show of pomposity—"what! Pray, Keller, do you see any thing that smacks of the *Pope* about me?"

"I don't know," replied Keller; "but at all events there is a great deal of the *Pretender*, and I always understood them to travel in company."

This was a kind of caustic wit which was not much cultivated in the higher convivial societies of that day, the members whereof used a more cordial species. But such sallies were always *repeated* with great glee when they did not affect the person who repeated them.

Norcott's mimickry was complete. This is a disagreeable and dangerous, because generally an *offensive* faculty. The foibles, absurdities, or personal defects of mankind are thus caricatured, and the nearer perfection the mimickry, the more annoying to the mimicked. Done in a man's presence, it amounts to a personal insult; in his absence, it is dramatic backbiting,—a bad quality in every point of view to cultivate, and such a weapon of ill-nature as every body should assist in blunting.

In a company where the late Lord Chief Baron Avonmore was a guest, Norcott was called on to show his imitative powers. He did so with great effect, taking off particularly well the peculiarities of the judges; and when he had finished, Lord

Avonmore said, with point, but good-humour, "Upon my word, Norcott, as you so ably exposed the absurdities of *eleven* of the judges, I think you did not act fairly by us in not giving also the *twelfth* of them" (his lordship's self).—Norcott did not utter a word more during the evening.

It is very singular, that a man with such a surplus of wit as Curran, never could write a good epigram—nor, with such an emporium of language, compose a pamphlet or essay that would pay for the printing; while a very eminent living friend of mine, high in the world—though not Curran's equal in either qualities—has written some of the most agreeable and classic *jeux d'esprits*, of the most witty and humorous papers, and most effective pamphlets, that have issued from the pen of any member of his profession during my time. I had collected as many as I could of this gentleman's productions and sayings (several printed and a few in manuscript); but, unfortunately, the whole was lost in a trunk of mine, (with a great number of my books and private papers and memoranda,) in 1812. I can scarce attempt to recollect any of them, save one or two, which may give some idea, but nothing more, of the agreeable playfulness of this gentleman's fancy. They have been long recorded by the Irish bar; and some of the English bar, who are not at present celebrated for their own impromptus or witticisms, and are too *wise* and *steady* to *understand* those of Ireland (unless in print and after due consideration), may be amused by reading and unriddling an Irish epigram, sent into the world by an English bookseller.*

A placard having been posted in the courts of law in Dublin by a bookseller for the sale of *Bibles*, the gentleman I allude to wrote instantly under it with his pencil—

> How clear is the case,
> He's mistaken the place,
> His books of devotion to sell :
>   He should learn, once for all,
>   That he'll never get call
> For the sale of his *Bibles* in *hell*.

Had the above *jeu d'esprit* been the impromptu of a beaten client, he would have got great credit for it; and in truth, I think, after a year or two of litigation in a court of justice, most clients would freely subscribe their names to the concluding epithet.

Another *jeu d'esprit* I remember, and so no doubt do all the bar of my standing who have any recollection left,—of whom, however, there is, I fancy, no great number.

There is a very broad and boisterous ferry be-

---

* An English gentleman once said to me very seriously, that he always preferred a London edition of an Irish book, as he thought, somehow or other, it helped to *take out the brogue.*

tween the counties of Wicklow and Wexford,
called Ballinlaw, which the Leinster bar, on circuit, were obliged to cross in a bad boat. At
times the wind was extremely violent between the
hills, the waters high, and the passage dangerous;
—yet the *briefs* were at the other side; and many
a nervous barrister, who on a simple journey
would have rode a high-trotting horse fifty miles
round-about rather than cross Ballinlaw when the
waves were in an angry humour, yet, being sure
that there was a golden mine, and a phalanx of
attorneys brandishing their white briefs on the
opposite shore—commending himself to Divine
Providence, and flinging his saddle-bags into the
boat—has stepped in after them; and if he had
any prayers or curses by heart, now and then pronounced a fragment of such in rotation as were
most familiar to him, on launching into an element
which he never drank and had a rooted aversion
to be upset in.

The curious colloquy of a boatman, on one of
those boisterous passages, with Counsellor Cæsar
Colclough, once amused such of the passengers as
had not the fear of death before their eyes.

Cæsar Colclough of Duffry Hall, a very eccentric, quiet character, not overwise, (he was afterward Chief Justice of Newfoundland,) was in the
boat during a storm. Getting nervous, he could
not restrain his piety, and began to lisp out, " O
Lord!—O Lord!" breathing an ardent prayer

that he might once more see his own house, Duffry Hall, in safety, and taste a sweet barn-door fowl or duck, of which he had fine breeds.

" Arrah! Counsellor," said the boatman, " don't be going on praying *that side,* if you plase; sure it's the *other lad* you ought to be praying to."

" What *lad* do you mean?" said Colclough with alarm.

" What lad! why, Counsellor, the old people always say, that the *devil* takes care of his *own;* and if you don't vex him by praying the *other way,* I really think, Counsellor, we have a pretty *safe* cargo aboard at this present passage."

The friend I alluded to, whose wit and pencil were always ready, immediately placed Cæsar in a much more classical point of view. Though he made him a downright idolater, yet he put him on a level with a mighty hero, or emperor—writing upon the back of a letter thus :

While meaner souls the tempest kept in awe,
Intrepid Colclough, crossing Ballinlaw,
Cried to the sailors (shivering in their rags)
You carry *Cæsar* and his *saddle-bags!*

Little did Julius Cæsar foresee before the birth of Christ that the first man at the Irish bar would, near two thousand years afterward, call to mind his exploits in Gaul on the waves of Ballinlaw, in the roaring of a hurricane. Should I meet him hereafter, I shall certainly tell him the anecdote.

COUNSELLOR LYSIGHT.

Edward Lysight, Esq., barrister-at-law—His peculiar talents—
A song of his contrasted with one of Moore's on the same subject—*Ounagh* and *Mary*—Pastoral poetry—" The Devil in
the Lantern "—A love story—" We're a' *noddin*"—Sketch
of Mr. Solomon Salmon and his daughter—Mr. Lysight's
nuptials with the latter—Sociality at Somers' Town—A morning call—All is not gold that glitters—Death of the counsellor and his lady.

AMONG the eccentric characters formerly
abounding at the Irish bar, was one whose species
of talent is nearly extinct, but whose singularities
are still recollected by such of his professional contemporaries as have had the good fortune to survive him.

Edward Lysight, a gentleman by birth, was
left, as to fortune, little else than his brains and
his pedigree. The latter, however, was of no sort
of use to him, and he seldom employed the former
to any lucrative purpose. He considered law as
his *trade*, and conviviality (to the cultivation
whereof no man could apply more sedulously) as

his *profession*. Full of point and repartee, every humourist and *bon vivant* was his patron. He had a full proportion of animal courage ; and even the fire-eaters of Tipperary never courted his animosity. Songs, epigrams, and lampoons, which from other pens would have terminated in mortal combat, being considered inherent in *his* nature, were universally tolerated.

Some of Lysight's sonnets had great merit, and many of his national stanzas were singularly characteristic. His " Sprig of shillelah and shamrock so green" is admirably and truly descriptive of the low Irish character, and never was that class so well depicted in so few words : but, to my taste, his sketch of a May morning is not to be exceeded in that cheerful colouring and natural simplicity which constitute the very essence and spirit of genuine pastoral. The beginning of the copy of verses called " Ounagh" offers an illustration of this ; and it is much to be lamented that, with strange inconsistency, the man did not write another line of it adapted for publication. The first verse is, however, in my mind, worthy of being recorded, and I give it as a sample either of my bad or good taste. All I am *sure* of is, that *I* admire it.

> 'Twas on a fine May morning,
>   When violets were springing O,
> Dew-drops the fields adorning,
>   The birds melodious singing O :

The green trees
Each soft breeze
Was gently waving up and down :
The primrose
That sweet blows
Adorned Nature's verdant gown :
The purling rill ·
Stole down the hill,
And softly murmur'd thro' the grove,
This was the time Ounagh stole out, to meet her
barefoot love.*

Lysight was, perhaps, not a poet in the strict acceptation of the term ;—but he wrote a great number of miscellaneous verses—some of them,

* Pastoral poetry, whether classic, amatory, or merely rural, owes its chief beauty to *simplicity.* Far-fetched points and fantastic versification destroy its generic attribute ; and their use reminds one of the fashion of *harmonising* the popular melodies of a country, in order that young ladies may screech them with more complicated execution.

Thus, I prefer, upon the whole, my deceased friend Lysight's words written to an old tune, to those of my celebrated living friend, Mr. Thomas Moore ; and think the *Ounagh* of the one likely to be quite as attractive a girl as the *Mary* of the other, notwithstanding all the finery wherewith the mention of the latter is invested. But our readers shall judge for themselves. We have given the commencement of Mr. Lysight's version : here followeth that of Mr. Moore's.

The day had sunk in dim showers,
But midnight now with " lustre meek "
Illumin'd all the pale flowers,
Like hope that lights the mourner's cheek.

in general estimation, excellent; some delicate, some gross. I scarce ever saw two of these productions of the same metre, and very few were of

> I said (while
> The moon's smile
> Play'd o'er a stream in dimpling bliss)
> The moon looks
> On many brooks—
> The brook can see no moon but this.
> And thus I thought our fortunes run,
> For many a lover looks on thee,
> While, Oh! I feel there is but one—
> One Mary in the world for me!—

" Had not my talented friend garnished the above ditty with a note, admitting that he had pilfered his *Irish* Melody from an *Englishman's* brains (Sir William Jones's), I should have passed over so extravagant an attempt to *manufacture simplicity.* I therefore hope my friend will in future either confide in his own supreme talents, or not be so candid as to spoil his song by his sincerity. " It is the devil (said Skirmish) to desert; but it's a d—d deal worse to *own* it!"

I think Dean Swift's sample of Love Songs (though written near a century ago) has formed an admirable model for a number of modern sonnets; it should be much esteemed, since it is copied by so many of our minstrels.

LOVE SONG BY DEAN SWIFT.

> Fluttering, spread thy purple pinions,
> Gentle Cupid, o'er my heart:
> I a slave in thy dominions—
> *Nature must give way to art,* &c. &c.

the same character. Several of the best poetical trifles in M'Nally's "Sherwood Forest" were penned by Lysight.

Having no fixed politics, or in truth *decided* principles respecting any thing, he was one day a patriot, the next a courtier, and wrote squibs both *for* government and *against* it. The stanzas relatively commencing,

> Green were the fields that our forefathers dwelt on, &c.

> Where the loud cannons rattle, to battle we'll go, &c.

and

> Some few years ago, though now she says no, &c.

were three of the best of his *patriotic* effusions ; they were certainly very exciting, and he sang them with great effect. He ended his literary career by a periodical paper in 1800, written principally against me, and called " The Lantern," for which and similar squibs, he received four hundred pounds from Lord Castlereagh. I sincerely wished him joy of the acquisition, and told him " if he found me a good chopping-block, he was heartily welcome to hack away as long as he could get any thing by his butchery." He shook me heartily by the hand, swore I was a " d—d good fellow," and the next day took me at my word by lampooning me very sufficingly in a copy of verses entitled " The Devil in the Lantern !" But I loved abuse, when it was incurred for opposing the Union ; and we never had a moment's coolness upon that or any other subject. Indeed, I really regarded him.

He attempted to practise at the English bar; but after a short time, told me he found he had not law enough for the King's Bench, was not dull enough for the Court of Chancery, and that before he could make way at the Old Bailey he must shoot Garrow, which would be extremely disagreeable to him. He therefore recurred to the periodicals; and though an indifferent prose writer, wielded his goose-quill with no small success. He showed me a *tariff* of his pieces in verse : it was a most pleasant document, and I greatly regret I did not keep a copy of it : he burned it, he told me, to light his candle with. So indifferent was he of the main chance throughout life, that he never adhered long to any pursuit after he found it was really likely to be productive.

In the year 1785, when I was at Temple, he called on me one morning at the Grecian Coffee-house, where I then lodged, and said, with much seeming importance—

" Barrington, put on your hat, and come along with me this moment. I want to show you a lady who has fallen in love with me."

" In love with *you*, Ned ?" said I.

" Ay, to insanity !" replied he.

" It must indeed be to *insanity*."

" Oh !" resumed he, gaily, " she is, I assure you, only considering what death she shall inflict on herself if I do not marry her. I Now, you know, I am as poor as a rat, though a *gentleman,* and her father is as rich as Crœsus, though a *blackguard:* so we shall be well matched. The blood, and the fat duly mixed, as Hogarth says, makes a right sort of pudding. So the thing is settled; and I'll have the twelve tribes of Israel at my beck in the course of Monday morning."

I thought he was distracted, and raving; but, however, immediately set out with him upon this singular expedition; and on our way to the Strand; where *the papa* resided, he disclosed to me all the circumstances of his amour.

"Barrington," said he, "the lady herself is not, to be sure, the most *palatable* morsel one might see in a circle of females; yet she is obviously of the *human* species; has the usual features in her face (such as they are), four fingers and a thumb on each hand, and two distinct feet with a proper number (I suppose) of toes upon each;—and what more need I expect, seeing she has plenty of the *shiners?*"

"True," said I: "as for beauty, those English girls, who *are* handsome, are too frolicksome: she'll stick the closer to you, because she has none."

"And what *advantage* will that be?" muttered Lysight, with a half-suppressed imprecation. "Her father pretends," continued he, "to be a *Christian,* and affects to keep a shop in the Strand;

under the name of ' *Salmon*, watchmaker :' but in
reality he is a d—d Jew, and only pretends to
be a Christian that he may transact affairs for certain Israelites of the city, who give him the devil's
own rate of commission!—I hope to be a *partner*
ere long!"

. . " Suppose he recéives *stolen goods*, Ned?" said
I. ."You'd cut but a queer figure at the *tail of a
cart* with a cat-o' nine-tails flourished over you."

" Father of Israel!" exclaimed Lysight, already
half a Jew, " you mistake the matter totally. No,
no! the maid-servant, whom I bribed with the
price of my last squib in the Chronicle, told me
every thing about Solomon Salmon—his dealings,
his daughter, and his great iron chest with eleven
locks to it : but as to *goods*, he never has fifty
pounds' worth of trinkets or watches in his shop—
only a few in the window, to *look* like trade. He
deals in the lending and borrowing way only—
all *cash* transactions, depend on it."

" For Heaven's sake, Ned," said I, " how did
you introduce yourself into the family of a He-
brew?"

" I met the girl three months ago," he replied,
." at a dancing-school at Somers' Town, set up by
an old Irish acquaintance, Terry M'Namara, with
whom I dine sometimes : he told me she was a rich
Jewess; so when I heard of her papa, I determined to know something more about his daughter, and stole frequently to Somers' Town, where

Mr. Solomon Salmon has a pretty cit cottage. There I hid behind a dead wall just in front, and when *she* came to the window, I nodded, and she ran away, as if offended. I knew this was a good sign with a woman. She soon returned to the window. I nodded again. Away went she a second time; but I heard a loud laugh, and considered that a capital sign : and in fact, she came a third time. Then I was sure, and nodded *twice*, whereupon she returned the salutation. Having carried on the *nodding* system sufficiently, I now ventured to speak to her on my fingers—an art which I had seen her dexterously practise at the dancing-school. ' My love !' fingered I ; at which she turned her back, but soon turned her face again. ' My love !' I repeated, still on my fingers. Off she scampered, but soon came back in company with the maid-servant (whom I therefore bribed next day). I now ventured to suggest an interview the following evening. The Jewess flushed at this proposal ; but on my repetition of it, held up *seven* of her fingers.

" Of course I was punctual at the time appointed, was admitted, and we swore eternal fidelity on the *Old* Testament. The maid betrayed us as soon as I ran short of hush-money, but repented afterward, when I gave her a fresh supply, and told me that her master, Mr. Solomon Salmon, had locked his daughter up. She had then attempted to throw herself out of a two-pair window for my sake; but the old Jew having caught her in the very act, she peremptorily told him she was determined to fall into a decay or consumption of the lungs, if he did not consent to her marrying the Christian counsellor.

"This he was in the sequel forced to agree to, or sacrifice his own virgin daughter, (like the king in the Bible,) besides whom he luckily has no other child to inherit his fortune, and the mother is at least twenty years past childbearing.

"At length all was settled, and we are to be actually married as Christians on Monday next. Little Egar of Hare Court has drawn up the marriage articles, and I am to have ten thousand now—that is, the interest of it during the Jew's life, payable quarterly: then twenty more, and *all the rest* on the mother's death: and in the mean time, half his commission on money dealings (to commence after a few months' instruction), together with the house in Somers' Town, where I shall reside and transact business."

All this Lysight told me with great glee and admirable humour.

"Egad, it's no bad hit, Ned," said I; "many a high-headed grand-juror on the Munster circuit would marry Solomon Salmon himself upon the same terms."

"You'll dine with me," said Lysight, "on Wednesday, at Somers' Town, at five o'clock? I'll give you a good turkey, and such a bottle of old black-strap as neither the Grecian nor the Oxford ever had in their cellars for any money."

" I'll surely attend a new scene, Ned," answered I.

I was accordingly most punctual. All appeared to be just as he had described. It was a small house, well furnished. Miss's visage, to be sure, though not *frightful*, was less *ornamental* than any article on the premises. The maid-servant was really a fine girl; the cook no bad *artiste*; the dinner good, and the wine capital. Two other Templars were of the party, and every thing went on well. About eight at night the old Jew came in. He appeared a civil, smug, dapper, clean, intelligent little fellow, with a bob-wig. He made us all welcome, and soon retired to rest, leaving us to a parting bottle.

The affair proceeded prosperously; and I often dined with my friend in the same cheerful manner. Ned, in fact, became absolutely domestic. By degrees he got into *the trade*; accepted all the bills at the Jew's request, to save *him* trouble, as old Salmon kept his own books; and a large fortune was accumulating every day, as was apparent by the great quantities of miscellaneous property which was sent in and as quickly disappeared; when one morning, Ned was surprised at three ugly-looking fellows entering his house rather unceremoniously and without stating their business. Ned immediately seized the poker, when his

arm was arrested gently by a fourth visitor, who
said :

"Easy, easy, Counsellor Lysight, we mean you
no harm or rudeness ; we only do our duty. We
are the *commissioners'* messengers, that's all. Gentlemen," said the *attorney*, as he proved to be, to
the three ruffians, "do your duty without the
slightest inconvenience to the counsellor."

₃₅ They then proceeded to seal up all the doors,
leaving Ned, wife, & Co. a bed-room only, to con-
sole themselves in. Mr. Solomon Salmon, in
truth, turned out both a Christian and a bankrupt;
and had several thousands to pay out of the sale
of about twoscore of silver watches and a few
trinkets—which constituted the entire of the splendid property he had so liberally settled on Mr.
Edward Lysight as a portion with his lady daughter.
Ned now found himself completely taken in,—
reduced, as he told me, to ten shillings and sixpence in gold, and four shillings in silver, but
acceptor of bills of exchange for Salmon & Co. for
more than he could pay should he live a hundred
years longer than the course of nature would permit
him. As he had signed no partnership deed, and
had no funds, they could not make him a bankrupt; and as the bills had not arrived at mercan-
tile maturity, he had some days of grace during
which to consider himself at liberty :— so he
thought absence and fresh air better than hunger
and imprisonment, and therefore *retreat* the wisest

course to be taken. He was right; for in some time, the creditors having ascertained that they could get nothing of a cat but its skin, (even could they catch it,) suffered him to remain unmolested on his own promise—and a very safe one—that *if ever he was able,* he would pay them.

He afterward went over to Dublin to the Irish bar, where he made nearly as many friends as acquaintances, but not much money; and at length died,—his widow soon following his example, and leaving two daughters, who, I believe, as teachers of music in Dublin, were much patronised and regarded.

Several years subsequently, being surprised that the creditors had let Lysight off so easily, I inquired particulars from a solicitor who had been concerned in the affairs of Salmon & Co., and he informed me that all the parties, except one, had ceased to proceed on the commission; and that he found the true reason why the alleged creditors had agreed to let Lysight alone was, that they had been all engaged in a piece of complicated machinery to deceive the unwary, and dreaded lest matters should come out, in the course of a strict examination, which might place them in a more dangerous situation than either the bankrupt or his son-in-law. In fact, the creditors were a knot; the bankrupt an instrument; and Lysight a tool.

Felix qui facit aliena periculum comtum.

FATALITIES OF MARRIAGE.

Speculations of the author on free-agency and predestination—
A novel theory—The matrimonial ladder—Advice to young
lovers—A ball in Dublin—Unexpected arrival of Lord G—
—His doom expressed—Marries the author's niece—Remarks on his lordship's character.

In a previous part of this volume, I promised
my fair readers that I would endeavour to select
some little anecdotes of tender interest, more particularly calculated for their perusal; and I now
proceed to redeem that promise, so far as I can.

Fatality in *marriages* has been ever a favourite
theme with young ladies who have promptly determined to resign their liberty to a stranger, rather than preserve it with a parent. I am myself
no unqualified fatalist; but have struck out a
notion of my own on that subject, which is, I
believe, different from all others;—and when I
venture to broach it in conversation, I am generally
ly assured by the most didactic of the company,
that (so far as it is comprehensible) it excludes

both sense and morality. Nevertheless it is, like my faith in supernaturals, a grounded and honest opinion : and in all matters connected with such shadowy things as spirits, fates, chances, &c. a man is surely warranted in forming his own theories—a species of construction, at any rate, equally harmless and rational with that castle-building in the air so prevalent among his wiser acquaintances.

It is not my intention here to plunge deep into my tenets. I only mean indeed to touch on them so far as they bear upon matrimony : and may the glance induce fair damsels, when first nourishing a tender passion, to consider in time what may be *fated* as the consequences of their *free-agency !*

The matrimonial *ladder* (if I may be allowed such a simile) has generally eight steps : viz. 1. Attentions ; 2. Flirtation ; 3. Courtship ; 4. Breaking the ice ; 5. Popping the question ; 6. The negotiation ; 7. The ceremony ; 8. The *repentance.*

The grand basis of my doctrine is, that free-agency and predestination are neither (as commonly held) inconsistent nor incompatible ; but, on the contrary, intimately connected, and generally copartners in producing human events: Every important occurrence in the life of man or woman (and matrimony is no *bagatelle*) partakes of the nature of both. Great events may ever be traced to trivial causes, or to voluntary actions ;

and that which is *voluntary* cannot, it should seem, be *predestined :* but when these acts of free-will are once. performed, they lead irresistibly to ulterior things. Our free-agency then becomes expended ; our spontaneous actions cannot be retraced; and then, and not before, the march of *fate* commences.

. The medical doctrine of remote and proximate causes of disease in the human body is not altogether inappropriate. to my dogma—since disorders which are *predestined* to send ladies and gentlemen on their travels to the other world, entirely *against* their inclinations, may frequently be traced to acts which were as entirely within their own option.

b I have already professed my intention of going but superficially into this subject just now ; and though I could find it in my heart considerably to prolong the inquiry, I will only give one or two marked illustrations of my doctrine, merely to set casuists conjecturing. There are comparatively few important acts of a person's life which may not be avoided. For example :—if any man chooses voluntarily to take a voyage to Nova Scotia; he gives *predestination* a fair opportunity of drowning him at sea, if it think proper ; but if he determines never to go into a ship, he may be perfectly certain of his safety in *that* way. Again :—if a general chooses to go into a battle, it is his free-agency which enables predestination to despatch him

there; but if, on the other hand, he keeps clear
out of it (as some generals do), he may set fatality
at defiance on that point, and perhaps return with
as much glory as many of his comrades had acquired by leaving their brains upon the field.
Cromwell told his soldiers the night before the
battle of Worcester, (to encourage them,) that,
" Every *bullet* carried its own *billet*."—" Why then,
by my sowl," said an Irish recruit, "that's the very
rason I'll *desert* before morning!" Marriage, likewise, is an act of free-agency; but, as I said before, being once contracted, predestination comes
into play, often despatching one or other of the
parties, either by grief, murder, or suicide, who
might have been safe and sound from all those
fatalities, had he or she never *voluntarily* purchased
or worn a plain gold ring.

Of the eight steps attached to the ladder of
matrimony already specified, *seven* (all lovers will
be pleased to remark) imply " free-agency;" but
the latter of these being mounted, progress to the
eighth is too frequently *inevitable*. I therefore
recommend to all candidates for the ascent,
thorough deliberation, and a brief pause at each
successive step:—for, according to my way of
thinking, the knot tied at the seventh interval
should be considered, in every respect, perfectly
indissoluble.

The principle of these few examples might extend to most of the events that chequer our pas-

sage through life; and a little unprejudiced reflection seems alone requisite to demonstrate that
" free-agency," may readily keep fate under her
thumb on most important occasions.

I cannot avoid particularising, as to matrimony,
an incident that came within my knowledge, and
related to individuals of rank who are still living.
The facts are well remembered, though they occurred nearly twenty years ago. Exclusive of the
intrinsic interest of the transaction, it may have
some weight with my fair readers.

About the year 1809, a ball, on an extensive
scale, was given by Lady Barrington in Dublin.
Almost every person of *ton* did her the honour of
participating in the festivity, and I think the Duke
of Wellington was present. : -

In the evening, I received a note from Sir
Charles Ormsby, mentioning that Lord G——,
son of my old friend the Earl of L——, had just
arrived. He was represented as a fine young
man ; and it was added that (though quite tired)
he might be prevailed on to attend Lady Barrington's ball, were I to write him a note of invitation.
Of course I did so with the greatest pleasure.
The Earl of L—— and I had been many years
intimate : the late Right Honourable Isaac Corry
was his close friend ; and before his lordship grew
too rich, he was my next door neighbour in Har-
court Street. We were, indeed, all three, boon
companions.

Lord 'G—— arrived at the ball, and a very good-looking fellow he certainly was—of about nineteen; his address corresponded with his mien, and I was quite taken with him, independently of his being my friend's son. Two very young relatives of mine—one my niece, Arabella E——, the other my daughter (now the Viscomtesse de F——,) did the juvenile honours of the party.

Sir Charles Ormsby, (who might have been termed a sort of *half-mounted* wit,) said to me, rather late; " Did you ever know such a foolish boy as G——? Before he had been half an hour in the room, he protested that ere three months were over, either one or other of your girls would be Lady G——; that it was a *doomed* thing;—though he could not exactly say *which* would be the bride —as he had not seen either from 'the time they were all children together."

The ball ended about day-break, and I was obliged immediately to set off for circuit. I had been engaged as counsel on the trial of Mr. Alcock for the murder of Mr. John Colclough (as mentioned Volume i.):

I finished my month's circuit at Wexford, where to my surprise I found Lord G——. I asked him his business there. He said he had been summoned as a witness on the above-mentioned trial; which I thought a very strange circumstance, as he could have known nothing whatsoever of the transaction. However, we travelled together to Dublin in my carriage; and on the way he spoke much of *destiny;* and of a cottage in County Wicklow, with every thing " rural." I did not then comprehend the young man's drift; but on my return, I found that his *free-agency* had been put in practice; and, in fact, very shortly after, Lord G—— was my nephew. *Fatality* now commenced her dominion; and a most charming gift from fatality had the young nobleman received in a partner juvenile, like himself, his equal in birth, and possessed of every accomplishment.

I had not at first been made acquainted with the cause of Lord G——'s visit to Ireland; but at length understood, with some surprise, that the Earl of L—— had placed his eldest son as an ensign in a marching regiment ordered to the continent. Thus, at the age of nineteen, he found himself in a situation unfavourable, as I think, to the fair and proper development of his mind and talents —uncongenial with the befitting pursuits for a nobleman's heir—and still less adapted to gratify the cravings of an ardent intelligent spirit, whose very enthusiasm was calculated, under such circumstances, to produce recklessness and evil.

The residue of this *novel* (for such, in all its details, it may fairly be denominated—and one of a most interesting and affecting cast) would afford ample material for observation : but it is too long, too grave, and perhaps too delicate, for investiga-

tion here.—Suffice it to add, that I saw Lord and
Lady G——, with their numerous and lovely family,
last summer on the continent—altered less than I
should have imagined, from the interval that had
elapsed.   In speaking of his lordship, I am re-
minded of the motto, " Every one has his fault :"
—but he has likewise great merits, and talent
which would have been higher had his education
been more judicious.   My friendship for him has
been strong and invariable ; and I think that fate
has not yet closed the book on his future renown
and advancement.

A WEDDING IN OLDEN DAYS. ·

Changes in the nuptial ceremony in Ireland—Description of
the *ancient* formula—Throwing the stocking—A lucky hit—
Reverse of the picture—Modern marriages—Coming of age
—Nuptials of the author's eldest brother—Personal description of the bride and bridegroom—Various preparations—
Dresses of the different members of the wedding-party—The
coach of ceremony—The travelling chaise—A turnpike dispute—Convenient temporary metamorphosis of the author
and two of his brothers—Circumstances preceding the marriage in question—A desperate lover—Disasters and blunders
—A "scene"—Major Tennyson Edwards—Marries a sister of the author—His fortunate escape from a ludicrous
catastrophe.

THERE are few changes in the manners and
customs of society in Ireland more observable
than those relating to marriage. The day has
been, within my recollection, when that ceremony
was conducted altogether differently from the present mode. Formerly, no damsel was *ashamed,*
as it were, of being married. The celebration
was joyous, public, and enlivened by every spe-

cies of merriment and good cheer. The bride
and bridegroom, bridesmaids, and bridesmen (all
dressed and decorated in gay and gallant costumes), vied in every effort to promote the pleasure they were themselves participating. When
the ceremony was completed, by passing round
a final and mystical word, " Amazement!"—every
body kissed the bride. The company then all
saluted each other: cordial congratulations went
round, the music struck up, and plenty of plum
cake and wine seemed to anticipate a *christening*.
The bride for a moment whimpered and coloured;
the mamma wept with gratification; the bridesmaids flushed with sympathy, and a scene was
produced almost too brilliant for modern apathy
even to gaze at. The substantial banquet soon
succeeded; hospitality was all alive; the bottle
circulated; the ball commenced; the bride led
off, to take leave of her celibacy; men's souls
were softened; maidens' hearts melted; Cupid
slily stole in, and I scarce ever saw a joyous
public wedding whereat he had not nearly expended his quiver before three o'clock in the
morning. Every thing cheerful and innocent combined to show the right side of human nature,
and to increase and perfect human happiness; a
jovial hot supper gave respite to the dancers and
time to escort Madam Bride to her nuptial-cham-
ber—whither, so long as company were permitted
to do so, we will attend her. The bed-curtains

were adorned with festoons of ribbon. The chamber was well lighted; and the bridesmaids having administered to the bride her prescriptive refreshment of white-wine posset, proceeded to remove her left stocking and put it into her trembling hand: they then whispered anew the mystical word before mentioned; and having bound a handkerchief over her eyes, to ensure her impartiality, all the lovely spinsters surrounded the nuptial couch, each anxiously expecting that the next moment would anticipate her promotion to the same happy predicament within three hundred and sixty-five days at the very farthest. The bride then tossed the prophetic hosiery at random among her palpitating friends, and whichever damsel was so fortunate as to receive the blow was declared the next maiden in the room who would become devoted to the joys of Hymen; and every one in company —both ladies and gentlemen—afterward saluted the cheek of the lucky girl. The ball then recommenced; the *future* bride led off; night waned;—and Phœbus generally peeped again ere the company could be brought to separate. Good-humoured tricks were also on those happy occasions practised by arch girls upon the bridegroom. In short, the pleasantry of our old marriages in Ireland could not be exceeded. They were always performed in the house of the lady's parents or of some relative. It would fill a volume were I to enumerate the various joyful and happy incidents I have witnessed at Irish weddings.*

. At one of the old class of weddings took place the most interesting incident of my early life, as

* How miserably has modern refinement reversed those scenes of happiness and hilarity—when the gentry of my native land were married in warm, cheerful chambers, and in the midst of animated beings, beloving and beloved! No gloom was there: every thing seemed to smile; and all thoughts of death or memoranda of mortality were discarded.

Now, those joyous scenes are shifted by sanctity and *civilisation*. Now, the female soul almost shudders—and it well may—on reaching the site of the connubial ceremony. The long, chilling aisle, ornamented only by sculptured tablets and tales of death and futurity, is terminated by the sombre chancel—whence the unpupilled eye and vacant stare of cold marble busts glare down on those of youth and animation, seeming to say, " .Vain, hapless couple! see me—behold your fate!—the time is running now, and will not stop its course a single moment till you are *my* companions!" Under such auspices, the lovers' vows are frozen ere they can be registered by the recording angel.

The cheerless ceremony concluded, the bridegroom solemnly hands the silent bride into her travelling chariot; hurries her to some country inn, with her pretty maid—perhaps destined to be a future rival; they remain there a few days, till yawning becomes too frequent, and the lady then returns to town a listless matron—to receive, on her couch of *ennui*, a string of formal congratulations, and predictions of connubial comfort, few of which are doomed to be so *prophetic* as the *bridal stocking* of her grandmother.

I stated in a former volume. The spectacle and events of that union never can be erased from my memory, and its details furnish a good outline wherefrom those of other marriages of that period, in the same sphere of society, may be filled up.

In those days, so soon as an elder son came of age, the father and he united to raise money to pay off all family incumbrances. The money certainly was raised, but the incumbrances were so lazy, that in general they remained *in statu quo.* The estates were soon clipped at both ends; the father nibbling at one, the son pilfering at the other, and the attorney at both. The rent-roll became short; and it was decided that the son must marry to " sow his wild oats," and make another settlement on younger children. Money, however, was not always the main object of Irish marriages :— first, because it was not always to be had; and next, because if it was to be had, it would so soon change masters, that it would be all the same after a year or two. Good family, good cheer, and beauty, when they could find it, were the chief considerations of a country gentleman, whose blood relatives, root and branch (as is still 'the case on the continent), generally attended the act of alliance, with all the splendour their tailors, milliners, and mantua-makers could or would supply.

My eldest brother (the bridegroom on the occa-

sion alluded to) was an officer of that once magnificent regiment the black horse, and fell most
vehemently in love with the sister of a brother-
officer, afterward Colonel E—— of Old Court,
County Wicklow. I have described some beau-
ties in my former volumes; but the charms of
Alicia E—— were very different from the dazzling
loveliness of Myrtle Yates, or the opening bloom of
Maria Hartpool. She was inferior to either in symmetry; but in interest had an infinite superiority
over both. Alicia was just eighteen: she had no
regular feature: her mouth was disproportionately
large; her lips were coral; her eyes destitute
of fire—but they were captivating tell-tales;
her figure was rather below the middle height, but
without an angle; and the round, graceful deli-
cacy of her limbs could not be surpassed. It was,
however, the unrivalled clearness of her pellucid
skin that gave a splendour and indescribable
charm to the contour of Alicia's animated face.
I may be considered as exaggerating when I declare, that her countenance appeared nearly trans-
parent, and her hands were more clear than may
well be imagined. Her address was still more
engaging than her person.

Such was the individual to whom my nut-brown
and unadorned D—— W——* was selected as
bridesmaid. My brother was gentlemanly, hand-

* See Vol. i.

some, and gallant, but wild; with little judgment
and a very moderate education.

It being determined that the wedding should be
upon a public and splendid scale, both families
prepared to act fully up to that resolution. The proper trades-people were set to work ; ribbon favours
were woven on a new plan ; in fact, all Dublin
heard of the preparations from the busy milliners,
&c.; and on the happy day, a crowd of neighbours
collected about my father's house in Clare Street,
to see the cavalcade, which was to proceed to Old
Court House, near the Dargle, where the ceremony was to be performed.

The dress of those days on such occasions was
generally splendid ; but our garments " out-He-
roded, Herod." The bridegroom, cased in white
cloth with silver tissue, belaced and bespangled,
glittered like an eastern caliph. My mother, a
woman of high blood and breeding, and just pride,
was clad in what was called a *manteau* of silvered
satin : when standing direct before the lights,
she shone out as the reflector of a lamp; and as
she moved majestically about the room, and curt-
seyed *à là Madame Pompadour*, the rustling of her
embroidered habit sounded like music appropriate
to the flow of compliments that enveloped her.
My father, one of the handsomest men of his day,
was much more plainly dressed than any of us.

The gilded coach of ceremony (which I noticed
in an early sketch) was put in requisition; and its

four blacks, Bully, Blackbird, the colt, and Stop-
ford (fourteen years of age), were all as sleek and
smooth as if cut out of ebony. Tom White and
Keeran Karry (postilions), with big Nicholas (the
footman), sported appropriate costumes ; and the
whole was led by Mr. Mahony, the butler, mounted
on Brown Jack, my father's hunter.

The cavalcade started off at a hand-gallop for
Bray, accompanied by the benediction of old
Sarah the cook, and Judy Berger the hereditary
house-keeper, who stood praying meanwhile, and
crossing their foreheads, at the door. An old travelling chaise of no very prepossessing appearance
(which had been rescued from the cocks and hens
in the country out-house), with a pair of hacks, was
driven by Matthew Querns the huntsman, and
contained the residue of the party—namely, my
two other brethren and self.

The more particular description of our attire
may strike certain *moderns* as somewhat ridiculous ; but that attire was in the *goût* of the
day, and covered as good proportions as those
of the new gentry who may deride it. The men
wore no stays ; the ladies covered their shoulders ;
and the first were to the full as brave, and the
latter at least as modest, as their successors. *Our*
wedding suits were literally thus composed. The
blue satin vests and inexpressibles were well
laced and spangled wherever there was any
room for ornament. The coats were of white

cloth with blue capes. Four large paste curls, white as snow with true rice powder, and scented strong with real bergamot, adorned our heads. My third brother, Wheeler Barrington, had a coat of scarlet cloth, because he was *intended* for the army.

In truth, greater luminaries never attended a marriage festivity. Our equipage, however, by no means corresponded with our personal splendour and attractions; and I thought the contrast would be too ridiculous to any observing spectator who might know the family. I therefore desired Matthew to take a short turn from the great rock road to avoid notice as much as possible; which caution being given, we crowded into the tattered vehicle, and trotted away as swiftly as one blind and one lame horse could draw such magnificoes. There were (and are) on the circular road by which I had desired Matthew Querns to drive us, some of those nuisances called turnpikes. When we had passed the second gate, the gate-keeper, who had been placed there recently, of course demanded his toll. "Pay him, French," said I to my brother. "Faith," said French, "I changed my clothes, and I happen to have no money in my pocket." "No matter," answered I, "Wheeler, give the fellow a shilling." "I have not a rap," said Wheeler.—"I lost every halfpenny I had yesterday at the royal cockpit in Essex Street."

By a sort of instinct I put my hand into my own pocket; but instinct is not money, and *reality* quickly informed me that I was exactly in the same situation. However, " no matter," again said I; so I desired old Matthew Querns to pay the turnpike. " Is it me pay the pike?" said Matthew—" me? the devil a cross of wages I got from the master this many a day; and if I did, do you think, Master Jonah, the liquor would not be after having it out of me by this time?" and he then attempted to drive on *without* paying, as he used to do at Cüllenaghmore. The man however grappled the blind horse, and gave us a full quantum of abuse, in which his wife, who issued forth at the sound, vociferously joined. Matthew began to whack him and the horses alternately with his thong whip; my brother French struggled to get out, and beat the pike-man; but the door would not open readily, and I told him that if he beat the turnpike man properly, he'd probably bleed *a few* himself; and that a single drop of blood on his fine clothes would effectually exclude him from society. This reasoning succeeded; but the blind horse not perceiving what was the matter, supposed something worse had happened, and began to plunge and break the harness. " You d—d gilt vagabonds," said the turnpike man, " such fellows should be put into the stocks or ducked at the broad stone beyond Kilmainham. Oh! I know you well enough! (looking into the carriage window :) what are yees but stage-players that have run away from Smock Alley, and want to impose upon the country-folk!—But I'll neither let yees back or forward, by ——, till you pay me a *hog* for the pike, and two and eightpence-halfpenny for every wallop of the whip that the ould green mummer there gave me, when I only wanted my honest dues.",

I saw fighting was in vain; but courtesy can do any thing with an Irishman. "My honest friend," said I, (to soften him,) "you're right; we are poor stage-players sure enough : we have got a loan of the clothes from Mr. Ryder—may Heaven bless him! and we're hired out to play a farce for a great wedding, that's to be performed at Bray to-night. When we come back with our money we'll pay you true and fair, and drink with you till you're stiff, if you think proper."

On this civil address the pike-man looked very kind : " Why, then, by my sowl its true enough," said he, " ye can't be very rich till ye get your entrance money; but sure I won't be out of pocket for all that. Well, faith and troth, ye look like decent stage-players; and I'll tell you what,' I like good music, so I do. Give me a new song or two, and d—mme but I'll let you off, you poor craturs, till you come back agin. Come, give us a chaunt, and I'll help you to mend the harness too!"

" Thank you, sir," said I humbly. " I can't

sing," said my brother Frènch, "unless I'm drunk!" "Nor I, drunk or sober," said Wheeler. "You *must* sing for the *pike*," said I to French; and at length he set up his pipes to a favourite song, often heard among the half-mounted gentlemen in the country when they were drinking; and as I shall never forget any incident of that (to me) eventful day, and the ditty is quite characteristic both of the nation generally and the half-mounted gentlemen in particular, (with whom it was a sort of charter·song,) I shall give it.

> D—n money—its nothing but trash :
> We're happy though ever so poor !
> When we have it we cut a great dash,
> When it's gone, we ne'er think of it more.
> Then let us be wealthy or not,
> Our spirits are always the same ;
> We're free from every dull thought,
> And the " Boys of old Ireland 's " our name !

I never saw a poor fellow so pleased as the pike-man; the words hit his fancy: he shook us all round, most heartily, by the hand; and running into his lodge, brought out a pewter pot of frothing beer, which he had just got for himself, and insisted on each of us taking a drink. We of course complied. He gave Matthew a drink too, and desired him not to be so handy with his whip to other pike-men, or they'd *justice* him at Kil-

mainham. He then helped up our traces; and
Matthew meanwhile, who, having had the last
draught, had left the pot no further means of
exercising its hospitality—enlivened by the liquor
and encouraged by the good-nature of the pike-
man, and his pardon for the *walloping*—thought
the least he could do in gratitude was to give the
honest man a sample of his own music, vocal and
instrumental : so taking his hunting horn from
under his coat (he never went a yard without it)
and sounding his best " Death of Reynard," he
sang a stave which was then the charter song of
his rank, and which he roared away with all the
graces of a view holloa :

> Ho ! ro ! the sup of good drink !
> And it's ho ! ro ! the heart wou'dn't think !
> Oh ! had I a shilling lapp'd up in a clout,
> 'Tis a sup of good drink that should wheedle it out.
> And it's ho ! ro ! &c. &c.

The man of the pike was delighted. " Why,
then, by my sowl, you ould mummer," said he,
" it's a pity the likes of you should *want* a *hog*.
Arrah ! here (handing him a shilling), maybe your
whistle would run dry on the road, and you'll
pay me when you come back, won't you ? Now
all's settled, off wid yees ! Success !—success !"
And away we went, as fast as the halt and blind
could convey us.

We arrived safe and in high glee, just as the prayer-book was getting ready for the ceremony. I apologised for our apparent delay by telling the whole story in my own manner. D— W— seemed wonderfully amused. I caught her eye : it was not like Desdemona's ; but she told me afterward, that my *odd* mode of relating that adventure first made her remark me as a singularity. She was so witty on it herself, that she was the cause of wit in me. She was indefatigable at sallies—I not idle at repartee ; and we both amused ourselves and entertained the company.

I sat next to D— W— at dinner ; danced with her at the ball ; pledged her at supper ; and before two o'clock in the morning my heart had entirely deserted its master.

I will here state, by way of episode, that great difficulties and delays, both of law and equity, had postponed the matrimonial connexion of my brother, Major Barrington (he bore that rank in the old volunteers), for a considerable time. There was not money enough *afloat* to settle family incumbrances, and keep the younger children from starving. A temporary suspension was of course put to the courtship. My brother in consequence grew nearly outrageous, and swore to me that he had not slept a wink for three nights, considering what species of *death* he should put himself to. Strong, and young, (though tolerably susceptible myself,) my heart was at that time my own, and I could not help laughing at the extravagance of his passion. I tried to ridicule him out of it. " Heavens !" said I, " Jack, how can you be at a loss on *that* score? You know I am pretty sure that, by your intended suicide, I shall get a step nearer Cullenaghmore. Therefore, I will remind you that there are a hundred very *genteel* ways by which you may despatch yourself without either delay or expense.

He looked at me quite wildly. In fact he was distractedly in love. Alicia was eternally on his lips, and I really believe, if his head had been cut off like the man's in Alonzo de Cordova, it would have continued pronouncing " Alicia," till every drop of blood was clean out of it. Reasoning with a mad lover is in vain, so I still pursued ridicule. " See," said I, " that marble chimney-piece at the end of the room ; suppose, now, you run head-foremost against it,—in all human probability you'll knock your brains out in a novel and not at all a vulgar way."

I spoke in jest, but found my hearer jested not. Before I could utter another word, he bent his head forward, and with might and main rushed plump at the chimney-piece, which he came against with a crash that I had no doubt must have finished him completely. He fell back and lay without a struggle ; the blood gushed, and I stood petrified. The moment I was able I darted out of the room, and calling for aid, his servant

Neil came.   I told him that his master was dead.

" Dead !" said Neil, " By —— he is, and *double dead* too !   Ah ! then, who *kilt* the major ?"

He took him up in his arms, and laid him on a sofa.   My brother, however, soon gave Neil the " retort courteous."   He opened his eyes, groaned, and appeared any thing but *dying*.   My fright ceased; he had been only stunned, and his head cut, but his brains were safe in their case.   He had luckily come in contact with the *flat* part of the marble : had he hit the *moulding*, he would have ended his love and misfortunes together, and given me, as I had said, a step toward Cullenaghmore.   The cut on his head was not material, and in a few days he was tolerably well again.   This story, however, was not to be divulged ; it was determined that it should remain with us a great secret. . Neil, his servant, we swore on a bible not to say a word about it to any body ; but the honest man must have practised some mental reservation, as he *happened* just only to *hint* it to his sweetheart, Mary Donnellan, my mother's maid, and she in a tender moment told the postilion Keeran, for whom she had a regard.   Keeran never kept a secret in all his life ; so he told the dairy-maid, Molly Coyle, whom he preferred to Mary Donnellan.   And the dairy-maid told my father, who frequented the dairy, and delighted to see Molly Coyle a-churning.   The thing at length became quite public; and my brother, to avoid raillery, set off to his regiment at Philipstown, whither I accompanied him. He still raved about taking the first favourable *opportunity* of putting himself to death, if the courtship were much longer suspended; and spoke of gallantly throwing himself off his charger at full gallop, previously fastening his foot in the stirrup. The being dragged head downwards over a few heaps of paving stones would certainly have answered his deadly purpose well enough; but I dissuaded him without much difficulty from that species of self-murder, by assuring him that every body, in such a case, would attribute his death to *bad horsemanship*, which would remain, on the records of the regiment, an eternal disgrace to his professional character. Many other projects he thought of; but I must here make one remark, which perhaps may be a good one in general— namely, that every one of those projects *happened* to originate *after dinner*—a period when Irishmen's chivalric fancies are at their most enthusiastic and visionary height.

At length, a happy letter reached the major, signifying that all parties had agreed, and that his Alicia, heart and hand, was to be given up to him for life, as his own private and exclusive property —"to have and to hold, for better for worse," &c. &c. This announcement rendered him almost as wild as his despair had done previously. When he received the letter, he leaped down a flight of

stairs at one spring, and in five minutes ordered
his charger to be saddled for himself; his hunter,
"Mad Tom," for me; and his chestnut, "Rainbow," for Neil. In ten minutes we were all
mounted and in full gallop toward Dublin, which
he had determined to reach that night after one
short stoppage at Kildare, where we arrived
(without slackening rein) in as short a time as if
we had rode a race. The horses were fed well,
and drenched with hot ale and brandy; but as
none of them were in love, I perceived that
they would willingly have deferred the residue of
the journey till the ensuing morning. Indeed,
my brother's steed conceiving that *charges* of
such rapidity and length were not at all military,
unless in *running away*, determined practically
to convince his master that such was his notion.
We passed over the famous race-ground of the Curragh in good style; but, as my brother had not
given his horse time to lie down gently and rest
himself in the ordinary way, the animal had no
choice but to perform the feat of lying down
whilst in full gallop—which he did very expertly
just at the Curragh stand-house. The only mischief occurring herefrom was, that the drowsy
charger stripped the skin, like rags, completely
off both his knees, scalped the top of his head,
got a hurt in the back sinews, and (no doubt without intending it) broke both my brother's collar-
bones. When we came up (who were a few hundred yards behind him), both man and beast were

lying very quietly, as if asleep;—my brother
about five or six yards before the horse, who had
cleverly thrown his rider far beyond the chance
of being tumbled over by himself. The result
was, as usual on similar occasions, that the horse
was led limping and looking foolish to the first
stable, and committed to all the farriers and
grooms in the neighbourhood. My brother was
carried flat on a door to the nearest ale-house;
and doctors being sent for, *three* (with bags of instruments) arrived from different places before
night, and, after a good deal of searching and fumbling about his person, one of them discovered
that both collar-bones were smashed, as aforesaid,
and that if either of the broken bones or splinters
thereof turned *inward* by his stirring, it might run
through the lobes of his lungs, and very suddenly
end all hopes of ever completing his journey: his
nose had likewise taken a different turn from that
it had presented when he set out :—and the palms
of his hands fully proved that they could do without any skin, and with a very moderate quantity of
flesh.

However, the bones were well arranged, a pillow strapped under each arm, and another at his
shoulder-blades. All necessary comforts were procured, as well as furniture from Mr. Hamilton,
whose house was near. I did not hear a word
that night about Alicia; but in due time the
major began to recover once more, and resumed

his love, which had *pro tempore* been literally knocked out of him. It was announced by the doctor that it would be a long time before he could use his hands or arms, and that removal or exercise might produce a new fracture, and send a splinter or bone through any part of his interior that might be most handy.

Though I thought the blood he had lost, and the tortures the doctor put him to, had rendered his mind a good deal tamer than it was at Maryborough, he still talked much of Alicia, and proposed that I should write to her, on his part, an account of his misfortunes; and the doctor in attendance allowing him the slight exertion of signing his name and address in his own handwriting, I undertook to execute my task to the utmost of my skill, and certainly performed it with great success. I commenced with due warmth, and stated that the " accident he had met with only retarded the happiness he should have in making her his wife, which he had so long burned for, but which circumstances till then had prevented," &c. &c. (The words I recollect pretty well, because they afterward afforded me infinite amusement.) The letter was sealed with the family arms and crest.

" Now, Jonah," said my brother, " before I marry I have a matter of some importance to arrange, lest it should come to the ears of my Alicia, which would be my ruin; and I must get you to see it settled for me at Philipstown, so as to prevent any thing exploding." He went on to give me the particulars of a certain *liaison* he had formed with a young woman there, an exciseman's daughter, which he was now, as may be supposed, desirous of breaking; and (though protesting that interference in such matters was not at all to my taste) I consented to write, at his dictation, a sort of compromise to the party, which he having signed, both epistles were directed at the same time, and committed to the post-office of Kilcullen bridge.

The amorous and fractured invalid was now rapidly advancing to a state of convalescence. His nose had been renovated with but an inconsiderable partiality for the left cheek; his collar-bones had approximated to a state of adhesion; and he began impatiently to count the days and nights that would metamorphose his Alicia from a spinster to a matron.

The extravagance of his flaming love amused me extremely: his aerial castles were built, altered, and demolished with all the skill and rapidity of modern architecture; while years of exquisite and unalloyed felicity arose before his fancy, of which they took an immovable grasp.

We were busily engaged one morning in planning and arranging his intended establishment, on returning to the sports and freaks of a country gentleman (with the addition of a terrestrial angel to do the honours), when, on a sudden, we heard rather a rough noise at the entrance of the little chamber wherein the invalid was still reclining upon a feather-bed, with a pillow under each arm to keep the bones in due position.   Our old fat landlady, who was extremely partial to the cornet,* burst in with her back toward us, endeavouring to prevent the entrance of a stranger, who, however, without the least ceremony, giving her a hearty curse, dashed into the centre of the room in a state of bloated rage scarcely conceivable—which was more extraordinary as the individual appeared to be no other than Captain Tennyson Edwards, of the 30th regiment, third brother of the beloved Alicia.   Of course we both rose to welcome him most heartily : this however he gave us no opportunity of doing ; but laying down a small mahogany case, which he carried in his hand, and putting his arms akimbo, he loudly exclaimed without any exordium, " Why, then, Cornet Jack Barrington, are you not the greatest scoundrel that ever disgraced civilised society ?"

This quere of course was not answered in the affirmative by either of us ; and a scene of astonishment on the one side and increasing passion on the other, baffled all common-place description : I must therefore refer it to the imagination of my readers.   The retort courteous was over and over

* My brother's *actual* rank in *the army.*

reiterated on both sides without the slightest attempt at any *éclaircissement*.

At length the captain opened his mahogany case, and exhibited therein a pair of what he called his " barking irons," bright and glittering as if both able and willing to commit most expertly any murder or murders they might be employed in.

" You scoundrel !" vociferated the captain to the cornet, " only that your bones were smashed by your horse, I would not leave a whole one this day in your body. But I suppose your brother here will have no objection to exchange shots *for* you, and not keep me waiting till you are well enough to be *stiffened !* Have you any objection (turning to me) ' to take a *crack ?* ' "

" A very considerable objection," answered I ; " first, because I never fight without knowing *why ;* and secondly, because my brother is not in the habit of fighting by proxy."

" Not know why ?" roared the captain. " There ! read that ! Oh ! I wish you were hale and whole, cornet, that I might have the pleasure of a *crack* with *you !*"

I lost no time in reading the letter ; and at once perceived that my unlucky relative had, in the flurry of his love, misdirected each of the two epistles just now spoken of, and consequently informed " the divine Alicia" that he could hold no further intercourse with her, &c.

A fit of convulsive laughter involuntarily seized me, which nothing could restrain; and the captain meanwhile, nearly bursting with rage, reinvited me to be shot at. My brother stood all the time like a ghost, in more pain, and almost in as great a passion as our visitor. He was unable to articulate; and the pillows fixed under each arm rendered him one of the most grotesque figures that a painter could fancy.

When I recovered the power of speaking (which was not speedily), I desired Tennyson to follow me to another room: he took up his pistol-case, and expecting I was about to indulge him with a *crack* or two, seemed somewhat easier in mind and temper. I at once explained to him the curious mistake, and without the least hesitation the captain burst into a much stronger paroxysm of laughter than I had just escaped from. Never did any officer in the king's service enjoy a victory more than Captain Edwards did this strange blunder. It was quite to his taste, and on our proposing to make the invalid as happy as exhaustion and fractures would admit of, a new scene, equally unexpected, but of more serious consequences, turned up.

A ruddy, active and handsome country girl came to the door, and sprang with rapidity from a pillion on which she had been riding behind a goodlooking rustic lad. Our landlady greeted her new customer with her usual urbanity. " You're wel-

come to these parts, miss," said Mrs. Mahony:
" you stop to-night—to be sure you do :—what do
you choose, miss?—Clean out the settle-bed parlour :—the chickens and rashers, miss, are capital,
so they are.—Gassoon, do run and howld the
lady's beast; go, avourneen, carry him in and
wipe him well—do you hear? and throw a wisp of
hay before the poor brute. You rode hard, miss,
so you did !"

" Oh! where's the cornet?" cried the impatient
maiden, totally disregarding Mrs. Mahony: for it
was Jenny ——— herself, who had come speedily
from Philipstown to forestall the happy moments
which my bewildered brother had, in his letter to
his Alicia, so delightfully anticipated. Nothing
could restrain her impatience; she burst into the
little parlour full on the astounded invalid, who
was still standing bolt upright, like a statue, in the
very position wherein we had left him. His loving Jenny, however, unconscious that his collar-
bones had been disunited, rushed into his arms
with furious affection. " Oh! my dearest Jack!"
cried she, " we *never* part *no* more! no, never—
never !" and tight, indeed, was the embrace wherewith the happy Jenny now encircled the astonished cornet; but, alas! down came one of the
pillows! the arm, of course, closed; and one half
of the left collar-bone being as ignorant as its
owner of the cause of so obstreperous an embrace,
and, wishing as it were to see what matter was

going forward in the world, instantly divorced itself from the other half, and thrusting its ivory end through the flesh, skin, and integuments (which had obstructed its egress), quickly appeared peeping through the lover's shirt.

The unfortunate inamorato could stand these accumulated shocks no longer, and sank upon the feather-bed in a state of equal astonishment and exhaustion, groaning pitiously.

Here I must again apply to the imagination of my reader for a true picture of the succeeding scene. Fielding alone could render a detail palatable; the surgeons were once more sent for to reset the collar: an energetic kiss, which his Jenny had imprinted on the cornet's nose, again somewhat disturbed its new position, and conferred a pain so acute, as to excite exclamations, by no means gentle in their nature, from the unresisting sufferer.

Suffice it to say, Jenny was with much difficulty at length forced away from her Jack, if not in a dead *faint*, at least in something extremely *like* one. An *éclaircissement* took place so soon as she came round; and the *compromise*, before hinted at, was ultimately effected.

Edwards asked a hundred pardons of my poor brother, who, worn out, and in extreme pain, declared he would as soon die as live. In fine, it was nearly a month more ere the cornet could travel to Dublin, and another before he was well

enough to throw himself at the feet of his dul-
cinea : which ceremony was in due season succeeded by the wedding* I have already given

* Irish marriages ran, some few years ago, an awkward risk
of being nullified *en masse*, by the decision of two English
judges. In 1826, I met, at Boulogne-sur-Mer, a young Hibernian nobleman, the eldest son of an Irish peer, who had arrived
there in great haste from Paris, and expressed considerable
though somewhat ludicrous trepidation on account of a rumour
that had reached him of his being *illegitimatised.* In fact, the
same dread seized upon almost all the Irish of any family there.

" I have no time to lose," said Lord ——, " for the packet
is just setting off, and I must go and inquire into these matters.
By Heaven," added he, " I won't leave one of the judges alive,
if they take my property and title ! I am fit for *nothing else,*
you *know* I am not; and I may as well be hanged as beggared !"

Scarce had his lordship, from whom I could obtain no explanation, departed, when another scion of Irish nobility, the
Honourable John Leeson, son to the late Earl of Miltown, joined
me on the pier. " Barrington, have you seen to-day's papers ?"
asked he.

" No," I answered.

" Where was your father married ?"

" In my grandfather's house," replied I, with some surprise.

" Then, by Jove," exclaimed Leeson, " you are an *illegitimate,* and so am I !—My father was married at home, at eight
o'clock in the evening, and that's *fatal.* A general outcry has
taken place among all the Irish at the reading-room."

He then proceeded to inform me of the real cause of the consternation—and it was no trivial one. Two very able and
honest English judges (Bayley and Park), on trying a woman for *bigamy,* had decided that, according to the English
law, a marriage in a private house, without special licence or in
canonical hours, was *void ;* and, of course, the woman was ac-

my account óf, and which left me much more un-
accountably smitten than ,my more fiery brother.

Captain Tennyson Edwards subsequently ran
away with the kind-hearted Jenny, and in three
or four years after, married one of the prettiest of
my six sisters. He was one of the drollest fellows
in the world on some occasions, and had once
nearly ended his days similarly (though more vul-
garly) to the traditional catastrophe of the Duke
of Clarence in the Tower. He persuaded a very
comely dairy-maid, at Old Court, that if she
would not abscond with him, he should end his
life in despair; and she would, in the eye of
Heaven, be guilty of his *murder:* and to convince her of his fixed determination to commit suicide for love of her, he put his head into a very

---

quitted, having been united to her first husband in Ireland
without those requisites. Had that decision stood, it would
certainly have rendered ninety-nine out of a hundred of the
Irish Protestants, men, women, and children—nobility, clergy,
and gentry—absolutely illegitimate ; it was a very droll mistake of the learned judges, but was on the merciful side of
the question before them ; was soon amended, and no mischief
whatsoever resulted from it :—though it was said that a great
number of husbands and wives were extremely *disappointed* at
the judges altering their decision. I seldom saw any couple
married in church in Ireland ; and in former times the ceremony
was generally performed between dinner and supper, when people are supposed to be vastly more in love with each other than
in the middle of the day.

high churn of butter-milk, which was standing in the dairy—when, the floor being slippery, his feet gave way, and he pounced down, head-fore-most and feet upward, clean into the churn; and had not the gardener been at hand on the instant, he would have expired by the most novel mode of extermination on record.

THE LAST OF THE GERALDINES.

Principles of domestic government discussed—How to rule a husband—Elizabeth Fitzgerald, of Moret Castle — Brings her son to see his father hanged by the Cahills—Enjoins him to revenge the outrage—Peculiar methods of impressing the injunction on the boy's memory—He grows to manhood—Mysterious disappearance of four of the Cahills—Mr. Jemmy Corcoran—Way of identifying a skeleton—Father Doran, and his *spiritual* theory — Squire Stephen Fitzgerald the son, and Squire Stephen Fitzgerald the grandson, of Elizabeth—Education, marriage, and personal description of the latter—The several members of his family described—Tom, the heir-apparent—A short life and a merry one—Jack, his successor—Moret Castle in its modern state—Miss Dolly Fitzgerald, and her sister Fanny—their respective merits—Matrimonial speculations—Curious family discussion as to the attractions of *hung* meat, &c.

In the early part of my life, the system of domestic government and family organization was totally different from that at present in vogue. The patriarchal authority was then frequently

exercised with a rigour which, in days of degene-
rate relaxation, has been converted into a fruitful
subject for even dramatic ridicule. In Ireland,
the "rule of the patriarchs" has become nearly
extinguished. New lights have shone upon the
rising generation; the "rights of women" have
become a statute law of society; and the old,
wholesome word *obedience* (by which all wives and
children were formerly influenced) has been reversed, by prefacing it with the monosyllable *dis*.

"Every body is acquainted," said an intimate
friend of mine to his wife, in my presence, "with
the ruinous state of obstinacy and contradiction
raging in modern times among the subordinate
members of families throughout the United Kingdom; as if the word *united* were applied to the empire only to satirise the *dis*united habits, manners,
politics, religion, and morality of its population.
There are," continued he, "certain functions
that must be exercised every day (two or three
times a day *if possible*) by persons of all descrip-
tions, who do not wish to leave this world within a
week at the very latest; but, unless on the absolute necessity of mastication for purposes of self-
support, I am not aware of any other subject
respecting which unanimity of opinion is even
affected among the individuals of any family
throughout the country."

The wife nodded assent, but spake not:—first,
because she hated all controversy; and second,

because though, on the subject of domestic supre-
macy, she was always sure of getting the worst of
the argument, she contented herself with having,
beyond doubt, the best of the practice.*

My friend's observations were, I think, just.   In
my time the change has been excessive; and to
enable my readers to form a better judgment of the
matter, I will lay before them a few authentic
anecdotes of rather antique dates.

In volume one I mentioned the illustrious exploits of my great-aunt, Elizabeth Fitzgerald, of
Moret Castle, and the heroic firmness wherewith
she bore the afflicting view of my great-uncle
Stephen, her husband, " dancing upon nothing "
(as the Irish phrase it) at the castle-gate, immediately under the battlements ; and though it is
possible there may exist some modern ladies who
might have sufficient self-possession to look on a

---

* Mrs. Mary Morton, of Ballyroan, a very worthy domestic
woman, told me, many years since, that she had but one way of
ruling her husband, which, as it is rather a novel way, and
may be of some use to my fair readers, I will mention in her
own words.

" You know," said Mrs. Morton, " that Tom is most horribly
nice in his eating, and *fancies* that both abundant and good
food is *essential* to his health.   Now, when he has been out of
temper with me, he is sure of having a very *bad* dinner ; if he
grumbles, I tell him that whenever he puts me into a *twitter*
by his *tantrums,* I always *forget* to give the cook proper
directions. This is sure," added she, " of keeping him in good
humour for a week at least !"

similar object without evincing those signs of in-
consolability natural to be expected on such an
occasion, yet, I will venture to say, few are to
be found who, like my aunt Elizabeth, would risk
their lives and property rather than accept of a
second husband. Nor do I believe that, since the
patriarchal government has been revolutionised by
the unnatural rebellion of wives and children,
there has existed one lady—young, old, or middle-
aged, in the three kingdoms, who could be persuaded to imitate the virtuous gentoos, and voluntarily undergo conflagration with her departed
lord and master.

My great-uncle had a son born unto him by
his magnanimous spouse, who was very young,
and in the castle at the time his father was *corded*
(*Hibernice*). Elizabeth led him to the castle top,
and showing him his dangling parent, cried, " See
there! you were born a Geraldine; the blood of
that noble race is in you, my boy! See—see the
sufferings of your own father! Never did a *true*
Geraldine forgive an enemy! I perceive your
little face gets flushed :—you tremble ; ay, ay, 'tis
for *revenge!* Shall a Cahill live ?"

" No, mother, no ! when I'm able, I'll kill them
all! I'll kill all the Cahills myself !" cried the lad,
worked on by the fury of his respectable mother.

" That's my dear boy !" said Elizabeth, kissing
him fervently. " Shall *one* live ?"

" No, mother, not one," replied the youngster.

" Man, woman, or child?" pursued the he-
roine.

" Neither man, woman, nor child," echoed her
precocious son.

" You are a Geraldine," repeated Elizabeth.
" Call the priest," added she, turning to a warder.

" He made a little too free, my lady mistress,"
said the warder, " and is not very fitting for duty,
saving your presence;—but he'll soon sleep it
off."

" Bring him up, nevertheless," cried Elizabeth :
—" I command you to bring up his reverence."

The priest was accordingly *produced* by Keeran
Karry. " Father," said the lady, " where's your
manual?"

" Where should it be," *answered* the priest
(rather sobered), " but where it always is, lady ?"
pulling, as he spake, a book out of a pocket in the
waistband of his breeches, where (diminished
and under the name of a *fob*) more modern clergy-
men carry their watches.*

---

* The priests then, to render mass *handy*, invariably kept
their manual in their breeches with a piece of strong green ribbon (having beads at the end of it) to lug it out by, resembling
the chain of a modern buckish parson's timepiece. They also
gave another very extraordinary reason for keeping their manual in their smallclothes—namely, that no *devil* would pre-

" Now, your reverence," said Elizabeth, "we'll *swear* the young squire to revenge my poor Stephen, his father, on the Cahills, root and branch, so soon as he comes to manhood.   Swear him !— swear him *thrice!*" exclaimed she.

The boy was duly sworn, and the manual reposited in the priest's smallclothes.

" Now, take the boy down and duck him, head over heels, in the horse-pond!" cried his mother.*

Young Fitzgerald roared lustily, but was nevertheless well soused, to make him remember his oath the better.   This oath he repeated upon the same spot, while his mother lived, on every anniversary of his father's murder ; and it was said by the old tenants, that " young Stephen" (though flourishing in more civilised times) religiously kept the vow as far as he could ;- and that, so soon as he came into possession of Moret, four of the ablest of the Cahills (by way of a beginning) were *missed* from the neighbourhood of Timahoe in one night—nobody ever discovering what had become

sume to come near them when he was sure he should have the mass to encounter before he could get at their carcases.

* When it was sought to make a child remember any thing long and circumstantially, it was the custom in Ireland either to *whip* him three or four times, *duck* him in cold water, or put him into a bag, with his face only out, and hang it up against a wall for a whole day.   Such an extraordinary and undeserved punishment made an impression on the fresh tablet of the youngster's mind never to be erased.

of them; indeed, the fewest words were considered far the safest.

The skeletons of four lusty fellows, however,
were afterwards found in clearing out a pit in the
Donane colliery, and many persons said they had
belonged to the four Cahills from Timahoe; but, as
the colliers very sapiently observed, there being
no particular marks whereby to distinguish the
bones of a Cahill from those of any other " boy,"
no one could properly identify them.

A bystander, who had been inspecting the relics, protested, on hearing this remark made, that
he could swear to *one* of the skulls at least (which
appeared to have been fractured and trepanned);
and he gave a very good 'reason for this assertion
—namely, that it was himself who had " cracked
the skull of Ned Cahill, at the fair of Dysart, with
a *walloper*, and he knew the said skull ever after.
It was between jest and earnest," continued Jemmy Corcoran, "that I broke his head—all
about a game-cock, and be d—d to it! and by
the same token, I stood by in great grief at Maryborough, while Doctor Stapleton was twisting a
round piece out of Ned Cahill's skull, and laying a
*two-and-eight-penny-halfpenny** (beaten quite thin
on the smith's forge) over the hole, to cover his
brains *any way.* The devil a brain in his sconce

* An Irish silver *half-crown* piece; the difference of English
and Irish currency.

but I could see plainly ; and the said *two-and-eight-penny-halfpenny* stayed fast under his *wig* for many a year, till Ned·pulled it off (bad luck to it !) to pay for drink with myself at Timahoe! They said he was ever after a little cracked when in his liquor : and I'm right sorry for having act or part in that same fracture, for Ned was a good boy, so he was, and nobody would strike him a stroke on the head at any rate after the *two-and-eight penny-halfpenny* was *pledged* off his skull."

Though Mr. Jemmy Corcoran was so confident as to the skull he had fractured, his testimony was not sufficient legally to identify a Cahill, and the four sets of bones being quietly buried at Clapook, plenty of masses, &c. were said for an entire year by Father Cahill, of Stradbally, to get their souls clean out of purgatory ; that is, if they were in it, which there was not a *clergy* in the place would *take on* to say he was " sartain sure of."*

* I recollect (at an interval of more than fifty years) Father Doran, of Culmaghbeg, an excellent man, full of humour, and well-informed, putting the *soul* in the most comprehensible state of personification possible : he said, the *women* could not understand what the soul was by the old explanations.

" I tell you all, my flock," said Father Doran, " there's not a man, woman, or child among you that has not his soul this present minute shut up in his body, waiting for the last judgment, according to his faith and actions. I tell you fairly, that if flesh could be seen through, like a glass window, you might see every one's soul at the inside of his body peeping out through the ribs, like the prisoners at the jail of Maryborough

This Stephen Fitzgerald,—who had killed the Cahills, sure enough, as became the true son and heir of the aforesaid Stephen, who was·hanged,— lived, as report went, plentifully and regularly at Moret.   No better gentleman existed, the old people said, in the quiet way, after once he had put the four Cahills into the coal-pit, as he promised his worthy mother Elizabeth, " the likes of whom Moret never saw before nor since, nor ever will while time is time, and longer too !"

Stephen had one son only, who is the principal subject of my present observations ; and as he and his family (two lovely boys and two splendid girls) were not exactly the same sort of people commonly seen now-a-days, it may not be uninteresting to give my readers a picture of them.

Stephen, the son of Elizabeth, had been persuaded by Mr. John Lodge, an attorney of Bull Alley, in the city of Dublin, (who married a maid-servant of my grandfather's at Cullenagh,) that the two-mile race-course of the Great Heath in Queen's County, which King George pretended was his property because it had been formerly taken from a papist Geraldine, now reverted to my great-uncle's family, in consequence of their being Protestants ; and Mr. Lodge added, that if Squire

through their iron bars : and the moment the breath is out of a man or woman, the soul escapes and makes off to be dealt with as it deserves, and that's the truth ;—so say your beads and remember your clergy !"

Stephen would make his son a counsellor, no doubt he would more aptly trace pedigrees, rights, titles, and attainders, and, in fine, get possession of several miles of the Great Heath, or of the race-course at any rate.

The advice was adopted, and Stephen the son was sent to the Temple in London, to study law; and while there, was poisoned at a cook's shop by the cook's daughter because he would not marry her. This poisoning (though it was not fatal) he always said, *stopped his growth* like witchcraft.

The father died in his bed; and my uncle, Stephen the counsellor, became a double relative from marrying Catherine Byrne, daughter of Sir John Byrne, Bart., of Timahoe Castle, and sister to my grandmother, heretofore mentioned. After he had studied Bracton, Fleta, Littleton, the Year Books, the three Cokes, and in short the *marrow* of the English law, he used to say that he got on very well with the *first* book, not so well with the *second,* worse with the *third;* and at length found that the more he read, the more he was puzzled, knowing less when he left off than when he began—as all the law books contradicted each other like the lawyers themselves: thus, after two years' hard work, he gave up all further attempts to expound, what he swore *fore God* was utterly inexplicable. He also relinquished his father's squabble with King George as to the race-course on the Great Heath; and, concentrating his search after knowledge upon one learned book, the " Justice of Quorum's pocket companion," commenced *magistrate*.   He was likewise a horse-racer, country gourmand, tippler, and farmer.   His wife, my aunt, was as ordinary a gentlewoman " as may be seen of a summer's day ;" but then, she was worthy in proportion.

As to my uncle's figure, nothing resembling it having ever been seen, at least by me, I cannot pretend to give any idea of it, save by an especial description. . He was short, (which he said was the effect of the poison,) and as broad as long—appearing to grow the wrong way.   He observed, touching this subject, that where there are *materials* for growth, if any thing does not advance in height, it spreads out like a *fir-tree*,* when the top shoot is broken off and it fills wide at the bottom.   He was not actually fat, nor particularly bony : I think his bulk consisted of solid, substantial flesh.' His face was neither extravagantly ugly, nor disproportioned to his body ; but a double, or rather treble chin descended in layers very nearly to the pit of his stomach, whence his

* This idea was a standing joke with him for some time, till old Kit Julian, the retired exciseman, (heretofore mentioned,) made a hit at my uncle, which put his comparison to an end. " By my troth, then, Counsellor," said Kit, " if you *are* like a fir, it is not a ' *spruce* fir ' any how." This sarcasm cut my uncle in the *raw ;* and it was said that he had an additional shaving day, and clean cravat every week afterward.

paunch abruptly stretched out, as if placed by
Nature as a shelf for the chin to rest upon. His
limbs each gained in thickness what it wanted in
length; so that it would seem impossible for him
to be *thrown down,* or if he were, he would roll
about like a ball. His hands (as if Nature exhibited the contrast for amusement's sake) were
thin, white, and lady-like; so much so, indeed,
that did he fall, they could not help him up again.
" Each particular hair" was almost of the thickness of a goose-quill; his locks were *queued* behind, and combed about once or twice a *month.*
His nostrils were always crammed with snuff,
(now and then discharged, as from a mortar, by
sneezing,) and his *chins* were so well dusted and
caked with that material, that the whole visage
at times appeared as if it were a magazine thereof.

My uncle's dress exactly matched his style of
person : he always wore a *snuff*-coloured coat and
breeches, with a scarlet waistcoat that had been
once bound with lace (the strings whereof remained, like ruins in a landscape); blue worsted stockings, and immense silver shoe and knee-buckles.
His hat was very large, with a blunt cock in front.
It had also once been fully laced; but, no *button*
had been seen on it since the year succeeding his
nuptials.

The fruits of my uncle's marriage were, as I
have said, two boys and two girls. The eldest of
these Geraldines, Tom, took to what ignorant doctors

call *poison*—but country gentlemen, *potation*. My uncle declared, he knew from his own experience that a " little learning was a dangerous thing;" and therefore thought it better that Tom should have *none at all!* Tom therefore studied nothing but " Carolan's receipt for drinking!" The art of writing his own name came pretty readily; but his penmanship went no further. At twenty-six he quarrelled with a vicious horse, which was easily offended. The animal, on his master's striking him with a whip, returned the blow with his hoof (a horse's *fist*); and on Tom being taken to his chamber and examined, it was found that he had left the greater part of his brains in the stable.

Jack, his brother, was now heir-apparent. His figure was nearly as grotesque, but only half the size of his father's; his eyes were of the most *cautious* description, one closely watching his nose, the other glancing quite *outward,* to see that no enemy approached. He loved liquor as well as Tom, but could not get down so much of it. Nevertheless, after a pretty long life, he was *concluded* by rather extravagant and too frequent doses of port and potsheen.

I have already given some account of the castle of Moret as it formerly appeared. When I last saw it, some dozen of years back, it presented nothing remarkable save its ivy covering. The dwelling-house, which as it stood in my uncle's time would have been worth detailing (had not every country gentleman's mansion been of a similar genus), had declined into an ordinary residence.   In Squire Stephen's day, it was low, long, dilapidated, dirty, old, and ugly—and had defied paint, plaster and whitewash for at least the better half of a century.   The barn, court, dunghill, pigeon-house, horse-pond, piggery, and slaughter-house, formed, as usual, the chief prospects from the parlour-windows; and on hot days the effluvia was so exquisite (they accounted it very *wholesome*) that one might clearly distinguish each several perfume.

My uncle never could contrive to stick on horseback, and therefore considered riding as a dangerous exercise for *any* gentleman.   He used to say (it was indeed one of his standing jokes) that jockeys and vulgar persons, being themselves *beasts*, might stick by virtue of mutual attraction upon their own species; but that ladies and gentlemen were, as a matter of course, always subject to tumble off.   He-bred and kept, notwithstanding, four or five race-horses, which he got regularly trained; and at every running upon the heath or curragh, he entered such of them as were qualified by weight, &c.: yet, singularly enough, though the animals were well bred and well trained, not one, during the whole of the five-and-twenty years that he kept them, ever won a plate, prize, or race of any description: for all that, he would never sell either for *any* price; and

when they got too old to run any more, they were
turned out to end their days unmolested in a
marsh and the straw-yard. It was said by those
competent to judge that some of these animals
were excellent; but that Squire Fitzgerald's old
groom used to give *trials*, and to physic the horses;
and that (through his people) they were *bought off*
when there was a probability of their winning.
However, my uncle, so that none of them were
distanced, was just as well pleased, exhibiting not
the least uneasiness at their failure. Indeed, he
never attended any of the races personally, or
betted a shilling upon the event of one—circumstances which remind me of a certain judge, who
was always sufficiently *gratified* by a simple *con-
viction* and by passing *sentence* on a culprit, eventually saving more lives by pardon than any two
of his colleagues.

I was very young when taken to my uncle's, for
a stay of some months, by my grandmother; but
at an age when strong impressions are sometimes
made upon the memory. I was a great favourite,
and indulged in every thing, even by my uncle;
and very frequently, afterward, while my aunt
lived at Moret in her widowhood, I visited there,
every visit reminding me of former times, and re-
calling persons and things that might otherwise
have been lost to my juvenile recollection. This
latter was the period when, having nobody of my
own age in the house to chatter to, I took delight

in hearing the old people about Moret tell their long traditionary stories, which, as I observed in my first sketch (Vol. i.) descended from generation to generation with hereditary exactness; and, to the present day, I retain a fondness for hearing old occurrences detailed.

My eldest female cousin, Miss Dolly Fitzgerald, was at least twelve years older than I when I was first taken to Moret by my grandmother; the second, Miss Fanny, ten. Never, sure, did two sisters present such a contrast. Dolly was as like her father as rather more height and an uncommonly fair skin would permit; her tongue was too large for the mouth, and consequently thickened her pronunciation; her hair was yellow; her feet were like brackets, and her hands resembled milk-white shoulders of mutton. Her features were good; but her nostrils and upper lip displayed considerable love of the favourite *comforter* of her father. She was very good-natured, but ignorance personified.

Her sister was as thin as the handle of a sweeping-brush, and had dark eyes twinkling like stars on a vapoury evening; with yellow skin, black hair, a mouth literally stretching across the face, (like a foss to protect her chin,) very red lips, and much more vivacity than comprehension. There were few sound teeth in the whole family, and none that a dentist would think worth the expense of dressing.

For these two amiable young ladies it was the principal object of my aunt to procure husbands, if possible, in the neighbourhood. But the squires were shy of matching into the family of so great an oddity as my uncle. They preferred getting wives among people who went on the jog-trot of the world like themselves.

On this point my uncle and aunt entirely differed; and during the discussions as to their differences, time ran on, nothing was done for the ladies, and Miss Dolly was in her six-and-twentieth year before she was fully emancipated from the discipline of the nursery and suffered to dine at papa's table. When that important period arrived, it was considered as a great epocha at Moret Castle; all the neighbours were invited, and Dolly's majority was formally announced. She was then given to understand she might thereafter dine at the great table, speak to any gentleman she pleased, and, in short, have full liberty to act entirely as she thought proper, *provided* she always *previously* consulted her father's will, and obeyed it without "questions asked." She was likewise enjoined to take especial care not to forget her pastry.*

On these free and happy terms, Dolly was to

---

* The Irish ladies in the country at that period were always taught the art of pie and dumpling making, as a necessary accomplishment; and a husband who liked a good table always preferred a *housekeeper* to a *gadder*. *Tempora mutantur!*

have the chariot for a day, and to set the world
on fire. The old carriage was accordingly cleared
for action from the dust accumulated upon it ; the
horses' tails were trimmed ; and the young lady
was to go to the church of Portarlington the ensuing Sunday — "Where," said my uncle to his
spouse, "fore gad, Kate, our Dolly will catch some
young fellow after the service is over, either in
the aisle or the churchyard. She'll have some proposals ; but, fore gad, it's not *every body* I'd give
her to."

"Don't be too sure, Stephen," rejoined my aunt.
"You keep your daughters as if they were haunches
of venison. It's not every body who has a taste
for meat that has been hung a fortnight in the
larder to give it a flavor. The men, I tell you,
like *fresh and fresh*, Stephen ; and be assured you
have kept Dolly too long to suit every man's
palate. I have always been telling you so, but
you are perpetually saying you'll be the *head* of
your *own family ;* so now you'll see the end of it !"

"Why, Kate, you were a good while in the
larder yourself at Timahoe before you got a husband," replied my uncle.

"I may thank the smallpox for that, Ste-
phen," retorted my aunt : "only for that enemy
I should never have been mistress of Moret Castle,
Counsellor Stephen being governor of it !"

"Well, you'll see that I'm right," said my
uncle. "I tell you, men who look out for wives

like a seasoned, obedient woman at the head of their families, and not your tittering, giddy young creatures, that have not had time to settle their brains or mature their understandings. No girl should be away from the eye of her natural guardian till she arrives at the full extent of her twenty-sixth year, like Dolly. You'll see now she'll do some *mischief* at the church or churchyard of Portarlington!"

" "Stephen," said my aunt, (who, by the bye, had her nose nearly stopped by the smallpox, which made her somewhat snuffle, and gave a peculiar *emphasis* to her vowels,) 'tis too late! Dolly knows nothing of the world. It would take a full year at the church and balls at Portarlington, the races of the Great Heath and green of Maryborough, the hurlings at the fort of Dunrally, and a month or two on a visit to our nephew, Jack Barrington, at Blandsfort, before she would learn enough to be able to converse with mankind on any subject—except darning your stockings, or turning off a kitchen-maid."

- My uncle started as much as his form would admit; cocked his eyebrows, and stared with all his might. " Fore gad, Kate, I believe you are out of your wits! Did you say Jack Barrington's of Blandsfort? Jack Barrington's! Why, you know very well, Kate, as every body knows, that there's nothing going on at that house but hunting and feasting; dancing all night, and rattling about all day, like mad people; and coshering with raking pots of tea, hot cakes, syllabubs, pipers, and the devil knows what! No, no. If Dolly were to get one month among her cousins at Blandsfort, I should never see a day's comfort after; topsy-turvy would go Moret! I'd never be master of my own house half an hour after Dolly had received a course of instruction at Jack Barrington's. I don't wish her to know too much of the world. No, no. 'Fore. Gad, Kate, Dolly never puts her foot, while she is a spinster, into Jack Barrington's house at Blandsfort."

Folks generally become mulish as their years advance, and my uncle enjoyed that quality in its greatest perfection.—The Misses Dolly and Fanny Fitzgerald were commanded, under the pain of displeasure, by their patri-archal father, Stephen, to abjure and give up all thoughts of the festivities of Blandsfort.

" 'Fore Gad, Kate!" said my uncle to their more conceding mother—" 'Fore Gad, Kate, you had better send the girls a visiting to the *antipodes* than be turning them upside down at Blandsfort. No rational man would have any thing to do with them afterwards.—There it is, only pull-haul and tear, and the devil take the hindmost!— eh?"

" And for Heaven's sake, Stephen," replied my aunt, (who was no cosmographer,) " what *family* are these *antipodes* whom you would send our daughters to visit in preference to their nearest relations ?—I never heard of them : they must be upstarts, Stephen. I thought I knew every family in the county."

" 'Fore Gad, Kate !" rejoined my uncle, laughing heartily, " your father, old Sir John, ought to be tied to the cart's tail for so neglecting your education. Why, Kate, the antipodes are at this moment standing on their heads immediately under you—upside down, just as you see a fly on the ceiling, without the danger of falling down from it."

" And for Heaven's sake, Stephen," said my puzzled aunt, " how do the ladies keep down their petticoats in that position ?"

" Ask Sir Isaac Newton that," said my uncle (who was not prepared for that interrogation). " But let me hear no more of the topsy-turvy of their cousins at Blandsfort. I'll send my daughters to church at Portarlington, Kate, where they cannot fail of being seen and much noticed."

" And that may not be much in their favour at present, Stephen," replied my aunt, who was not blind to her progeny—" at least, until they are a little better rigged out than in their present nursery dresses, Stephen."

" Rig away, rig away, Kate !" said my uncle, " rig away ; you may make them as tawdry as jackdaws, so as you don't turn their heads at Jack Barrington's."

In fine, they were made sufficiently glaring, and, accompanied by aunt in the resuscitated post-

chaise, made their first *début* at the church of
Portarlington.   Of course they attracted universal
notice : the ladies congratulated my aunt on her
showy girls; the parson on their *coming of age;*
and the innkeeper declared they were the most
genteelest of all the new subscribers to his ball
and supper at the market-house.

The ladies returned to Moret highly delighted
with their cordial reception in the church-yard,
and Mrs. Gregory, the head mantua-maker of the
county, was immediately set to work to fit out the
ladies in the newest taste of Dublin fashions, pre-
paratory to the next ball.

Now, Portarlington had been a very small village in the Queen's County until the French Protestant emigrants, on the revocation of the Edict
of Nantes, made a settlement there, (it was said,
from the enormous quantity of fine frogs gene-
rated in that neighbourhood,) and there they
commenced schoolmasters and mistresses, with
a good reputation, which they ceased not to keep
up, until in time it became an established semi-
nary.   Here the numerous schools and academies
were always ready to pour out their hobbardehoys
and misses in their teens to the dances and assem-
blies ; but very few mature gentlemen assisted
at these coteries, and it was the customary prayer
of all the young ladies going to those balls—" If
I cannot get a *man* for a partner, O Heaven, in
thy mercy, send me a big boy !"

Suffice it to say, that my cousins, at the first ball, outglared all the females in the room put together; my aunt's old rings and hereditary paraphernalia had been brought fully into requisition. But, unfortunately, Providence sent them that night neither a grown man partner nor a big boy in the shape of a man partner, and, after having sat as full-blown wall-flowers the whole night, they returned to Moret highly discouraged, that their rose-colour satin and family Dresdens, which cut all the other girls out of feather, had no better result than the going home again, my philosophical aunt telling them all the way home—" that balls were no places to catch husbands at, there was so much variety; and I assure you, Dolly," said my aunt, " men, now-a-days, look more at a girl's purse than her flounces, and you'll have nothing very showy in that way whilst your father and mother are alive, Dolly."

My poor cousin Dolly's feet also, after three balls more (dead failures) got so crimped and cramped by tight shoes, to restrain her fat brackets within reasonable boundaries, that corns, bunnions, callosities, &c., showed a plentiful harvest the ensuing summer, and, conspiring with her winter chilblains, and tortures to match, put my poor cousin's jigging out of the question for the remainder of her existence.

My cousin Fanny, whose feet were only bone and gristle, made numerous exhibitions, both in

the minuet and rigadoon, and for the same purpose; but no wooers for the Miss Fitzgeralds of
Moret Castle made their advances; not a sigh was
exploded for either of the demoiselles, though the
church, the balls, the races at the great heath,
and hurlings at the fort of Dunnally, were all as-
siduously attended for the laudable purpose aforesaid; all in vain; and after a two years' vigorous
chase, the game was entirely given over, and my
cousins slunk back into cover, where, in all human probability, they would have remained during their lives, had not Heaven sent down a putrid
fever to bring my uncle Stephen up to it, as all
the old ladies asserted (to please the widow),
although old Julian, the exciseman, ungratefully
remarked, that "there must have been a great
number of vacancies in heaven, when they called
up the counsellor there." However, before her
weeds got rusty, my aunt, shaking a loose leg,
after having been forty years handcuffed and linked
to Counsellor Stephen, set out with the entire
family for the great city of Dublin, where, no
doubt, the merits, if not the beauty of my cousins,
with a more proximate reversion, would be duly
appreciated.

However, neither their merit nor beauty, nor
the reversion, could exorcise the spirit of celibacy,
which still pursued them from Moret. Jack,
their brother, married a mantua-maker; and my
poor uncle not being a Mahomedan, and, of

course, not having any houri in the clouds to solace
his leisure hours, and finding himself lonesome
without his old Kate, Providence again showed
its kindness towards him, and sent down a pulmo-
nary consumption to Dublin, to carry my aunt
up to her well-beloved Stephen.   My unfortunate
cousins were now left orphans, of only forty and
forty-one years of age, to buffet with the cares of
the world, and accept the brevet rank of old
maidens, which they certainly did, with as much
good-humour and as little chagrin as are generally
exhibited on those occasions.   Their incomes were
ample for all their purposes, and they got on to
the end of their career very comfortably.   Dolly
chose three lap-dogs and a parrot for her fa-
vourites, and Fanny adopted a squirrel and four
Tom-cats to chase away her ennui.   But those
animals having a natural antipathy to each other,
got into an eternal state of altercation and hostility,
the parrot eternally screeching, to make peace between them.   So a maid-servant, who understood
the humour of poodles, cats, &c. &c., was hired
to superintend and keep them in peace and
proper order.

   This maid of natural history got great ascendancy; and, as she was what is termed in Ireland
a swaddler, (in England a canter or psalm-singer,)
she soon convinced my cousins that there was
no certain road to salvation, save through the
preachers and love-feasts of those societies.   Of

course a plate was laid ready for some lank
pulpiteer at dinner, every day, and my cousins
became thorough-paced swaddlers (singing ex-
cepted). But, as years would still roll on, and
they could not be always swaddling, and saving
their souls, some extra comfort was, as customary,
found necessary for their languid hours. The
maid of natural history therefore suggested that,
as solid food and weak Bourdeaux were not of the
best efficacy for feeble appetites, which her mistresses were beginning to show symptoms of, a
glass of cordial, now and then, in the morning,
might restore the tone of their stomachs. Of consequence, a couple of liqueur bottles were prepared, and always properly replenished; the ladies
found their liquid appetites daily increase: the
preacher got the whole bottle of wine to himself;
Lundy Foot's most pungent was well crammed
into my cousins' nostrils, as an interlude, till
snuffling was effected; and the matter went on
as cheerily as possible between the dogs and
cats, the preacher, snuff, and the cordial comforts, till an ill-natured dropsy, with tappings to
match, sent my cousin Dolly to my uncle Stephen;
and some other disorder having transmitted cousin
Fanny the same journey to her mother, I anticipated very great satisfaction in opening the last will
and testament of the survivor; whereupon, all things
being regularly prepared, with an audible voice
I read the first legacy, bequeathing "her body to

the dust, and her soul to God," in most pious and
pathetic expressions, and of considerable lon-
gitude.   The second legacy ran : " Item—to my
dear cousin, Jonah Barrington, I bequeathe my
mother's wedding-ring and my father's gold
sleeve-buttons, as family keepsakes ; also all my
father's books and papers of every description,
except bonds, or any securities for money, or con-
tracts;" and so far looked favourable, till, casting
my eye over the third legacy, to the wonder of
the company, I stopped short, and handing it
cautiously to the swaddling preacher (who was
present), begged he would be so kind as to read
it himself.   This office he coyly accepted, and performed it in a drawling whine, and with heavy sighs,
that made every body laugh, except myself.   In
fine, cousin Fanny, after her " soul to God, and her
body to the dust," (the latter of which legacies she
could not possibly avoid,) as to all her worldly
substance, &c., bequeathed it " to such *charitable* purposes as her maid Mary might think
proper, by and with the spiritual advice and assistance of that holy man, Mr. Clarke."   This
pious philosopher never changed a muscle at his
good fortune.   The will, indeed, could be no surprise either to him or Mrs. Mary.   With the aid
of the orator's brother, who was an attorney, (and
got snacks,) they had prepared it according to
their own satisfaction ; and cousin Fanny executed it one evening, after her cordial and prayers

had their full operation; and, in a few days more, her disorder put a conclusive termination to any possibility of revoking it.

This affair had its sequel exactly as any rational person might have anticipated. The preacher and Mrs. Mary, after a decent mourning, united their spiritual and temporal concerns, and became flesh of the flesh and bone of the bone; in which happy state of husband and wife (which happy state they had been in many months before the *ceremony* was thought necessary) they remained nearly two years, when His Reverence, happening to light on a younger and handsomer swaddler, and legatee, after beating Mrs. Mary almost to a jelly, embarked with his new proselyte for America, where, changing his name, curling his hair, colouring his eyebrows, &c. &c., he turned quaker, and is at this moment, I have learned, in good repute at meeting, and solvency as a trader, in the city of Philadelphia.

The entire of my uncle Stephen's library and manuscripts, with the exception of the year books, Newcastle on the Manége, seven farriery and several cookery books, I gave to my friend, old Lundyfoot, to envelope his powder in; and most of my books being well impregnated, or rather populously inhabited by divers minute and nearly impalpable maggots, probably added some poignancy to the sneezing qualities of his celebrated preparation.

I recollect a whimsical expression used by Davy Lander, an Irish counsellor, whom I brought with me to hear the will read.

" By my soul, Barrington," said Lander, " she was right enough in bequeathing her soul to God, out of hand, or the devil would certainly have taken it as *heir-at-law!* But I hope he has the reversion."

That branch of the Geraldines is now entirely extinct, having ended with my cousin Fanny, the swaddler; and nothing now remains but the old castle, its celebrated ivy tree, St. Bridget's stone, and my legends, to preserve even the recollection of Moret.

HANGING AN ATTORNEY BY ACCIDENT.

The attorney's corps of yeomanry, and their strange appellation—Eccentric loyalty in Dublin—The Fogies—Sir John
Ferns, and his anti-rebel resolve—Aide-de-Camp Potterton and the other members of Sir John's chivalrous party—
Tragi-comic incidents attending their martial progress—Ad-
mixture of discretion with bravery—Discovery of a suspicious lurker, and zealous anxiety for his immediate execution—Process of suspension—Attorney Walker's accidental
participation in the captive's lot—Respective demeanor of
the two sufferers—Appearance of the enemy in sight—The
attorney relieved from his situation—Conclusion of the day's
adventures.

A HANGING match of a very curious nature occurred a few days after the breaking out of the
same rebellion in Dublin, and its relation will
form an excellent companion to that of Lieutenant H———'s mode of execution (*ante*).

The attorneys' corps of yeomanry, horse and
foot, were at that period little less than 800 or
900 strong ; and I really believe it might, in an
enemy's country, (or even in a remote district of
its own,) have passed for as fine a " pulk of Cossacks" as ever came from the banks of the Don
or the Danube.

In Ireland, every thing has its *alias* denomination;—in the regular army, certain regiments are honoured by the titles of the " King's *own*," the " Queen's *own*," or the " Prince's *own*," &c. Many of the Irish yeomanry corps, in 1798, were indulged with similar distinctions; not indeed by the King himself, but by his majesty's sovereign mob of Dublin. For example, the attorneys' regiment was christened, collectively, the "*Devil's* own;" the infantry part of it, the *Rifle* Brigade; and the cavalry, the *Chargers;* the Custom-house corps, Cæsar's (*seizer's*) army, &c. &c. &c. The pre-eminent titles thus given to the attorneys, (who are gentlemen by *Act of Parliament,*) were devised by one Mr. Murry, a cheese and oilman in Great George Street, whose premises (as he deposed) were stormed one night by a patrol of that legal corps, and divers articles of the first quality—food and luxury, cheeses, hams, tongues, anchovies, Burton ale, and bottled porter, &c. were abstracted against his will therefrom, and feloniously conveyed into, and concealed in, the bodies, bowels, and intestines, of divers ravenous and thirsty attorneys, solicitors, and scriveners; and thereby conveyed beyond the reach or jurisdiction of any search warrants, replevins, or other legal process. A more curious deposition did not appear during the whole of those troublesome times, than that sworn by Mr. Murry, cheese and oilman, and annexed to a petition to parliament for *compensation*. However, the

parliament, not considering Mr. Murry to be an
extra-loyalist (but which the attorneys certainly
were, and *ultra* into the bargain), refused to
replenish his warehouse. In consequence whereof, Mr. Murry decided upon his own revenge by
nicknaming the *enemy*, wherein he succeeded
admirably.

Here I cannot avoid a little digression, by
observing, that so strong and enthusiastic was
the genuine loyalty which seized upon the
nobility, gentry, and clergy of Dublin at that
period, that even the young gentlemen of Merrion
Square, who had so far advanced toward their
grand climacteric as to exceed threescore, formed
a strong band of volunteers, who proved their
entire devotion to king and country, by first
parading every fine evening, then drinking tea and
playing whist, and afterwards patrolling all Merrion Square—east, west, north, and south; and if
there had been any more sides, no doubt they
would have patrolled them also. They then, in a
most loyal manner, supped alternately at each
other's houses. They were commanded by Lord
Viscount Allen, who was surnamed the "*Bog of
Allen,*" from his size and substance, and contrasted with the Lieutenant-Colonel, Mr. Wes-
tenra, (father of the present Lord Rossmore,) who,
having no flesh of his own, was denominated "the
Commissary." This company, as a body, were
self-intitled the *Garde du Corps*, alluding to their

commander Lord Allen ; and as they could have (by the course of nature) but a short period either to fight or run away, and life, like every other commodity, when it runs rather short, becomes the more valuable, so they very wisely took most especial care of the remnants of their own, as *civilians :* and, of a wet or damp night, I have with great pleasure seen a score, at least, of our venerable *Garde Grenadier* gallantly patrolling Merrion Square, and marching in a long file of sedan-chairs, with their muskets sticking out of the windows ready to deploy and fire upon any rebel enemy to church or state, who should dare to oppose their progress and manœuvres.

The humorists of that day, however, would not consent to any *Gallic* denomination for these loyal yeomen, whom they rather chose to distinguish by a real Irish title; viz. the *Fogies,**—a term meaning, in Hibernian dialect, " a bottle that has

---

* Few gentlemen in Ireland made more " *Fogies* " than the good and witty Sir Hercules Langrish, one of that corps, and who was said to have been the godfather of his company.

Sir Hec's idea of " *Fogies* " may be collected from an anecdote Sir John Parnell, chancellor of the exchequer, used to tell of him with infinite pleasantry.

Sir John, one evening immediately after dinner, went to Sir Hercules on some official business : he found him in the midst of revenue papers, with two empty bottles and a glass standing immediately before him. " What the deuce, Sir Hec !" said Sir John, " why, have you finished these two already ?"—" To be sure I have," said Sir Hec ; " they were only claret."— " And was nobody helping you ?" said Sir John. " Oh, yes,

no liquor in it." This excellent corps, in due
time, however, died off without the aid of any
enemy, and, I fear, not one of them remains to
celebrate the loyalty of the defunct. I therefore
have taken upon myself that task, (so far as my
book can accomplish it,) for which I shall, doubtless, receive the heartfelt thanks of their sons and
grandchildren.

I shall now proceed to the misfortunes of an
attorney, neither deserved nor expected by that
loyal yeoman : the anecdote, however, should remain as a caution and warning to all hangmen
by profession, and other loyal executioners, down
to the latest posterity.

The regiment of attorneys, &c. (or, as the
malicious Mr. Murry called them, the "Devil's
own") was at that time extremely well commanded; the cavalry (or "chargers") by a very
excellent old fox-hunting solicitor, Arthur Dunn ;
the infantry, (or rifle companies,) by Mr. Kit
Abbot, a very good, jovial, popular practitioner.

Both commanders were loyal to the back-bone ;
they formed unbending buttresses of church and
state, and had taken the proper obligation, " to
bury themselves under the ruins of the Weavers'
Hall and Skinners' Alley, sooner than yield one
inch of the *Dodder River* or the *Poddle Gutters* to
any *Croppy* or democratic papist."

---

yes !" said Sir Hercules ; " see there, a bottle of port came to
my assistance ; there's his *fogy*."

After the rebellion broke out, some of these true and loyal attorneys, feeling that martial law had totally superseded their own,—and that, having nothing to do in the *money*-market, their visits to the *flesh*-market were proportionably curtailed ; credit having likewise got totally out of fashion, (as usual during rebellions,)— they bethought themselves of accomplishing some military achievement which might raise their renown, and perhaps at the same time " raise the wind ;" and, as good luck would have it, an opportunity soon turned up, not only of their signalising their loyalty, but also (as they imagined without much hazard) of a *couple of. days' feasting* at free quarters.

This adventure eventually had the fortunate result of procuring a bulletin in several of the Dublin newspapers, though it did not seriously give the gallant yeomen half the credit which their intrepidity and sufferings had merited.

Sir John Ferns,* who had been sheriff, and the

---

* Sir J. Ferns had one quality to an astonishing extent, which I can well vouch for, having often heard and seen its extraordinary effects.

His singing voice, I believe, never yet was equalled for its depth and volume of sound. It exceeded all my conceptions, and at times nearly burst the tympanum of the ear, without the slightest discord !

Yet his falsetto, or feigned voice, stole in upon the bass without any tones of that abrupt transition which is frequently perceptible amongst the best of songsters : his changes, though as most celebrated wine-merchant of Dublin, was at that period justly admired for his singing—his luxurious feasts—insatiable thirst—and hard-going hospitality : his amarynth nose, with cheeks of Bardolph, twinkling black eyes with a tinge of blood in the white of them, rendered any further sign for his wine-vaults totally unnecessary.

, This Sir John (like the Earl of Northumberland in Cheviot Chase) had made some vow, or cursed some curse, that he would take his sport three summer days, hanging or hunting rebels, and burning their haunts and houses about the town of Rathfarnan, where he had a villa. All this he was then empowered and enabled to do, by virtue of martial law, without pain or penalty, or lying under any compliment to judges or juries, as in more formal or legal epochas. He accordingly set about recruiting well-disposed and brave asso-ciates to join him in the expedition, and most for-tunately hit upon Attorney James Potterton, Esq., in every point calculated for his aide-de-camp. The troop was quickly completed, and twenty

---

it were from thunder to a flute, had not one disagreeable tone with them.

, This extreme depth of voice was only in perfection when he was in one of his singing humours; and the effect of it (often shivering empty glass) was of course diminished in a large, and altogether inoperative in a very spacious room ; but, in a moderately low and not very large chamber, its effect was miraculous.

able and vehement warriors, with Captain Sir John Ferns at their head, and Mr. James Potterton, (who was appointed sergeant,) set out to hang, hunt, and burn all before them where they found disloyalty lurking about Rathfarnan.

The troop was composed of five attorneys; three of Mr. John Claudius Beresford's most expert yeomen, called *manglers,* from his riding-house; two grocers from the guild of merchants; an exciseman, and a master tailor; a famous slop-seller from Poolbeg-street; a buck parson from the county of Kildare; one of Sir John's own bottlers, and his principal corker; also a couple of sheriff's officers. Previously to setting out, the captain filled their stomachs gullet-high with ham, cold round, and cherry bounce; and being so duly filled, Sir John then told them the order of battle.

"I sent to the landlord of the yellow house of Rathfarnan, many months ago," said Sir John, "a hogshead of my capital *chateau margot,* for which he has never paid me; and as that landlord now, in all probability, deserves to be hanged, we can at least put up with him at nights; drink my *chateau;* do military execution in the days, which will report well to Lord Castlereagh; and at all events, the riding and good cheer can do us no harm." This was universally approved of; and, led by this gallant and celebrated vintner, the troop set off to acquire food and fame about the environs of the capital.

' Sergeant Potterton, who was a very good-humoured and good-natured attorney, with a portion of slang dryness and a sly drawl, diverting enough, afterwards recited to me the whole of their adventure, which campaign was cut a good deal shorter than the warriors premeditated.

" No man," said Attorney Potterton, " could be better calculated to lead us to any burning excursion than Sir John. You know, Counsellor, that every feature in his face is the picture of a conflagration ; and the people swear that when he bathes, the sea *fizzes,* as if he was a hot iron.

" But," continued Sergeant Potterton, " Counsellor Curran's story of Sir John's nose setting a cartridge on fire, when he was for biting off the end of it, has not one word of truth in it."

This troop had advanced on their intended route just to the spot where, a few nights before, the Earl of Roden had received a bullet in his night-cap, and had slain some rebels, when Sergeant Potterton espied a rebel skulking in what is called in Ireland a brake or knock of furze. Of course the sergeant immediately shouted out, in the proper military style—" Halloa, boys !—halloa !—hush !—hush !—silence !—halloa ! Oh ! by——, there's a nest of rapparee rebels in that knock. Come on, lads, and we'll slice every mother's babe of them to their entire satisfaction. Now, draw, boys !—draw !—cock !—charge !" said the grocers. " Charge away !" echoed the attorneys ;·

and without further ceremony they did charge the
knock of furze with most distinguished bravery :
but, alas! their loyal intentions were disappointed;
the knock of furze was found uninhabited ; the
rebels had stolen off, on their hands and feet, across
a ditch adjoining it ; and whilst the royal scouters
were busily employed cutting, hacking, and twisting every furze and tuft, in expectation that a rebel
was behind it, of a sudden a certain noise and
smoke, which they had no occasion for, came
plump from an adjoining ditch. "Halloa!—halloa!—I 'm hit, by ——!" said one. "I 'm grazed,
by the ——!" said another. "I heard the slugs
whiz like hailstones by my head !" swore a third.
"O; blood and ——z!" roared out Sergeant Potterton the attorney, "I 've got an *indenture* in my
forehead."—"This is nothing 'else but a fair ambush," said Malony the bailiff, scratching his cheek,
through which a couple of slugs had made an illegal
entry to visit his grinders. "Church and state
be d——d!" said the buck parson, *inadvertently*,
on seeing a dash of blood on his waistcoat. "Oh,
murder! murder!" cried the slop-merchant. "Oh,
Mary Ann, Mary Ann! why did I not stay fair
and easy at Poolbeg-street, as you wanted me,
and I would not be massacred in this manner ?"
Many of the combatants actually fancied themselves mortally wounded, at least, and all flocked
round Captain Sir John Ferns for orders in this
emergency. "Halloa!" roared the captain;

" Halloa, boys, wheel—wheel—eel—l—boys ! I
say, wheel—l—l !", But being too brave to specify
whether,,to the right, or left, or front, or rear,
every wheeler wheeled according to his own taste
and judgment ; some to right and others to left,
by twos, threes, fours, and single files, as was
most convenient ; of course the poor horses, being
equally uncertain as the riders, absolutely charged
each other in one *mélange*—heads and tails—helter
skelter—higgledy piggledy—rumps and foreheads
all toulting and twisting, to the great edification of
the gentlemen rebels, who stood well hid behind
the ditch, charging for another volley. '   ⟩

Sir John standing bravely in the centre to rally
his men, his nose like the focus of a burning-glass
collecting its rays, was himself a little astounded
at seeing the number who appeared wounded and
bleeding after so short an encounter. For this
surprise the captain no doubt had very good
cause : his charger had, in truth, got a bullet
through his nostrils, and not being accustomed to
twitches of that kind, he began to toss up his
head, very naturally, in all directions, dispersing
his blood on the surrounding warriors ; whilst, there
being no particular tint by which the blood of a
Christian or an attorney and that of a horse are
distinguished on a field of battle, every gallant
who got a splash of the gelding's *aqua vitæ* from
his nose and nostrils, fancied it was his own
precious gore which was gushing out of some hole

bored into himself, in defence of the church and state; to both of which articles he gave a smothered curse for bringing him into so perilous and sanguinary an adventure.

However, they wisely considered that the greatest bravery may be carried too far, and become indiscretion. By a sort of instinctive coincidence of military judgment, therefore, without waiting for a council of war, word of command, or such ill-timed formalities, the whole troop immediately proved in what a contemptible point of view they held such dangers; and to show that they could turn a battle into a matter of amusement, commonly called a horse-race—such as was practised by the carbineers at the battle of Castlebar (*ante*), Captain Ferns, Sergeant Potterton, and the entire troop, started from the post, or rather the knock of furze, at the same moment, every jockey trying whose beast could reach a quarter of a mile off with the greatest expedition. This was performed in a time incredibly short. The winner, however, never was decided; as, when a halt took place, every jockey swore that he was the last—being directly contrary to all horse-races which do not succeed a *battle*.

When the race was over, a council of war ensued, and they unanimously agreed, that as no rebel had actually appeared, they must of course be defeated, and that driving rebels out of the furze was, in matter of fact, a victory.

After three cheers, therefore, for the Protestant ascendancy, they determined to follow up their success, and scour the neighbourhood of all lurking traitors.

With this object (like hounds that had lost their game), they made a cast to get upon the scent again ; so at a full hand-gallop they set out, and were fortunate enough to succeed in the enterprise. In charging through a corn-field, the slop-seller's horse, being rather near-sighted, came head foremost over some bulky matter hid amongst the corn.—" Ambush !—ambush !" cried Sir John :— " Ambush ! ambush !" echoed his merry men all. Sergeant Potterton, however, being more foolhardy than his comrades, spurred on to aid the poor slop-trader : in getting across the deep furrows, his gelding took the same summersets as his less mettlesome companion, and seated Sergeant Potterton exactly on the carcass of the slopman, who, for fear of worse, had laid himself very quietly at full length in the furrow ; and the sergeant, in rising to regain his saddle, perceived that the slop-man's charger had stumbled over something which was snoring as loud as a couple of French-horns close beside him. The sergeant promptly perceived that he had gotten a real prize : it was, with good reason, supposed to be a drunken rebel, who lay dozing and snorting in the furrow, but, certainly, not dreaming of the uncomfortable journey he was in a few minutes to travel into a world that, before he fell asleep, he had not the least idea of visiting.

"Hollo! hollo! hollo! Captain, and brave boys," cried Attorney Potterton : " I 've got a lad sure enough ; and though he has no arms about him, there can be no doubt but they lie hid in the corn: so his guilt is proved ; and I never saw a fellow a more proper example to make in the neighbour-hood !" In this idea all coincided. But what was to be done to legalize his death and burial, was a query. A drum-head court-martial was very properly mentioned by the captain ; but on con-sidering that they had no drum to try him on, they were at a considerable puzzle, till Mr. Ma-lony declared " that he had seen a couple of gentlemen hanged in Dublin on Bloody-bridge a few days before, without any trial, and that by martial law no trial was then necessary for hanging of any body." This suggestion was unanimously agreed to, and the rebel was ordered to be im-mediately executed on an old leafless tree, (which was at the corner of the field, just at their posses-sion,) called in Ireland a rampike.

It was, however, thought but a proper courtesy to learn from the malefactor himself *whom* they were to hang. He protested an innocence, that no loyal man in those times could give any credit to ; he declared that he was Dan Delany, a well-known brogue-maker at Glan Malour ; that he was going to Dublin for leather ; but the whisky

was too many for him, and he lay down to sleep
it off when their hands waked him. " Nonsense!"
said the whole troop, " he 'll make a most beneficial example!"

Nothing now was wanting but a rope, a couple
of which the bailiff had fortunately put into his
coat-case for a magistrate near Rathfarnan, as
there were no ropes there the strength of which
could be depended upon, if rebels happened to
be fat and weighty, or hanged in couples.

. This was most fortunate; and all parties lent
a hand at preparing the cravat for Mr. Dan Delany, brogue-maker. Mr. Walker happened to
be the most active in setting the throttler, so as
to ensure no failure. All was arranged; the rebel
was slung cleverly over the rampike; but Mr.
Walker, perceiving that the noose did not run
glib enough, rode up to settle it about the neck
so as to put Mr. Delany out of pain, when, most
unfortunately, his own fist slipped inadvertently
into the noose, and, whilst endeavouring to extri-
cate himself, his charger got a smart kick with the
rowels, which, like all other horses, considering as
an order to proceed, he very expertly slipped from
under Attorney Walker, who was fast, and left him
dangling in company with his friend the brogue-
maker, one by the head, and the other by the
fist; and as the rope was of the best manufacture,
it kept both fast and clear from the ground, swing-
ing away with some grace and the utmost security.

The beast being thus freed from all constraint, thought the best thing he could do was to gallop home to his own stable (if he could find the way to it), and so set out with the utmost expedition, kicking up behind, and making divers vulgar noises, as if he was ridiculing his master's misfortune.

He was, however, stopped on the road, and sent home to Dublin, with an intimation that Captain Ferns and all the troop were cut off near Rathfarnan; and this melancholy intelligence was published, with further particulars, in a second edition of the Dublin Evening Post, two hours after the arrival of Mr. Walker's charger in the metropolis.

Misfortunes never come alone. The residue of the troop in high spirits had cantered on a little. The kind offices of Mr. Walker to Mr. Delany being quite voluntary, *they* had not noticed his humanity; and, on his roaring out to the very extent of his lungs, and the troop turning round, as the devil would have it, another tree intercepted the view of Mr. Walker, so that they perceived a very different object.—" Captain, Captain," cried out four or five of the troop, all at once, " Look there ! look there !" and there did actually appear several hundred men, attended by a crowd of women and children, approaching them by the road on which the rebel had been apprehended. There was no time to be lost ; and a second heat of the horse-race immediately took place, but without waiting to be started, as on the former occasion; and this course being rather longer than the last, led them totally out of sight of Messrs. Walker and Delany.

The attorney and rebel had in the mean time enjoyed an abundance of that swing-swang exercise which so many professors of law, physic, and divinity practised pending the Irish insurrection; nor was there the slightest danger of their pastime being speedily interrupted, as Captain Ferns' troop, being flanked by above three hundred rebels, considered that the odds were too tremendous to hold out any hopes of a victory: of course a retrograde movement was considered imperative, and they were necessitated, as often happens after boasted victories, to leave Messrs. Walker and Delany twirling about in the string, like a pair of fowls under a bottle-jack.

. But notwithstanding they were both in close and almost inseparable contact, they seemed to enjoy their respective situations with a very different demeanour.

The unpleasant sensations of Mr. Delany had for a considerable time subsided into a general tranquillity, nor did his manner in the slightest degree indicate any impatience or displeasure at being so long detained in company with the inveterate solicitor; nor indeed did he articulate one sentence of complaint against the boisterous conduct of his outrageous comrade.

The attorney, on the contrary, not being blessed with so even a temper as Mr. Delany, showed every symptom of inordinate impatience to get out of his company, and exhibited divers samples of plunging, kicking, and muscular convulsion, more novel and entertaining than even those of the most celebrated rope-dancers ; he also incessantly vociferated as loud, if not louder than he had ever done upon any former occasion, though not in any particular dialect or language, but as a person generally does when undergoing a cruel surgical operation.

The attorney's eyes not having any thing to do with the hanging matter, he clearly saw the same crowd approaching which had caused the retrograde movement of his comrades ; and, as it approached, he gave himself entirely up for lost, being placed in the very same convenient position for piking as Absalom (King David's natural son) when General Joab ran him through the body without the slightest resistance ; and though the attorney's toes were not two feet from the ground, he made as much fuss, floundering and bellowing, as if they had been twenty.

The man of law at length became totally exhausted and tranquil, as children generally are when they have no strength to squall any longer. He had, however, in this state of captivity, the consolation of beholding (at every up glance) the bloated, raven-gray visage of the king's enemy, and his disloyal eyes bursting from their sockets, and full glaring with inanimate revenge on the loyalist who had darkened them. A thrilling horror seized upon the nerves and muscles of the attorney : his sins and clients were now (like the visions in Macbeth, or King Saul and the Witch of Endor) beginning to pass in shadowy review before his imagination. The last glance he could distinctly take, as he looked upward to Heaven for aid, (there being none at Rathfarnan,) gave a dismal glimpse of his once red-and-white engrossing member, now, like the cameleon, assuming the deep purple hue of the rebel jaw it was in contact with, the fingers spread out, cramped, and extended as a fan before the rebel visage; and numbness, the avant-courier of mortification, having superseded torture, he gave himself totally up to Heaven. If he had a hundred prayers, he would have repeated every one of them; but, alas! theology was not his forte, and he was gradually sinking into that merciful insensibility invented by farriers, when they twist an instrument upon a horse's nostrils, that the torture of his nose may render him insensible to the pains his tail is enduring.

In the mean time the royal troop, which had most prudentially retreated to avoid an overwhelming force, particularly on their flank, as the enemy approached, yielded ground, though gradually. The enemy being all foot, the troop kept only

a quarter of a mile from them, and merely retreated a hundred yards at a time, being sure of
superior speed to that of the rebels,—when, to
the surprise of Captain Ferns, the enemy made
a sudden wheel, and took possession of a church-
yard upon a small eminence, as if intending
to pour down on the cavalry, if they could
entice them within distance; but, to the astonishment of the royal troopers, instead of the Irish
war-whoop, which they expected, the enemy set
up singing and crying in a most plaintive and inoffensive manner. The buck parson, with Malony
the bailiff, being ordered to reconnoitre, immediately galloped back, announcing that the enemy
had a coffin, and were performing a funeral; but,
both swearing that it was a new ambush, and the
whole troop coinciding in the same opinion, a
further retreat was decided on, which might be
now performed without the slightest confusion.
It was also determined to carry off their dead, for
such it was taken for granted the attorney must
have been, by the excess of his agitation, dancing
and plunging till they lost sight of him, and also
through the contagion and poisonous collision of
a struggling rebel, to whom he had been so long
cemented.

In order, therefore, to bring off the solicitor,
dead or alive, they rallied, formed, and charged,
sword in hand, towards the rampike, where
they had left Attorney W—— and Mr. Delany in

so novel a situation, and where they expected no loving reception.

In the mean time, it turned out that the kicking, plunging, and rope-dancing of the attorney had their advantages ; as, at length, the obdurate rope, by the repeated pulls and twists, slipped over the knot of the rampike which had arrested its progress, ran freely, and down came the rebel and royalist together, with an appropriate crash, on the green sod under their gibbet, which seemed beneficently placed there by nature on purpose to receive them.

The attorney's innocent feet, however, still remained tightly moored to the gullet of the guilty rebel, and might have remained there till they grew or rotted together, had not the opportune arrival of his gallant comrades saved them from mortification.

To effect the separation of Attorney W—— and Mr. Delany was no easy achievement : the latter had gone to his forefathers, but the rope was strong and tight, both able and willing to have hung half a dozen more of them, if employed to do so. Many loyal pen-knives were set instantly at work; but the rope defied them all; the knot was too solid. At length Sergeant Potterton's broad-sword, having assumed the occupation of a saw, effected the operation without any accident, save sawing across one of the attorney's veins. The free egress of his loyal gore soon brought its proprietor to his sense of existence ; though three of the fingers had got so clever a stretching, that the muscles positively refused to bend any more for them, and they ever after retained the same fan-like expansion as when knotted to Mr. Delany. The index and thumb still retained their engrossing powers, to the entire satisfaction of the club of Skinners' Alley, of which he was an active alderman.

The maimed attorney was now thrown across a horse and carried to a jingle,* and sent home with all the honours of war to his wife and children, to make what use they pleased of.

Captain Ferns' royal troop now held another council of war, to determine on ulterior operations; and, though the rebel army in the church-yard might have been only a funeral, it was unanimously agreed that an important check had been given to the rebels of Rathfarnan; yet that prudence was as necessary an ingredient in the art of war as intrepidity ; and that it might be risking the advantage of what had been done, if they made any attempt on the yellow house, or the captain's *Bourdeaux*, as they might be overpowered by a host of pot-valiant rebels, and thereby his Majesty be deprived of their future services.

They therefore finally decided to retire upon

* A jingle is a species of jaunting-car used in the environs of Dublin by gentry that have no other mode of travelling.

Dublin at a sling-trot—publish a bulletin of the battle in Captain Giffard's Dublin Journal—wait upon Lords Camden and Castlereagh, and Mr. Cooke, with a detail of the expedition and casualties,—— and, finally, celebrate the action by a dinner, when the usual beverage, with the anthem of " God save the King," might unite in doing national honour both to the liquor and to his Majesty, the latter being always considered quite lonesome by the corporators of Dublin, unless garnished by the former accompaniment.

This was all carried into effect. Lieutenant H————, the walking gallows, (*ante*) was especially invited ; and the second metropolis of the British empire had thus the honour of achieving the first victory over the rebellious subjects of his Majesty in the celebrated insurrection of 1798.

FLOGGING THE WINE-COOPERS.

Account of the flagellation undergone by the two coopers—
Their application to the author for redress—'Tit for tat, or
giving *back* the compliment—Major Connor, and his disincli-
nation for attorneys—His brother, Arthur Connor.

An anecdote, amongst many of the same genus,
which I witnessed myself, about the same period,
is particularly illustrative of the state of things in
the Irish metropolis at the celebrated epocha of
1798.

Two wine-coopers of a Mr. Thomas White, an
eminent wine-merchant, in Clare Street, had been
bottling wine at my house in Merrion Square. I
had known them long to be honest, quiet, and in-
dustrious persons : going to their dinner, they returned, to my surprise, with their coats and waistcoats hanging loose on their arms, and their shirts
quite bloody behind. They told their pitiful story
with peculiar simplicity :—that as they were passing

quietly by Major Connor's barrack, at Shelburn
House, Stephen's Green, a fellow who owed one
of them a grudge for beating him and his brother
at Donnybrook, had told Major Connor that " he
heard we were black rebels, and knew well where
many a pike was hid in vaults and cellars in the
city, if we chose to discover of them ; on which
the Major, please your honour, Counsellor, without
stop or stay, or the least ceremony in life, ordered
the soldiers to strip us to our buffs, and then tied
us to the butt-end of a great cannon, and—what
did he do then, Counsellor dear, to two honest poor
coopers, but he ordered the soldiers to give us fifty
cracks a-piece with the devil's cat-o'-nine-tails,
as he called it; though, by my sowl, I believe
there were twenty tails to it—which the Major
said he always kept saftening in brine, to wallop
such villains as we were, Counsellor dear!   Well,
every whack went thorough my carcase, sure
enough; and I gave tongue, because I couldn't
help it : so, when he had his will of us, he ordered us to put on our shirts, and swore us to
come back in eight days more for the remaining
fifty cracks, unless we brought fifty pikes in the
place of them.   Ah, the devil a pike ever we had,
Counsellor dear, and what 'll we do, Counsellor,
what 'll we do ?"

" Take this to the Major," said I, writing to
him a note of no very gentle expostulation.
" Give this, with my compliments ; and if he does

not redress you, I'll find means of making him."

The poor fellows were most thankful; and I immediately received a note from the Major, with many thanks for undeceiving him, and stating, that if the wine-coopers would catch the fellow that belied them, he'd oblige the chap with a cool hundred, from a new double cat, which he would order for the purpose.

The Major strictly kept his word. The wine-coopers soon found their accuser, and brought him to Major Connor, with my compliments; who sent him home in half-an-hour with as raw a back as any brave soldier in his Majesty's service.

Learning also from the coopers that their enemy was an attorney's clerk, (a profession the Major had a most inveterate and very just aversion to,). he desired them to bring him any disloyal attorneys they could find, and he'd teach them more justice in one hour at Shelburn Barracks, than they'd practise for seven years in the Four Courts.

The accuser, who got so good a practical lecture from Major Connor, was a clerk to Mr. H. Hudson, an eminent attorney, of Dublin.

The Major's brother, Arthur, was under a state prosecution, and incarcerated as an unsuccessful patriot—but one to whom even Lord Clare could not deny the attributes of consistency, firmness, and fidelity. His politics were decidedly sincere. Banished from his own country, he received high promotion in the French army; and, if he had not been discontinued from the staff of his relative, Marshal Grouchy, the battle of Waterloo (from documents I have seen) *must* have had a different termination. This, however, is an almost inexcusable digression.

THE ENNISCORTHY BOAR.

Incidents attending the first assault of Wexford by the rebels, in 1798—Excesses mutually committed by them and the royalists—Father Roche—Captain Hay, and his gallant rescue of two ladies—Mr. O'Connell in by-gone days—Painful but ludicrous scenes after the conflict at Wexford—Swinish indignity offered to a clergyman—A pig of rapid growth—Extraordinary destination of the animal—Its arrival and special exhibition in London—Remarks on London curiosities—Remarkable success of the Enniscorthy boar—Unhappy disclosure of the animal's previous enormities—Reaction on the public mind—His Majesty's comments on the affair—Death of the swinish offender, in anticipation of a projected rescue by the London Irish.

A MOST ludicrous incident chanced to spring out of the most murderous conflict (for the numbers engaged) that had occurred during the merciless insurrection of 1798 in Ireland.

The murdered victims had not been effectually interred, the blood was scarcely dry upon the hill, and the embers of the burned streets not yet entirely extinguished in Enniscorthy, when, in company with a friend who had miraculously escaped the slaughter, and Mr. John Grogan, of Johnston, who was then seeking for evidence amongst the conquered rebels, to prove the injustice of his brother's execution, I explored and noted the principal occurrences of that most sanguinary engagement. I give them, in connexion with the preposterous incident which they gave rise to, to show in one view the *mélange* of fanaticism, ferocity, and whimsical credulity, which characterised the lower Irish at that disastrous epocha, as well as the absurd credulity and spirit of true intolerance which signalised their London brethren, in the matter of the silly incident which I shall mention.

The town of Enniscorthy, in the county of Wexford, in Ireland, (one of the first strong possessions that the English, under Strongbow, established themselves in,) is situate most beautifully on the river Slaney, at the base of Vinegar Hill; places which the conflicts and massacres of every nature, and by both parties, have marked out for posterity as the appropriate sites of legendary tales, and traditional records of heroism and of murder.

The town is not fortified; and the hill, like half a globe, rising from the plain, overlooks the town and country, and has no neighbouring eminence to command it.

The first assault on this town by the rebels,

and its defence by a gallant, but not numerous garrison, formed one of the most desperate, heroic, and obstinate actions of an infatuated people. It was stormed by the rebels, and defended with unflinching gallantry ; but captured after a long and most bloody action, during which no quarter was given or accepted on either side. Those who submitted to be prisoners only preserved their lives a day, to experience some more cold-blooded and torturing extinction.

The orange and green flags were that day alternately successful. But the numbers, impetuosity, and perseverance of the rebels, becoming too powerful to be resisted, the troops were overthrown, the rout became general, and the royalists endeavoured to save themselves in all directions : but most of those who had the good fortune to escape the pike or blunderbuss were flung into burning masses, or thrown from the windows of houses, where they had tried to gain protection or conceal themselves.

The insurgents were that day constantly led to the charge, or, when checked, promptly rallied by a priest, who had figured in the French revolution in Paris—a Father Roche. His height and muscular powers were immense, his dress squalid and bloody, his countenance ruffianly and terrific ; he had no sense either of personal danger, or of Christian mercy. That day courage appeared contagious, and even his aged followers seemed to have imbibed all the ferocity and blind desperation of their gigantic and fearless pastor.

The streets through which the relics of the royal troops must traverse to escape the carnage were fired on both sides by the order of Father Roche, and the unfortunate fugitives had no chance but to pass through volumes of flame and smoke, or yield themselves up to the ferocious pikemen, who chased them even into the very body of the conflagration.

My accompanying friend had most unwittingly got into the town, when in possession of the army, and could not get out of it on the sudden assault of the rebels. He had no arms. Many of them knew him, however, to be a person of liberal principles, civil and religious; but he with difficulty clambered to a seat high up in the dilapidated castle; where, unless as regarded the chance of a random shot, he was in a place of tolerable safety. There he could see much; but did not descend till the next morning; and would certainly have been shot at the windmill on Vinegar Hill had not the Catholic priests of his own parish vouched for his toleration and charity; and above all, that he had, early that year, given a large sum towards building a chapel and endowing a school for the cottagers' children.

His description of the storm was extremely exciting; and the more so, as it was attended by an occurrence of a very interesting nature.

It was asserted by some of the loyal yeomen who were engaged, that the rebels were commanded, as to their *tactics*, by Captain Hay, of the ——— dragoons, who had been some time amongst them as a prisoner; a report countenanced by the disaffection of his family. This gave rise to charges against Captain Hay of desertion to the rebels, and high-treason. He was submitted to a court-martial; but an act of the most gallant and chivalrous description saved him from every thing but suspicion of the criminality imputed.

Mrs. Ogle and Miss Moore, two of the most respectable ladies of Wexford, happened to be in Enniscorthy, when it was assaulted, without any protector, and subject to all the dangers and horrors incidental to such captures. They had no expectation of escape, when Captain Hay, in the face of every species of danger, with a strength beyond his natural powers, and a courage which has not been exceeded, placing them on a horse before him, rushed into the midst of a burning street, and, through flames and shots, and every possible horror, bore them through the fire in safety; and, although he sadly scorched himself, proceeded in conveying and delivering them safe to their desponding relations. Mr. Ogle was member for the county. The act was too gallant to leave any thing more than the suspicion of guilt, and the accused was acquitted on all the charges.

Very shortly afterwards his eldest brother was executed at Wexford, his father died, while another brother, also deeply implicated, was not prosecuted, and figured many years afterwards as secretary to the Catholic Committee; but he was neither deep enough nor mute enough for Mr. Daniel O'Connell, who, at that day, was, by-the-by, a large, ruddy young man, with a broad and savoury dialect, an imperturbable countenance, intrepid address, *et præterea nihil*. He was then more fastidious as to his approbation of secretaries than he afterwards turned out to be.*

Amongst the persons who lost their lives on that occasion was the Rev. Mr. Haydn, a very old and highly respected clergyman of the Established Church: he was much more lamented than the thirty priests who were hanged at the same period. He was piked or shot by the rebels in the street, and lay dead and naked upon the Castle Hill, till duly consumed by half-starving dogs, or swine of the neighbourhood, that marched without invitation into the town, to dine upon any of the combatants who were not interred too deep to be easily rooted up again.

After the rebellion had entirely ended, it was

---

* Mr. O'Connell was called to the bar, Easter, 1798, on or about the same day that Father Roche was hanged. He did not finger politics in any way for several years afterwards, but he studied law very well, and bottled it *in usum—jus habentis* may be added or not.

remarked in the neighbourhood, that what the peasants call a "slip of a pig," who had been busy with his neighbours carousing in Enniscorthy, as aforesaid, had, from that period, increased in stature and corresponding bulk to an enormous degree, and far outstripped all his cotemporaries, not only in size, but (so far as the term could be applicable to a pig) in genuine beauty. At length his growth became almost miraculous ; and his exact symmetry kept pace with his elevation.

This young pig was suffered to roam at large, and was universally admired as the most comely of his species. He at length rose to the elevation of nearly a heifer, and was considered too great a curiosity to remain in Ireland, where curiosities, animate and inanimate, human and beastly, are too common to be of any peculiar value, or even excite attention. It was therefore determined to send him over as a present to our Sovereign—as an olive-branch, so to speak, for the subdued and repentant rebels of Enniscorthy, and a specimen which, being placed in the Tower, might do great honour to the whole race of domestic swine, being the first tame gentleman of his family that ever had been in any royal menagerie.

This Enniscorthy miracle was accordingly shipped for Bristol, under the care of a priest, two rebels, and a showman, and in due season arrived in the metropolis of England. Regular notice of his arrival was given to the king's proper officers at the Tower, who were to prepare chambers for his reception, though it was maliciously whispered that the "olive branch," as the priest called the pig, was intended only second-hand for his Majesty; that is to say, after the party and showman should have pursed every loose shilling the folks of London might be tempted to pay for a sight of so amiable an animal. The pig took admirably; the showman (a Caledonian by birth) was economical in the expenditure, and discreet in his explanations. The pig became the most popular show at the east end; Exeter Change even felt it. However, fate ultimately restored the baboons and tigers to their old and appropriate rank in society.

This proceeding, this compliment of the *olive branch*, was neither more nor less than is generally used in the case of our most celebrated generals, admirals, and statesmen, (and occasionally our most gracious Sovereigns,) who, being duly disembowelled, spiced, swaddled, and screwed up in a box, with a white satin lining to it, (well stuffed, to make it easy,) are exhibited to their compatriots of all ranks, who can spare sixpence to see an oak trunk, covered with black, and plenty of lacquered tin nailed on the top of it. But here the pig was seen alive and merry, which every body (except testamentary successors) conceives has much the advantage over any thing that is inanimate.

I had myself, when at Temple, the honour of paying sixpence to see the fork which belonged to the knife with which Margaret Nicholson attempted to penetrate the person of his Majesty, King George the Third, at St. James's; and the Dean and Chapter of Westminster, through their actuaries, receive payment for showing the stone heads of patriots, poets, and ministers, whom they have secured in their tabernacle; Sir Cloudesley Shovel, who was drowned as an admiral; Major André, who was hanged as a spy; and Mr. Grattan, who should have been buried in Ireland.

There can be little doubt that the greatest men of the present day, for a British shilling, before much more of the present century is finished, will be exhibited in like manner.

The thing has become too public and common. In early days, great men, dying, required to be buried in the holiest sanctuary going. Sometimes the great bust was transferred to Westminster Abbey; but, of late, the monuments are becoming so numerous, the company so mixed, and the exhibition so like a show-box, that the modern multiplication of Orders has made many Knights very shy of wearing them. Thus the Abbey has lost a great proportion of its rank and celebrity; and I have been told of a gentleman of distinction, who, having died of a consumption, and being asked where he wished to be buried, replied, " any where but Westminster Abbey."

To resume, however, the course of my narra-

tive—the celebrity of the "olive branch" every
day increased, and the number of his visitors so
rapidly augmented, that the priest and showman
considered that the day when he should be committed to the Tower would be to them no trifling
misfortune. Even the ladies conceived there was
something musical in his grunt, and some tried to
touch it off upon their pianos. So gentle, so sleek
and silvery were his well-scrubbed bristles, that
every body patted his fat sides. Standing on his
bare feet, his beautifully arched back, rising like a
rainbow, overtopped half his visitors; and he became so great and general a favourite, that, though
he came from Ireland, nobody even thought of
inquiring whether he was a papist or protestant
grunter!

One day, however, the most unforeseen and
grievous misfortune that ever happened to so fine
an animal, at once put an end to all his glories,
and to the abundant pickings of his chaplain.

It happened, unfortunately, that a Wexford
yeoman, who had been at the taking and retaking
of Enniscorthy, (a theme he never failed to expa-
tiate on,) and had been acquainted with the pig
from his infancy, as well as the lady sow who
bore him, having himself sold her to the last proprietors, came at the time of a very crowded
assembly into the room; and, as Irishmen never
omit any opportunity of talking, (especially in a
crowd, and, if at all convenient, *more* especially

about themselves,) the yeoman began to brag
of his acquaintance with the hog, the storming of
the town, the fight, and slaughter; and, unfortunately, in order to amuse the company, by sug-
gesting the cause of his enormous bulk and stature,
mentioned, as a national curiosity, that the people
in Ireland were so headstrong as to attribute his
growth to his having eaten the Rev. Mr. Haydn, a
Protestant clergyman of Enniscorthy, after the
battle; but he declared to the gentlemen and ladies
that could not be the fact, as he was assured
by an eye-witness, a sergeant of pikemen amongst
the rebels, that there were several dogs helping
him, and some ducks out of the Castle court.
Besides, the parson having been a slight old gentleman, there was scarcely as much flesh on
his reverend bones as would have given one
meal to a hungry bull-dog. This information,
and the manner of telling it, caused an instantaneous silence, and set every English man and
woman staring and shuddering around him, not
one of whom did the pig attempt to put his snout
on. The idea of a *Papist* pig eating a *Protestant*
parson was of a nature quite insupportable; both
church and state were affected: their praises
were now turned to execration; the women put
their handkerchiefs to their noses to keep off the
odour; every body stood aloof both from the pig
and the showman, as if they were afraid of being
devoured. The men cursed the Papist brute,

and the rebellious nation that sent him there; every one of them who had a stick or an umbrella gave a punch or a crack of it to the " olive branch;" and in a few minutes the room was cleared of visitors, to the astonishment of the yeoman, who lost no time in making his own exit. The keepers, now perceiving that their game was gone, determined to deliver him up, as *Master Haydn,* to the lieutenant of the Tower, to be placed at the will and pleasure of his Majesty.

The chaplain, showman, and two amateur rebels, now prepared to return to Wexford. Though somewhat disappointed at the short cut of their exhibition, they had no reason to find fault with the lining their pockets had got. The officers of the Tower, however, had heard the catastrophe and character of the " olive branch," and communicated to the lieutenant their doubts if he were a fit subject to mix with the noble wild beasts in a royal menagerie. Several consultations took place upon the subject; the lord chamberlain was requested to take his Majesty's commands upon the subject in council: the king, who had been signing some death-warrants and pardons for the Recorder of London, was thunderstruck and shocked at the audacity of an Irish pig eating a Protestant clergyman; and though no better Christian ever existed than George the Third, his hatred to pork from that moment was invincible, and became almost a Jewish aversion.

"The Tower! the Tower!" said his Majesty, with horror and indignation. "The Tower for an Irish hog that ate a pious Christian!—No, no—no, no, my lords.—Mr. Recorder, Mr. Recorder—here, see, see—I command you on your allegiance—shoot the pig, shoot him—shoot, Mr. Recorder—you can't hang.—Eh! you would if you could, Mr. Recorder, no doubt. But, no, no—let me never hear more of the monster. A sergeant's guard—shoot him—tell Sir Richard Ford to send his keepers to Ireland to-night—to-night if he can find them—go, go—let me never hear more of him—go—go—go—go—shoot him, shoot him!"

The Recorder withdrew with the usual obeisances, and notice was given that at six next morning a sergeant's guard should attend to shoot the "olive branch," and bury his corpse in the Tower ditch, with a bulky barrel of hot lime to annihilate it. This was actually executed, notwithstanding the following droll circumstance that Sir Richard Ford himself informed us of.

Sir Richard was far better acquainted with the humour and management of the Irish in London, than any London magistrate that ever succeeded him: he knew nearly all of the principal ones by name, and individually, and represented them to us as the most tractable of beings, if duly come round and managed, and the most intractable and obstinate, if directly contradicted.

The Irish had been quite delighted with the honour intended for their compatriot, the Enniscorthy boar, and were equally affected and irritated at the sentence which was so unexpectedly and so unjustly passed on him ; and, after an immediate consultation, they determined that the pig should be rescued at all risks, and without the least consideration how they were to save his life afterwards. Their procedure was all settled, and the rescue determined on, when one of Sir Richard's spies brought him information of an intended rising at St. Giles's to rescue the pig, which the frightened spy said must be followed by the Irish firing London, plundering the Bank, and massacring all the Protestant population— thirty thousand choice Irish being ready for any thing.

Sir Richard was highly diverted at the horrors of the spy, but judged it wise to prevent any such foolish attempt at riot, by anticipating his Majesty's orders ; wherefore, early in the evening, a dozen policemen, one by one, got into the hog's residence, with a skilful butcher, who stuck him in the spinal marrow, and the " olive branch," scarcely brought life to the ground with him. The rescue was then out of the question, and in a very short time Doctor Haydn's Gourmand was not only defunct, but actually laid ten feet under ground, with as much quick-lime covered up over his beautiful body as soon left hardly a bone to discover the place of his interment.

Sir Richard told this anecdote, as to the execution, &c. with great humour. The Irish used to tell Sir Richard that a pig was dishonoured by any death but to make bacon of; that God had sent the breed to Ireland for that purpose only; and that, when killed for that purpose, they considered his death a natural one!

THE END.

PRINTED BY A. J. VALPY, RED LION COURT, FLEET STREET.

ImTheStory.com

Personalized Classic Books in many genre's

Unique gift for kids, partners, friends, colleagues

Customize:

- Character Names
- Upload your own front/back cover images (optional)
- Inscribe a personal message/dedication on the
  inside page (optional)

Customize many titles Including
- Alice in Wonderland
- Romeo and Juliet
- The Wizard of Oz
- A Christmas Carol
- Dracula
- Dr. Jekyll & Mr. Hyde
- And more...

CPSIA information can be obtained at www.ICGtesting.com
Printed in the USA
LVOW10s1937271013

358805LV00024B/1433/P